AF564488

GROWTH AND HUMAN DEVELOPMENT

Economic Thoughts of Wassily W. Leontief

GROWTH AND HUMAN DEVELOPMENT

Economic Thoughts of Wassily W. Leontief

Edited by

DR. INDERJEET SINGH

DR. ANIL KUMAR THAKUR

On behalf of
INDIAN ECONOMIC ASSOCIATION

DEEP & DEEP PUBLICATIONS PVT. LTD.

F-159, Rajouri Garden, New Delhi - 110027

GROWTH AND HUMAN DEVELOPMENT:
Economic Thoughts of Wassily W. Leontief

ISBN 978-81-8450-041-7

Typeset by SHRI GANESH COMPOSERS, R-3/120, Balaji Chowk, Mohan Garden, New Delhi.

Printed in India at MAYUR ENTERPRISES, WZ-Plot No. 3, Gujjar Market, Tihar Village, New Delhi-110018.

Published by DEEP & DEEP PUBLICATIONS PVT. LTD., F-159, Rajouri Garden, New Delhi-110027. Phones: 25435369, 25440916.
E-mail: deep98@del3.vsnl.net.in
Sales Showroom: 2/13, Ansari Road, Daryaganj, New Delhi-110002
Phone/Fax: 23245122

Contents

SECTION II

HUMAN DEVELOPMENT

SECTION III

STRUCTURE AND STRUCTURAL CHANGE

SECTION IV

ENVIRONMENT AND INTERNATIONAL TRADE

Preface

The Indian Economic Association (IEA) organizes its annual conference every year. A conference volume containing papers on all themes of the conference is published and distributed to its members. These themes are debated at length in the conference. After the conference, IEA publishes theme-wise volumes in the form of books. IEA held its Eighty-ninth Annual Conference at Kurukshetra University, Kurukshetra, Haryana. This publication is based on the contributions made to the conference theme: *'Economic Thoughts of Wassily W. Leontief"*. The synoptic view of these papers is available in the opening chapter entitled, 'Introduction'. We hope that the readers will find this work both interesting and useful.

We acknowledge and put on record, the contribution of Professor Inderjeet Singh, for making this publication, a reality. We are thankful to Dr. Anil Kumar Thakur, for the keen interest taken by him in this publication. Our thanks are to the authors of papers without whose cooperation this work could not have been published in time. Last, but not the least, we are thankful to the publishers for bringing this volume in time and in an elegant manner. Although, every effort has been done to make this volume a perfect one, but still if any lapses are there, we should be excused by our readers.

PROF. K.C. REDDY
Indian Economic Association

Introduction

Modern economic development cannot be satisfactorily explained in terms of labour and capital alone. Different factors have been identified as determinants of growth in different growth models. According to some descriptive theories of economic growth, a purely structural change will raise the level of per capita income when there is a shift from sectors of the national economy that requires more labour per unit of output to sectors that requires less of it, other things being equal. Other theories consider capital as the main key to development. The process of capital is interacting and cumulative: once the process gets started, it feeds itself on the own steam. As the economy moves from lower to higher stages of development, there occurs a shift from simpler to more modern and complicated techniques of production. The technological changes bring about an increase in per capita income, either by reducing the amount of inputs per unit of output or by yielding more output for a given amount of input. Technological change of an economy therefore refers to changes in the input-output relations of production activities. Input-output relations and their dynamics at a disaggregated level can be analyzed using the input-output framework. This input-output framework is due to Wassily Leontief.

Professor Wassily W. Leontief (1905-1999), a Nobel Laureate, was both a theorist and an empiricist *par excellence*. He produced excellent pieces of work as a habit. Although he worked in many diverse areas of economics, there is a common thread into all his works, and that was his passion for general equilibrium. Although, he is mainly known for input-output analysis, he also made very fundamental contributions to pure theory of economics. He wrote on diverse subjects like environment, population growth, automation, defence and so on. He wrote in his nineties also. It is not an easy job to put his lifetime contributions at one place. At its Annual Conference of 2005, Indian Economic Association, decided to devote a full session of following year's conference to the theme, 'Economic Thoughts of Wassily Leontief'.

Content and quality-wise this session was very rich and the book is an outcome of learned contributions to this session. There are sixteen papers in all. Five papers deal with the review of Leontief's life and works and rest of the papers are related to extension and application of the input-output technique to diverse areas. The book has been divided into four sections: the opening section deals with economic thoughts of Wassily Leontief; next section deals with human development; third section is related to structural change; and the last section deals with environment, service sector and international trade. The book is a good collection on input-output framework and its application to diverse areas.

The paper by Shri Prakash is a succinct review of Leontief's input output Economics in retrospective perspective. Leontief's input-output Economics filled up empty boxes of theory with empirical contents and empirics, bare of theory, with theoretical contents. It endowed General Equilibrium Analysis with a powerful method to transform it into a computable model. It has enriched practically all branches of economics with theoretical paradigms matched with empirical applications. In generality and relevance, Leontief's contribution may be compared with Einstein's theory of relativity.

Biography and a synoptic review of works of Professor Wassily W. Leontief, has been done by Inderjeet Singh and Reena Singh. Leontief qualified his first degree from Russia, moved to Berlin for doctoral research and then to United States where he came in interaction of emerging schools of thought. The paper argues that he was both a theorist and an empiricist. It adds that works of Leontief are revolutionary and not just an evolutionary outcome of historicity.

Biswajit Chatterjee and Ram Pratap Sinha make a comparative discussion of the two complimentary approaches to the input-output framework—the Leontief model and the Ghosh model. In both the approaches, the interdependence between the individual sectors of the given system is described by a set of linear equations. The Leontief model derives the sectoral outputs from exogenously specified final demands. It is the final demand vector that drives the model. The Ghosh model derives the sectoral outputs from the exogenously specified value-added (comprising of payments to primary factors such as labour and capital). Thus while the Leontief input-output model is demand-driven, the Ghosh model is supply driven. However, the presence of variable returns to scale and technological progress severely limit the application of the input-output approaches.

V. Anbumani and M. Saravanakumar have reviewed the life and the input-output technique of Wassily Leontief. The paper reviews the achievements of Leontief in a chronological manner. As per the argument, the important innovation has given, to economic science, an empirically useful method to highlight the general interdependence in the production system of a society. One of the advantages of input-output analysis is its use in different types of economic systems: decentralized market economics with mainly private enterprise as well as centrally planned economies dominated by public ownership. The paper underscores some important problems relating to the input-output technique.

A comprehensive review of Indian contribution to Leontief's input-output economics has been done by Shalini Sharma. The review has been organized along the thematic lines, since review of individual contributions would have made it difficult to take a holistic view. The review highlights the enormity of Indian contribution to theory, methodology and empirical applications of input-output models to practically every branch of economic analysis. It concludes that Indian contributions to this area of economics are comparable to the American and Dutch contributions.

Another paper by Shri Prakash attempts to push forward the threshold of input-output modeling to encompass human development index within its analytical framework and it enriches human development index estimation by encompassment of input-output modeling. The paper gives an alternative approach to the conventional principal component analysis and Kendall's method of ranking of rank sums. An alternative method of factor/

principal component analysis has been used to determine objectively a system of weights to be assigned to different factors/ variables used in human development index. The method incorporates: rank correlation analysis; concordance analysis; and rank sums. The empirical prognostication of the model has been done by using the input-output table for the year 1993-94.

Human resource development depends on innate capabilities, skills and knowledge of people. Economics have not yet developed any objective technique for the measurement of innate capabilities of individuals. Human development indices often ignore this factor completely. R. Hemalatha extends the basic Leontief framework to augment the human development index by taking innate capabilities as a key factor to human development dynamics.

Decomposition model, to determine the employment and productivity components of growth, has been developed by Shri Prakash and Brinda Balakrishnan. The model has been empirically implemented with input-output tables of Indian economy for 1988-89 and 1993-94. The results show the relative contribution of growth of productivity and employment along with the impact of change in technology on the growth of income. For five out of nine broad sectors of the Indian economy, productivity growth has been dominated by human capital. In three sectors, the productivity has been dominated by technology.

Sri Lanka has been the first South Asian country to embark on a liberalization program. In this context it must be remembered that in the areas of conventional market failure the government has actively intervened to build up a reputation through its accomplishments in the domain of literacy and health. Notwithstanding this fact, rapid growth is still the single-most sought-after criterion in the economy. Partha Pratim Ghosh, Arpita Dhar and Debesh Chakraborty have done a simulation exercise on the Sri Lankan economy using a Keynes-Leontief-Klien framework. The paper underscores the growth dynamics of the Sri Lankan economy.

Paramita Dasgupta and Debesh Chakraborty have made an attempt to study the structural changes of the Indian economy over the decade of the 1980's and the 1990's. Along with the conventional input-output open model, the structural relationships have also been studied with an augmented input-output framework, which is expected to be a more suitable model for exploring the structure of a developing country like India. In the augmented model the final private consumption demand of the non-durable consumer goods is endogenised while the other components of final demand are treated as exogenous. The study reveals that India's production structure is neither traditional nor a highly modernized one. The study also concludes that the Indian economy has not experienced any major structural change during the decade of the 1980's and 1990's, even after adoption of reform measures during this period.

India has accepted the economic policy of liberalization, privatization and globalization since 1991 and the rate of growth of gross domestic product gradually approaching nine percent per annum. For sustainability of this high rate of growth, it is necessary to study the structure of Indian Economy. Vijay S. Sathe has analyzed the structure of Indian economy using the input-output framework. The study, using the 115 sector transaction matrix, analyses the indices of the total linkages, forward linkages and backward linkages.

Orissa is one of the backward States of the economy. Widespread unemployment and poor industrial base are mainly responsible for the existence of high incidence of poverty in the state. However, the state is rich in physical and human resources. The way-out from this impasse necessitates proper planning. Using the input-output approach Aditya Kumar Patra has analyzed the structure of Orissan economy. For analysis, the various linkage patterns have been studied. The results show that Orissa is a primary producing economy where method of production has not much roundabout. But various producing sectors are intensively interrelated; hence, steps should be taken for the encouragement of some key sectors.

Conventionally, the basic input-output model deals with industrial products and services but Pushpa Ranade has analyzed the economic thoughts of Leontief with special reference to environment. Leontief extended the technique to include a pollution abatement sector. He estimated pollution coefficients. He related tons of pollutants to some unit of value of industrial output. According to Leontief, the system can be easily extended to cover the relationship between the net output of pollutants on one hand and public health and corresponding demand for health care on the other. The cost of elimination of pollutants originating in various sectors can be paid for either directly by the final users or by the producing sectors in which they are being generated. The paper elaborates the various cost and pricing related issues of environment in input output framework.

B.P. Chandramohan has further extended the environmental dimension of Leontief formalism by taking the example of emissions. Every economic activity has pollution as its by-product or undesired output. Often the link between the undesired by-products and the physical relationships that govern the day-to-day economic activities is unnoticed. The technical interdependence between the desirable and undesirable outputs can be described in terms of structural coefficients. The paper shows how the externalities can be incorporated into the conventional input-output analysis which yields results to some questions raised by undesirable environmental effects of the competing economies.

The excess growth of tertiary sector coupled with state-of-the-art technology has got its own implications for the future development patterns of the system. Inderjeet Singh, Parmod Kumar and Anju Bansal trace the service sector dynamics in India using the Leontief framework. In India, the share of tertiary sector in the gross domestic product has crossed the fifty percent mark. The nature and role of this excessive tertiarization has become a matter of concern. The work is an attempt to analyze the structure, linkage pattern and dynamics of the tertiary sector growth in India and its implications for the future.

Leontief's one of the monumental contribution to economics was the Leontief Paradox. The Leontief paradox was the total reversal of Heckscher-Ohlin theory of international trade. Leontief paradox came into lime light in 1956 when Leontief used the 1947 input-output tables of the US economy. He again repeated the test in 1956 for US imports and exports data for the year 1951. Deepa Rawat and Shyam Sunder Singh Chauhan have worked on the relevance of Leontief Paradox in the modern international trade. The paper, after a detailed analysis, concludes that despite all the criticism and drawbacks of the Leontief paradox, the fact remains that it was a major study of its times, that questioned the static Heckscher-Ohlin theory and provided a different path for analyzing international trade with all its complexities.

The papers have been arranged according to themes. The book is expected to encourage discussion and research on the matter and will be useful for academia.

Often words are too weak to serve as a mode of expressing ones inner feelings, especially the sense of indebtedness and gratitude. We must place on record our sincerest gratitude to learned teacher, Dr. Shri Prakash, who gave the first lesson on Leontief Economics and motivated the first author for doctoral research on the same. Our sincerest thanks are to Indian Economic Association for giving us an opportunity to serve the association by editing this work.

DR. INDERJEET SINGH
DR. ANIL KUMAR THAKUR

List of Contributors

1. **Aditya Kumar Patra**, Lecturer in Economics, Kalinga Mahavidyalaya, G. Udayagiri, Orissa.
2. **Anju Bansal**, Lecturer in Economics, Baba Farid College, Deon (Bhatinda), Punjab.
3. **Arpita Dhar**, Economics Department, Jadavpur University, Kolkata, W. Bengal.
4. **B.P. Chandramohan**, Reader, Economics Department, Presidency College, Chennai.
5. **Brinda Balakrishnan**, Research Scholar, Birla Institute of Management Technology, Greater Noida, UP.
6. **Biswajit Chatterjee**, Professor of Economics, Jadavpur University, Kolkata, West Bengal.
7. **Debesh Chakraborty**, Professor of Economics, Jadavpur University, Kolkata, West Bengal.
8. **Deepa Rawat**, Reader, Economics Department, Agra College, Agra.
9. **Inderjeet Singh**, Professor of Economics, Punjabi University, Patiala, Punjab.
10. **M. Saravanakumar**, Research Scholar, Economics Department, Bharathiar University, Coimbatore.
11. **Paramita Dasgupta**, Economics Department, Ananda Chandra College, Jalpaiguri.
12. **Parmod Kumar**, Lecturer, Economics Department, Punjabi University, Patiala.

13. **Partha Pratim Ghosh**, Economics Department, St. Xavier College, Kolkta.
14. **Pushpa Ranade**, Lecturer, Siddhivinayak Arts and Commerce College, Pune.
15. **R. Hemalatha,** Center Head, ICFAI National College, Faridabad, Haryana.
16. **Ram Pratap Sinha,** Assistant Professor, Economics Department, A.B.N. Seal (Govt.) College, Coochbehar.
17. **Reena Singh**, Reader, Economics Department, M.M.H. College, Ghaziabad UP.
18. **Shalini Sharma,** Assistant Professor, IILM Academy of Higher Leraning, Greater Noida.
19. **Shri Prakash**, Dean (Research) and Editor, Business Perspectives, Birla Institute of Management Technology, Greater Noida.
20. **Shyam Sunder Singh Chauhan**, Head, Economics Department, Govt. Girls (PG) College, Sirsaganj, Firozabad, U.P.
21. **V. Anbumani**, Reader, Economics Department, Bharathiar University, Coimbatore.
22. **Vijay S. Sathe**, Former Principal and HOD, S.B. City Collage, Nagpur.

SECTION I

LEONTIEF ECONOMICS

Leontief's Input-Output Economics in Retrospect

SHRI PRAKASH

INTRODUCTION

Leontief ranks among the greatest economists of all times. Award of Nobel Prize was the recognition of his lasting contribution to Economic Theory. Leontief's greatness is manifested by his (i) Creativity and originality culminating in the invention of input-output economics, concepts, theories and methods; (ii) Influence and leads to others for further research in the area, and (iii) Empirical applications (Prakash, 2003, Prakash and Sharma, 2005). This survey attempts to recapitulate the broad features of Leontief's Input-Output Economics.

CONTEXT OF INPUT-OUTPUT ECONOMICS

The depression, technological and institutional development made both classical and neo classical theories and their assumptions woefully irrelevant after First War (Prakash, 1984).

German Historical School challenged the universality of theory and its relevance to reality. List rejected the generality of policy and highlighted even the need for economic laws/policies in tune with space-time. Veblen explained facts in terms of institutional framework. But none offered meaningful results. Empirical analysis showed no general tendency/proposition and remained descriptive. Similarly, 'Statistical Economists' generated volumes of data without endowing these with meaning. They neither could raise explanation/understanding of the observed phenomena nor did they match theory with empirics.

End of Marginalist Approach

As Mathur (1969, p. 2) points out 'main economic questions of marginal character susceptible to partial analysis with ceteris paribus has been destroyed'. Assumptions of Neo-classical Economics of Menger, Bohmbawerk, Walras, Wicksteed, Wicksell, Jevons, Cournot and Marshall became tenuous after First War. Keynes filled up some gaps left by supply side economics. Still theories could not explain empirical reality and many facts had no underlying theory. This left boxes of empiricism empty without theoretical contents and theoretical, boxes empty without facts. Leontief (1953) highlights this chasm between theory and reality and gap between data and methods of classification and analysis thus "why is it that despite such prodigious accumulation of building material the edifice which we are supposed to be erecting still seems to be in a stage of preliminary excavations. Some tell us that all we have to do is to hand in some more bricks and mortar. Is it possible that what is needed even more is a workable working procedure? Without giving them any detailed specifications, how can one expect our suppliers to deliver materials which will actually fit together?" Leontief's model filled up empty boxes of theory with empiricism and theoretically empty boxes of empiricism with a unique theory, novel data classification technique and innovative method (Cf. Mathur, 1969).

Leontief fused sectoral inter-dependence organically into theory, theory into empirics and method into data. This made input-output analysis tremendously popular among economists, planners and policy-makers across the globe. Leontief, in fact, ignited a revolution in economists' approach to theory and empirical analysis to make economics an empirical science. He developed a powerful method of determining the solution of General Equilibrium Model to capture both visible and invisible and direct and indirect effects of change. No other theory or method could achieve this.

PRECEDENTS AND INTERPRETATIONS OF INPUT-OUTPUT MODEL

We consider hereunder interpretations of so-called fore-runners of Leontief's model.

Quesnay's Model

Francois Quesney's *Tableu Economique* is the first economy wide general equilibrium model. The model focuses on inter-dependence of three economic agents and their operations. Natural sector supplies land. Landowners are the rentier class. Farmers' Agriculture produce (food and raw materials), Craftsmen's/artisans'/industrialists' manufactured goods, made from raw (agro) materials and their money values enter into 'stationary circular flows in the economy' which are conceived being similar to the 'flow of blood through human body' (Harvey, 1578-1657). It is an open triple sector static model, crudely approximating input-output type model. As against application of Leontief's model to real economies, Physiocrats illustrated their model with fictitious data, embodying analysis of fragile inter-group inter-relations. It has no theoretical, methodological and empirical resemblance to Leontief's model.[1] It may be a pretender to be general equilibrium model.

Marxian/Material Balance Model and Leontief

Material Balance Approach, evolved through Trial and Error for Consistency Planning, is cited as a crude version of Leontief's model. According to Mathur, "In the Soviet Union economists were struggling to quantify the socially necessary labours" for production of each commodity and 'Marxian scheme describing the inter-relations between capital and consumer goods industries'. The first 'required tracing of labour contents of both capital and current inputs backwards and the latter was a classification of demand according to use, while they were devising process of commodity classification'. But they failed 'to achieve either of their objective' (1969). We slightly differ from Mathur. During his association with Gosplan Authority, Leontief might have noted: (i) Want of scientific method and Ad-hocism underlying MBA; and (ii) Its sterility due to want of theoretical base. These facets might have prompted him to invent input-output economics. MBA used commonsense logic and pragmatism for exhaustive data collection, classification, reconciliation of facts and testing consistency among output targets and available supplies to avoid bottlenecks/surpluses so as to conform to commodity balances.[2] It stands no comparison with Leontief's Model that embodies a general theory, encompasses a scientific method, theoretical and conceptual schemata of aggregation and enormous empirical applications.

Walras Model and Leontief

Walras Hicks-Pareto General Equilibrium Model is much closer to Leontief's model than Quesnay's and Marxian/MBA models. Leon Walras envisaged the economy as a whirlpool of interdependencies on which he based his General Equilibrium Model. He determined quantities and prices in terms of *a Numerari.*

Pareto-Wald-Cassel-Hicks extended Walras' Model, which could not be applied to real economies due to following factors: Marginal analysis required the use of differentiation for optimization, which imposed twin conditions of continuity and double differentiability of variables. Economic variables are discrete which change catastrophically in chaotic manner, making marginal conditions un-observable. Then, no practical procedure was evolved to determine marginal coefficients empirically. Economy-wide data for consumption/production, prices were not available. Focus on inter-firm and inter-personal relations accentuated the difficulty further. During Walras' time, profession was dominated by economists not knowing mathematics to understand his model. Such difficulties discouraged empirical application. Since applications of Walrasian model had not been attempted, there was no demand for data. Then, no computational devices had been developed till then. The want of empirical applications made his work appear to the contemporaries as a Magic Castle of Magnificent Grandeur and Splendour, erected on Sand Dunes having no practical relevance (Prakash, 1983).

But enormity of Walarsian contribution to economics made Schumpeter calls it the *'Magna Carta of Economics'*.

Walrasian general equilibrium model was over-shadowed by Marshall's Partial Equilibrium Analysis. Mathur describes Marshall's *'Principles of Economics'* as *'Magnus Opus'*. Marshall's analytics were considered both empirically manageable and relevant. Leontief's Economics has, however, now been in currency for nearly six and a half decades.

Still some economists consider Leontief's model to have used the theoretical framework of Walras-Pareto Model. But Leontief developed more aggregative, theoretical, methodological and empirical model different from model of Walras. The view that 'Leontief's attempt was indeed to render the Walrasian system, which had a remote majesty but was empirically unworkable, to manageable proportions by constructing a model of inter-industrial' interdependence' (Bharadwaj, 1969) is difficult to accept. This is a limited view of Leontief's contribution. It reduces Leontief's model to a special case of Walras model. Alternatively, it becomes a modified version of Walrasian model to make it empirically implemental. This glosses over the novelty of method of determining solution, differential theoretical paradigms, and vast empirical applications.

Keynes in Input-Output Framework

This interpretation may prompt one to interpret Leonteif's model as a modified version of Keynes' model of interdependence of consumption, investment and income. Treatment of these variables as representing one sector each will transform Keynes' model into a Leontief type three sector open/closed model. Assumption of constancy of average propensity to consume coupled with treatment of investment exogenously will make Keynes' model an open model. If both consumption and investment are treated endogenously with income, having constant consumption and investment coefficients, model shall be similar to closed model. Conversion of Keynes' model into input-output framework will highlight the synthesis of joint and separate working of Multiplier and Accelerator Principles (Prakash and Chowdhury, 1993).

COMPARATIVE EVALUATION

These interpretations do not tally with the context, rationale and contents of Leontief's model. Unlike Walras, Leontief filled up the gap between theory and facts and offered an empirically Computable General Equilibrium model, backed by a powerful method.

Walras' general equilibrium model's theoretical focus on inter-firm inter-personal dependencies is more micro than macro and it could not be empirically implemented. Marxian/MBA model ended up with the accumulation and classification of massive data without theory. Physiocratic model focused on highly aggregative three-fold inter-sector and inter-group flows of goods and money on the basis of exogenously determined agriculture output. It was only slightly more disaggregate than two sector Marxian model and classical single sector models of growth. Physiocrats relied on hypothetical data for illustrating their theory. This made Leontief to observe (1953, p. 9), "The concentration of theories without facts, on the one side, has for long time been confronted by a parallel accumulation of facts without theories, on the other" (pp. 1-2). Chasm between theory and facts makes him exclaim 'One hundred and fifty years ago, when Quesnay first published his famous scheme, his contemporaries and disciples acclaimed it as the greatest discovery since Newton's Laws. The idea of general inter-dependence among the various parts of economic system has become by now the very foundation of economic analysis. Yet when it comes to the practical application of this theoretical tool, modern economist must rely, exactly as Quesnay did, upon fictitious numerical examples'. It may be added that theoretical speculations enhanced the empirical vacuum further and empirical investigations brought more data for classification and accumulation without addition to theory, further widening the gulf (Cf. Mathur, 1969).

Leontief's model is more detailed than Marxian-Physiocratic models but much less detailed than Walrasian model. Physiocratic and Walrasian models use hypothetical numerical figures for illustration; Leontief's model is applied to real economies. Conceptually, input-output analysis can accommodate any level of details and number of sectors.

Quesnay-Walras-Pareto theory of an Inter-dependent multisectoral economy describes 'a Static General Equilibrium' relating to a state that can exist only if the 'effects of all economic forces have already been worked out' and such 'values of mutually related variables' have been determined which 'have no inherent tendency to change'. Such a motionless economy does not exist in real life. This difficulty is theoretical as distinct from data and computational difficulties. But Leontierf's theory relates to 'an inter-dependent multi-sectoral economy, operating under specific laws, that govern its responses to any induced or actual change observed at the given instant'. 'Such an economy has no time to alter its fixed coefficients so as to rule out any observed change in data leading to the activation of substitution process in the short-run (Mathur, 1969, p. 4). To use J.K. Mehta's notion, 'it is a snap shot picture with a video camera of an economy in motion at a given instant.

Process/Factor Substitutability

Leontief has often been criticized for excluding factor substitution possibility from his model. Leontief (1953, p. 39) explains that a 'large number of phenomena, which in economic discussions are referred to as instances of factor substitution, prove upon closer examination to conceal the non-homogenous character of the conventional industrial classification'. Besides, once the choice of techniques of production has been exercised, factor proportions become fixed until the technology is changed. Rationality requires the choice of the best technology relative to resource constraints and other limitations (Cf. Dorfman *et. al.*, 1962).

Assumptions and Basic Features

Leontief's focus on inter-sector/industry inter-dependence drastically reduced the unknowns and equations of the Walrasian model. But the number and nature of sectoral division of economy depends on data limitations, problems of aggregation, purpose of study and computational facility.

Methodological Innovation

Determination of gross output in terms of given final demand vector through matrix inversion simplified the methodological problem. Leontief makes an innovative use of Vector and Matrix Algebra, eliminating limitations of differential calculus and associated assumptions of continuity and double differentiability. It also moves the analysis away from marginal analysis and can be worked out easily from actual data.[3] 'At the outset of the 1930s study of multi-sectoral production itself suggested to Wassily Leontief a most 'beautiful, simple and powerful use of matrix algebra, which was thus brought into economics at the same moment as it was brought (By MaxBorn) into quantum physics'. 'Leontief by expression of the genetic tree of inter-industry production as a matrix equipped it at once with the whole armoury of manipulation, which constitute the matrix algebra. His input-output analysis fuses theoretical clarity, mathematical manipulation and statistical fact into a tool of great beauty and practical power, one of the most impressive that economists have ever offered to the statesman, and to already in world use. It is the paradigm of genuine and worthwhile econometrics' (Shackle, G.L.S.).

Synthesis of Theory and Empirical Applications

Leontief's (1953) synthesis of theorizing, both explicit and implicit, and statistical data collection, measurement and classification provided the means by which 'statistical data collected fill in the 'empty boxes' of the theory. Hypothetical production and consumption equations gain explicit meaning as soon as the symbolic algebraic signs are replaced by observed numerical values. Once an empirical foundation is thus established, the value generalities of abstract theoretical, statements will acquire concrete empirical significance (Mathur, 1965).

He assumed that production takes place under Constant Returns to Scale with invariant input proportions, that is, 'Fixed Technical Coefficients of Production'. He also ruled out the possibility of joint production, making every sector correspond to one single homogeneous good and each good to one industry only. He excluded the possibility of factor substitution. But Leontief did not use the Walarasian assumption of limited factor/ input supplies. He assumed labour as the only exogenously given primary factor. This left the scope for treating capital accumulation endogenously, while labour is kept outside in the open dynamic model.

Sectoral aggregation makes it feasible to determine specific variables' endogenously from a single point observation(s). In the static 'open and dynamic models', matrix equation has one degree of freedom, which facilitates a unique mathematical and empirical solution in terms of Leontief Inverse for given final demand.

He distinguishes intermediate from final demand. From accounting point of view, output is exhausted between final and intermediate uses. Each component of demand may be specified as a separate vector. Intermediate demand is represented by a square n × n matrix; n depends on (a) purpose of study, (b) availability of data, (c) computational facility, and (d) approximation of assumption of one to one correspondence between industry and product. Sub-vectors of final demand determine the dimension of dependence of output on the given component. Within the simplifying assumptions, Hawkin-Simon conditions are formally stated for solution of Static Model. The stability and uniqueness depend upon the invariance of technology and given demand. The solution of Leontief's Closed Model depends on Solow-Brauer conditions. For solution of Leontief's Dynamic Model, Mathur (1967) used Perron-Frobinius Theorem to show the existence of at least one positive Frobinius root with the reciprocal of the least positive root corresponding to the maximal growth of output. Positivity of X, A and F, rules out both trivial and meaningless solutions. Input-Output model ensures compatibility between gross output, fixed input coefficients and final demand (Prakash, 1992). Unlike 'Physiocritic inter-sector-inter-group and Marxian labour-capital interdependence' being rooted in natural and socio-economic forces, Leontief's interdependence is technology determined. The input coefficients define the forward and backward linkages.

OPEN STATIC MODEL

The model in matrix form may briefly be recapitulated as follows:

$$X = (I-A)^{-1} F \tag{1}$$

and

$$X_o = A_o X = A_o (I-A)^{-1} F \quad (2)$$

where A is matrix of technical coefficients of production, a_{ij}: $A = (a_{ij})$, X is column vector of outputs, F is vector of final demand, $(I-A)^{-1}$ is Leontief Inverse, A_o is row vector of labour coefficients, and X_o is total labour required, where subscript o denotes labour/household sector.

Equation 2 may be re-specified as follows: X_0 is column vector of employment of labour, and A_0 is diagonal matrix of labour coefficients. Obviously, $A_0(I-A)^{-1}$ furnishes estimates of direct and indirect requirements of labour per unit of final demand. No element of Leontief inverse can be negative, since $(I-A)^{-1} = I + A + A^2 + \ldots,$

Matrix A has all non-negative elements and I is an identity matrix. Thus, inter-industry demand, AX for sectoral/commodity production is distinguished into n elements. F may be expressed as an identity:

$$F = C + G + I + E \quad (3)$$

where, C, G, I, and E are vectors of consumption, government expenditure, investment and exports net of imports. Each term of 3 is a column vector.

CLOSED STATIC MODEL

The closed model determines short run effect of policy or impact of change in any variable/value within the system upon the non-changing components of rest of the economy at that instant. This makes closed model similar to Marshallian partial model: 'While Marshall's *centeris paribus* probably implied the constancy of all other economic variables, in this formulation it confines itself only to all other economic relations (coefficients), while quantities and prices of all the commodities are allowed to adjust to the situation' (Mathur, 1969, p. 6). Closed model focuses on 'structural change in a given industry, and in ones which are directly affected by it so as to introduce them in the coefficients of input-output model'. For a closed economy, shut off to all outside transactions, households are conceived to produce service called 'labour'. Consumption is perceived as commodity inputs into household sector's non-technological process yielding labour as output. Abstracting from all elements, except C, equation 1 may be reformulated as follows:

$$\hat{X} - \hat{A}\hat{X} = 0 \tag{4}$$

where $\hat{X}$ is an augmented gross output vector, having X_0 units of labour as n + 1th element, and A is n + 1 × n + 1 augmented A matrix, n + 1th row consists of sector wise labour coefficients, a_{oi}, i =1, . . . n, and n + 1th column comprises of a_{io}, average consumption of i per unit of gross output of labour.

Consumption coefficients are fixed since consumption changes if income will change. Household income rises only when production/productivity increase. But production/productivity, and hence, labour coefficients do not change in the instant/short run. Uniform wage rate in all sectors implies similar consumption pattern for all wage earners producing homogenous labour. But it the marginal rather than average fixed coefficients, since marginal and average values are equal in equilibrium.

MARXIAN MODEL IN INPUT-OUTPUT FRAMEWORK

What Marxists failed to achieve could be realized through Leontief's model. Modified equation 4 gives an estimate of labour contents of current inter-industry demand. Assuming constant labour coefficients for all output components, labour and output vectors are decomposed as follows:

$$X_o = X_o^1 + X_o^2 \tag{5}$$

$$X = X^1 + X^2 \tag{6}$$

X^1_0 is labour output for $X^1 \simeq F$; and X^2_0, for $X^2 \simeq AX$:

$$X_o^2 = A_o X^2 = A_o AX = A_o A (I-A)^{-1} F \tag{7}$$

X_0^2 may be an over estimate due to double counting of indirect component of intermediate inputs used for final demand. Consideration of unit level operation will eliminate it. Thus, relation 7 is an approximation. Labour requirements of capital are determined similarly:

$$X^3_o B = A_o (I\text{-}A)^{-1} B \qquad (8)$$

When super-script 3 denotes labour required for producing all capital goods at unit level, A_o is row vector of labour coefficients and B is column vector of capital coefficients: $b_j = \Sigma_i b_{ij}$.
where b_{ij} is ith good needed as capital for one unit of jth good.

DYNAMIC MODEL

Stock matrix is incorporated in the structural equation and final demand in the dynamic model is net of investment. Current output is assumed to be at full capacity. Hence, investment relates to additional output:

$$X = (I\text{-}A\text{-}GB)^{-1} C \qquad (9)$$

where $\Delta X = GX$, G is diagonal matrix of sectoral growth rates, B is stock matrix and C is final demand.

LEONTIEF'S DUAL (PRICE) MODEL

Dual of Leontief's Primal Model deals with prices. In real part of the economy, final demand depends on prices and incomes (value added). For eliminating circularity, final demand is determined exogenously. In the monetary part, wages and profits approximate administered prices that affects commodity prices. Forces that govern value-added, are therefore, treated exogenously. Prices are determined within the model in terms of given value-added vector. Leontief has explained the relationship between sectoral value-added and prices, "as a practical problem in a 'comparative instantaneous analysis', this is the utmost we can go" (Mathur, 1969, p. 9).

In classical model used by Mathur, value-added comprises of wages and profits/interest whose rates are equalized in the economy in long-run equilibrium. Mathur's Price Model for input-output system conforms to these conditions (1965). These prices are 'Shadow/Accounting Prices'. Andras Brody and Morishima propounded different price theories. Morishima assumes value added to consist of Wages, Interest and Profits at uniform rates for all sectors.

Dynamic Price Model shall be

$$P = WA_0 (I - A - rB)^{-1} \tag{10}$$

where, W and r are uniform wage and interest rates. The Classical economists recognized only labour and capital as factors of production.

DIVERSE FIELDS OF APPLICATIONS

World wide continuous use of Leontief's models in increasing number of fields and countries enriched input-output economics.

Input-Output Tables

Initially, lot of time, labour and money were devoted by individual researchers to construct input-output tables which were not available. Leontief compiled 8×8 input-output table for US and performed calculations on desk computer. The government agencies have now constructed input-output tables for almost all countries.

Foreign Trade

Leontief used his model to empirically test the prediction of Hescher-Ohlin theorem of foreign trade. Leontief's (1953) analysis of external trade ended up with *'Leontief Paradox'*. He found that US was importing capital intensive and exporting labour intensive goods. This runs counter to the prediction of Hescher-Ohlin theorem that the foreign trade of countries should be in conformity with their factor endowments. Capital abundant countries should export capital intensive goods. To resolve the paradox Leontief used normalised units for estimating labour contents of trade. Productivity was used for Normalisation.

It may be added that Leontief's contribution is not confined only to Leontief paradox. His most important and incisive contribution to this filed is (i) his demonstration that Hescher-Ohlin theory is empirically testable; (ii) he thoroughly transformed the two country-two commodity Hescher-Ohlin model into a multi-country, multi-commodity computable model, and (iii) Model was extended to analyse inter-country interdependence also.

It may however be noted that the productivity is the resultant of the configuration of operations multiple factors. Investment in R&D, R&D manpower and the technology they develop is only one factor. Investment in health and education is another. Whereas, investment in health, education, and training and R&D manpower leads to human capital augmentation, investment in research and development and resultant development of technology is labour displacing but resource productive augmenting. All these factors result in increased resource productivity. Leontief had attempted to take these into account in the process of resolving his own paradoxical findings.

It may however be noted that labour and capital are not the only productive resources of a country. Natural resources are equally imported. Human capital, comprising of health, knowledge and skills, as distinct from labour directly affect production and productivity. K.N. Prasad (1969) endogenised natural resources in his foreign trade model but he found that the estimated pattern of trade did not support Leontief paradox. Bhardwaj and Bhagwati (1969) endogenized human capital, but they also discovered that the pattern of Indian exports conformed to the prediction of Hescher-Ohlin theorem.

For evaluating empirical relevance of either Leontief Paradox or Hescher-Ohlin theorem in modern economies of 21st century, the following have to be kept in view in order to make suitable adjustments:

(i) Assumptions of immobility and hence no tradability of land, labour and technology does not hold true. Hence, the backward technology can be up-graded by technology imports and capital/labour scarcity can be overcome through imports in order to bring factor endowment on power.

(ii) Advance managerial techniques and organizational decision making are also imported when MNCs set house in developing countries, so even soft technology endowment of countries also tend to converge in long-run.

(iii) Re-exports for gaining value addition through further processing reflects differential factor requirement than those associated with the rest of activities. This may probability been put forward and an explanation of high import intensity of Indian exports.

(iv) Market demand and urgency of foreign exchange requirements may often force developing countries to exports goods the production of which may not be inconformity with their factor requirements.

Regional Analysis

Input-output models have been applied to Theories of Regional Development, Location and Transport. Results of Leontief's Regional Input Output Model fell short of expectations even for short-run analysis. Leontief-Strout Gravity Model furnished better results. Mathur applied modified Leontief-Strout Gravity Model to analyse benefits of regional cooperation (1979).

Dynamic Inverse

Dynamic Inverse represents theoretical and empirical advance through its backward and forward for planning, growth and forecasting. 'So at last the core of the notions of 'productive advance' of F. Quesnay, 'expanded reproduction' of Marx and 'roundabout production' of Bohm-Bawberk has got a measurable content' (Mathur, 1969). We may add that this provides base for examining (i) Prebish-Singer-Myrdal Balanced Growth Theory, and (ii) Dynamic Dual Hirshmanian Static Unbalanced Growth Theory. Residentiary Linkage effect of both consumption multiplier and investment accelerator (Prakash, 1992) is another off-shoot. Consequences of accumulation of capital of specific technological complex could now be analyzed meaningfully. Modified specification leads to the derivation of Leontief-Von Neuman trajectories.

Output Price Forecasting Model

Models of Forecasting of output and prices have now been developed for numerous countries. This has involved development of demand forecasting models as well.

Human Resource and Human Capital

The role and contribution of human capital in development have also been studied that have resulted in the evolving of highly specialized matrices (See Tinbergen & Correa, 1965, Richard Stone, 1967, Prakash, 1976).

CONCLUSION

In our view, Leontief's invention of input output economics has been more Revolutionary even than the 'Keynesian Revolution'. It is theoretically more comprehensive, exhaustive, empirically implementable and logically persuasive than Marshall's *Magnus Opus,* Marshallian partial equilibrium model may be treated as a special case of Leontief's general equilibrium model. It is more empirical than empirical econometrics. It matches mathematical-theoretical rigor of Cournot-Jevons-Walras' Mathematical Economics. Leontief's contribution is comparable to that of Smith-Ricardo-Mill of classical school, Menger-Bohmbawerk-Wicksel-Wicksteed of Austrian School, Cournot-Walras-Jevons-Parteto-Hicks of utility and general equilibrium schools. This survey highlights input output as a sea of confluence of different strands of theory and diverse streams of thought. If the replacement of many by one general theory and numerous by single method is taken as criterion of scientific development, then Leontief's Input Output Economics stands as an outstanding among the contributions of several generations of economists. His contribution may be comparable to Einstein's Theory of Relativity.

NOTES

1. For presentation of Quesnay's Tableu in Input Output Framework, See Prakash, 1983.
2. This view is in contrast to Mathur's postulation that 'in the Soviet Union economists were struggling with a revolutionary zeal to quantify the "Socially Necessary Labour" for production of each commodity and the Marxian scheme describing the inter relations between capital and consumer goods industries. They could achieve neither. They stumbled upon yet another way of arranging data called Material Balances' (p. 2, 1969). In our view, the Soviet economists used the material balances as the base of reconciliation of actual output to targets

and inputs required for their production so as to remain within the realm of consistency.

3. This also promoted the use of difference rather than differential equations which, several times, were employed in conjunction with linear algebra.

REFERENCES

Bharadwaj, R. (1969), "Methodological Survey of the Application of Input Output In Developing Countries", In Mathur and Venkatramaina, P. (Eds.) *Economic Analysis in Input-Output Framework,* Vol. II, Input Output Research Association.

Chennery, H.B. (1954) "Interregional and International Input-Output Analysis. In Barna, Tibor", (Ed.), *The Structural Interdependence of the Economy,* John Wiley, New York.

Dorfman, R., Solow, R.M. and Samuelson, P.A. (1958), *Linear Programming and Economic Analysis,* New York.

Hicks, J.R. (1939), *Value and Capital,* Cheap Edition.

Leontief, W.W. (1953), *The Structure of American Economy,* 1919-39, Oxford.

Leontief, W.W. and Strout, A. (1963), "Multiregional Input-Output Analysis", In Barna, Tibor (Ed.) *Structural Interdependence and Economic Development.*

Leontief, W.W., *Input-Output Relations,* In Netherlands Economic Institute (Editor).

Mathur, P.N. (1969), "Input-Output Framework for Explorations in Theoretical and Empirical Research", In Mathur, P.N. and Venkatramaina, P. (Eds.) *Economic Analysis in Input-Output Framework,* Vol. II, Input-Output Research Association.

Mathur, P.N. (1965), "A Modified Leontief Dynamic Model and Related Price System", *Econometric Annual of Indian Economic Journal.*

Mehta, J.K. (1959), *Studies in Advanced Economic Theory,* S. Chand & Co., Delhi.

Morishima, M. (1958), "Prices Interest and Profits in Dynamic Leontief System", *Econometrica,* XXVI.

Prakash, S. (1983), *Historical Evolution of Quantitative Economcis,* UGC Workshop on Development of Model Course Structure, Mysore Universwity, Mysore.

Prakash, S. (2003), *Originality and Social Science Research,* Mimeographed, BIMTECH, Greater Noida.

Prakash, S. (1984), *Leontief's Static and Dynamic Models—Some Experiments,* Working Paper, Economics Department, NEHU, Shillogn.

Prakash, S. and Chowdhury, Sumitra (1993), "Consumption of Forest Produce and Deforestation in India", *The Journal of Quantitative Economics.*

Prakash, S. (1992), "Dynamic Backward and Forward Linkages As the Base of Convergence of Unbalanced to Balanced Growth", *International Journal of Development Planning Review*, Vol. VI.

Prakash, S. and Sharma, Shalini (2005), "Intellectual Property Rights: Conceptual and Theoretical Paradigms", *Business Perspectives*, Vol. 6, No. 1.

Shackle, G.L.S., *The Years of High Theory*, pp. (7-9).

Wonacot and Wonacot, *Canadian-American Economic Interdependence*.

Professor Wassily W. Leontief: Life and Works

INDERJEET SINGH AND REENA SINGH

INTRODUCTION

"We are what we repeatedly do. Excellence then, is not an act, but a habit", said Aristotle. Professor Wassily W. Leontief was both a theorist and an empiricist *par excellence*. He produced excellent pieces of work as a habit. Although he worked in many diverse areas of economics, there is a common thread into all his works, and that is his passion for general equilibrium. Although he is mainly known for input-output analysis, he has also made very fundamental contributions in pure theory of economics. He wrote on diverse subjects like environment, population growth, automation, defence and so on. He wrote in his nineties also. It is not a comfortable job to classify his contributions and place them into neat boxes. The paper is an attempt to put his life-time works briefly in a simplest possible way.

BIOGRAPHY

Professor Wassily W. Leontief was born into an academic family on August 5, 1905 in St. Petersburg in Russia. His father was a Professor of Economics in the University of St. Petersburg. His daughter Svetlana Alpers is now an Emeritus Professor of Art History at the University of California at Berkeley. He studied economics, philosophy and sociology at the University of St. Petersburg during 1921 to 1925, and received the degree of Learned Economics in 1925. Being a *Menshevik* (non-communist socialist) and vocal in his criticism of the new regime in Russia, he spent some time in prison during his student years (Lahiri, 2000). Soon after doing his first degree he left Soviet Union and went to University of Berlin, the then centre of academic excellence. For his doctoral dissertation he worked under supervision of Werner Sombart and Laidslaus von Bortkiewicg on the topic, *"The Economy as a Circular Flow"*, and completed it in 1928. Leontief started his professional life at Institute of World Economics, University of Kiel, and started working on the derivation of statistical demand and supply curves. For two years (1929-30) he had been the advisor to the Ministry of Railroads in China. In 1931 he moved to National Bureau of Economic Research in New York and then in 1932 to Harvard University. His career in the universities of the U.S. reached its apex when Schumpeter invited him to Harvard University, where Leontief became the mathematical economist and a primary source of influence on neoclassical economists such as Paul Samuelson and Robert Solow (Baumol and Raa, 2002). He was married in 1932 to Estelle Marks, a poet. For a long time, he was the Director of the Harvard University Research Project until 1973 and then joined New York University in 1975 to set-up the Institute of Economic Analysis. The Nobel Prize in Economic Sciences was awarded to him in 1973. It followed a series honors: President of American Economic Association in 1970 and 1971; Honorary Fellow of Royal Statistical Society; Corresponding Fellow of the British Academy; Doctor of the University New York; Officer of the French Legion d' Honneur; and so on. He used to enjoy trout fishing. It is really remarkable that even in his nineties, he was writing in journals. In his last three months, he wrote an article with his former student of Harvard, Professor Robert Solow (Garifield, 1986). He breathed his last on 5 February, 1999.

WORKS OF LEONTIEF

Leontief was both a theorist and an empiricist *par excellence.* He produced excellent pieces of work as a habit (refer to appendix). He not only spanned the twentieth century, he was also one of its most creative economists. He was the first to put the concept of economic system being an aggregation of interrelated parts in which each part is system in itself. In this context, he emphasized that micro and macro-economics are different depictions of the same system, different part of which are studied in fields of specialization such as economic growth, spatial and environmental economics, and monetary economics. His work opened up entirely new and highly fruitful directions to the practitioners of economics discipline. His contributions are wider than input-output analysis. His representation of the economy as a complex system with many dimensions enables us to inter-relate all this, to unite pure theory with policy issues and to connect micro data with national statistics.

Although Leontief worked in many diverse areas of economics, there is a common thread to all his works, and that was his love for general equilibrium. It is not an easy job to classify his contributions and place them into neat boxes. Yet, it is possible roughly speak of three main interrelated types. *First,* there is, of course, the theory of input-output analysis, which is, in itself, a major leap forward from the work of the predecessors who led up to Leontief's analysis. *Secondly,* he was able to quantify the models with the aid of empirical data for an economy, enabling the model to serve as a guide to concrete policy decisions as well as contributing to pure understanding. *Thirdly,* Leontief took the applications far beyond that, sometimes in totally unexpected directions.

Leontief's Revolutionary Advance in Historical Perspective

Although, Leontief entirely by himself constructed an operational framework that is now used throughout the discipline and all over the world, his work fits in with that of a chain of predecessors. The chain of historicity runs right from Quesnay to

Marx to Bortkiewicz to Leontief. Leontief's work can be seen as a culmination of a sequence that runs from the beginning of a systematic economic literature to the end of twentieth century.

The relationship between Tableau and the input-output has been debated a lot in the economic literature (Phillips, 1955). And here there is a linkage considerably more continuous than is generally recognized. But Leontief has also repeatedly been linked with a much earlier contribution, the physiocratic *Tableau Economique* (1758-59), the work of that early economist Francois Quesnay. Quesnay was not the first to make it rather both William Petty and Bernard de Mandeville also contributed a lot in this development (Kuczynsky and Meek, 1972). The Tableau more or less disappeared from the economic literature half a century after Du Pont de Nemours left France for United States.

The Tableau was later rediscovered by Karl Marx when he characterized the Tableau as "incontestably the most brilliant idea of which political economy had hitherto been guilty." (Sweezy, 1942, p. 75). In fact, he translated the logic of the Tableau into his structure of "simple reproduction" under capitalism, and then used it in attempting to solve what he called "the transformation problem." He used the concept for derivation of the numerical relationships between his two concepts, value and surplus value, and the price and profit variables of standard economic analysis. Marx argued in Capital (Vol. III, Ch. IX) that his solution would have been imperfect and the task of providing the first fully defensible way of dealing with the problem was left to Laidslaus von Bortkiewics (1868-1931), a distinguished Polish mathematical statistician (Bortkiewicz, 1907).

In the historicity of events Bortkiewicz has relevance for two reasons. First, he gave the logic for solution for Marxian model of simple reproduction based on Quesnay's work. Secondly, he has been the Co-Advisor of Leontief in Post-graduate degree research thesis at Berlin. First Advisor admitted that he could not cope up with Leontief's mathematics (Baumol and Raa, 2002). Bortkiewicz, the teacher of Leontief at Berlin, linked him to the chain that started from the times of Quesnay. This is how the chain is completed from Quesnay to Marx to Bortkiewicz to Leontief. The story seems to be fascinating and one must not be mislead as it puts Leontief in the position of a writer who merely carried previous traditions one step further. Leontief's work was a revolutionary contribution and was a giant leap further, well beyond anything that the previous links in the historic chain had provided.

In the context of above historic roots of what Leontief added to the work was truly revolutionary. The work of Quesnay, Marx and Bortkiewicz had its limited and specified purpose, and none had any empirical connection. Quesnay used his table largely to support the view that manufacturing is a sterile activity and that only agriculture offers a surplus. Marx explicitly translated Quesnay's work into a static two-sector model. But the works of Leontief proved to be a system that is blend of theory, modeling rigour and wide array of applications.

Early Works on Pure Theory

Although Leontief is mainly known for input output analysis, he also made very fundamental contributions in pure theory of economics. When Leontief moved to Berlin, the then centre of academic excellence, for ten years he was a creator of valuable research papers in theory. A full decade (1925-35), he concentrated on research that had a rigour of theory and none of his work during this period dealt with input-output technique. This theoretical grinding helped Leontief to go deeper the discipline when the fast paced idea generation was in full swing. This was the time when world faced the hard realities of inter-war period and the great depression. It was the phase when the other economists of the century, J.M. Keynes and J.R. Hicks were in the process of completing their monumental works. Following is the brief review Leontief's works on the theoretical side.

In the national income theory, the problem of "double counting" was first raised by Leontief (1925) in connection with errors being done at Soviet Statistical Office. He argued that outputs are distributed between intermediate demand (industries) and final demand (such as households) and that only the latter should be included. This paper is considered the first input-output study, particularly by the Soviets after Stalin, when input-output analysis was no longer viewed as a 'bourgeois' tool.

As already said, that one of his first projects at the University of Kiel, in the late 1920s, was on the "derivation of statistical demand and supply curves." He was the one of the first, along with Elmer and Ragnar Frisch, to discuss the issue of simultaneous estimation of demand and supply curves and the problem of identification, etc. (Richmond, 1976).

In the year 1936, two major contributions of Leontief were again a milestone in economic theory relating to: (a) modern price index theory; and (b) dynamics and Keynes. Modern price index theory still makes use of his first contribution (Leontief, 1936a). His work on aggregation and index numbers has also had a lasting impact on the subject. This work lead to what is commonly known as the Leontief aggregation theorem, which provides a sufficient condition under which it is legitimate to aggregate over commodities in consumer preferences. This theorem has had many applications (Dixit and Norman, 1980). Modern macro-economics, with emphasis on dynamics, draws its origin from the Leontief's critique of Keynes (Leontief, 1936b). In this work he emphasized that Keynes underplayed the importance of the role of investment and that it should be viewed as a productive input and not just a component of demand.

As an innovator of "Separability Condition", he was motivated a lot by the production analysis. In this context, his deepest theoretical work, however deals with the structure of functional relationships. (Leontief, 1947). The economy is a system that transforms resources into final goods and services, in which he considered whether it is possible to distinguish stages of a production process. In other words, can distinct sectors of activity be identified? And, if so, what conditions should guide us in this process? Thus, he was also one of the early contributors to the theory of aggregation of production relations (Leontief, 1947). Although he never used the word like 'structural' or 'reduced form', yet he derived the condition under which one can identify structural mathematical relationships from a reduced-form one. There is a definite link between Leontief's work and the analysis of identification in econometrics (Richmond, 1976).

Further his most striking and unexpected application was that to international trade (1953), where "the Leontief paradox" has, for evident reasons, generated a huge theoretical and empirical literature seeking to shed light on the puzzling result and to draw out its implications for the field. Leontief was deeply interested in international trade. His empirical research on the pattern of trade in the United States led to the well known Leontief Paradox (Leontief, 1953). The paradox contradicts the Heckscher-

Ohlin prediction that a country abundant in a factor should export the good which uses the factor more intensively. Here lies the advancement over the predecessors. Over the predecessors Leontief's works offered anything like this degree of flexibility and rich diversity of application. Late the analysis was left open for others to find unexpected applications of the analysis, taking off still other and very different directions. This paradox had been a source of motivation for many researchers.

The roots of use of game theory in modern macro-economics again can be traced back to Leontief's model of wage bargaining (Leontief, 1946). Later in his life, he wrote on diverse subjects like environment, population growth, automation, defence, etc. His purely theoretical work continued much after the appearance of his first input-output study.

Static Input-Output Model

The closed input-output model was Leontief's breakthrough in relating general equilibrium theory to the data for an economy. The input-output matrix encompasses the data for all branches of the economy, including consumption coefficients. Leontief's closed model came as his first input-output study (Leontief, 1936c). As per this model, all outputs are also used as inputs. Industries produce commodities using commodities as well as factor inputs. Households produce these factor inputs using commodities. This, of course, is very much in the spirit of the contemporaneous work of Neumann (1945). Algebraically, it entails the following flow:

$$x_i = x_{i1} + x_{i2} + \ldots + x_{in} + y_i \ (i = 1, 2, \ldots, n),$$

where x_i and y_i are respectively the levels of production and final use of good i, n is the number of goods and x_{ij} is the amount of i required as intermediate input to produce x_j amount of good j. Here the basic assumption is that the input output coefficients ($a_{ij}=x_{ij}/x_j$) are constants. On the basis of this assumption, one can write the system in matrix notation as $\mathbf{x} = \mathbf{Ax} + \mathbf{y}$, where $\mathbf{x}$ and $\mathbf{y}$ are the vectors of production and final use and $\mathbf{A}$ is an $n \times n$ non-negative matrix, the Leontief matrix. The basic problem here is to find an output vector that solves the system for a given final demand. The solution is given by $\mathbf{x} = (\mathbf{I}-\mathbf{A})^{-1}\mathbf{y}$. Having obtained the output levels, one can compute the input requirements. Here the $(I-A)^{-1}$ is called Leontief inverse. Matrix **A** gives the direct and $(I-A)^{-1}$ gives the total input output coefficients.

Then the model was also used to analyze pricing. Assuming perfect competition, the zero-profit condition determines the prices as a row eigenvector of the matrix. The treatment of investment was a weak element in the closed model. Investment is represented in a manner similar to household consumption which can indeed be treated appropriately as an instantaneous activity. However, Neumann (1945) circumvented the problem by assuming balanced growth.

Dynamic Input-Output Model

Leontief originally started with a closed static system and then moved to an open system so as to meet the practical requirements of policy-making decisions. The open input-output model was probably the first attempt in dealing with a substantial set of simultaneous economic interrelationships, nothing like that had ever been done before. The open input-output model was launched in 1941 (Leontief, 1941) and studied in 1977 (Leontief, 1977). He allowed the investment part of the final use vector to be endogenous and distinguished between: investment in fixed capital and investments in working capital (or inventories).

In a simplest format, this formulation assumes that at any time t, unit expansion of capacity in a sector requires fixed amount of all commodities and that whole of these amounts are made available from the respective productions in the same time unit. Another assumption, here is that there is a full capacity utilization. Formally, it is assumed that the investment use of good i for the expansion of in sector j is given by:

$$b_{ij}\,[x_j(t+1) - x_j(t)],$$

where b_{ij} is a non-negative parameter. The total investment use of good i is for the expansion in sector j is given by:

$$\Sigma_{j=1...n} b_{ij}\ [x_j(t + 1) - x_j(t)],$$

and the dynamic input output model, in matrix notation, is given by:

$$\mathbf{x}\,(t) = \mathbf{A}\mathbf{x}\,(t) + \mathbf{B}\,[\mathbf{x}\,(t + 1) - \mathbf{x}\,(t)] + \mathbf{y}\,(t),$$

Where the final use vector **y** (t) is net of investment use and **B** is *nxn* capital coefficient matrix. Later several modified versions this model found substantial practical applications in development planning literature. The techniques have been applied to subjects as heterogeneous as international trade, economics of the environment, energy and productivity. Using the Leontief inverse, studies have gone much beyond the simple direct effects.

CONCLUSION

Economics discipline owes a great deal to Professor Wassily Leontief. He was pioneer, he is for Economics what is Einstein for Physics. His contributions are vast not only from the view point of his writings; rather his works influenced other economists. Being sketchy in our approach we have been able to highlight only a fraction of this vastness.

REFERENCES

Baumol, W.J. and Raa, T.T. (2002), "Wassily Leontief: In Applreciation", *Journal of Economic and Social Measurement*, 26. pp. 1-10.

Bortkiewicz, L. Von (1907), "On Correction of Marx's Fundamental Theoretical Construction in the Third Volume of Capital", in *Jahrbucher fur National oknomie and Statistik*, July, translated by Paul M. Sweezy in, *Karl Marx and the Close of his System*, New York: Augustus M. Kelley, 1949, pp. 199-221.

Dixit, A.K. and Norman, V. (1980), *Theory of International Trade*, Cambridge: Camridge University Press.

Garfield, E. (1986), "Wassily Leontief: Pioneer of Input-Output Analysis", *Current Contents*, Vol. 9, pp. 272-81.

Kuczynsky, M. and R.L. Meek (1972), *Quesnay's Tableau Economique*. London: Macmillan.

Lahiri, S. (2000), "Professor Wassily Leontief, 1905-1999", *The Economic Journal*, 110, Nov., pp. 695-707.

Leontief, W. (1925), "Die Bilanz der Russischen Volkswirtschaft – Eine methodologische Untersuchung", Weltwirtschaftliches Archiv 22, No. 2, 338-44. Later English translation: "The Balance of the Economy of the USSR", in *Foundations of Soviet Strategy for Economic Growth, Selected Short Soviet Essays*, 19024-1930, N. Spulber, ed., Indiana University Press, Bloomington, 1964, pp. 88-94.

Leontief, W. (1936a), "Composite Commodities and the Problem of Index Numbers", *Econometrica*, 4, No. 1, pp. 39-59.

—— (1936b), "The Fundamental Assumptions of Mr. Keynes' Monetry Theory of Unemployment", *Quarterly Journal of Economics*, 51, No. 1, 192-97.

—— (1936c), "Quantitative Input and Output Relations in the Economic System of the United States", *Review of Economics and Statistics*, 18, No. 3, pp. 105-25.

—— (1941), *The Structure of the American Economy*, 1919-29, Harvard University Press, Cambridge, 1941.

—— (1946), "The Pure Theory of the Guaranteed Annual Wage Contract", *Journal of Political Economy*, 54, No. 1, 76-69.

—— (1947), "A Note on the Interrelation of Subsets of Independent Variables of a Continuous Function with Continuous First Derivatives", *Bulletin of the American Mathematical Society*, 53, No. 4, pp. 343-50.

—— (1953), "Domestic Production and Foreign Trade: the American capital position re-examined", *Proceedings of American Philosophical Society*.

—— (1977), *The Future of the World Economy*, with A.P. Carter and P. Petri, 1977.

Neumann, J.V. (1945), "A Model of General Equilibrium", *Review of Economic Studies*, 13, No. 1, pp. 1-9.

Phillips, A. (1955), "The Tableau Economique as a Simple Leontief Model", *Quarterly Journal of Economics*, pp. 137-44.

Sweezy, P.M. (1942), *The Theory of Capitalist Development*, Oxford University Press, New York.

Richmond, J. (1976), "Aggregation and Identification", *International Economic Review*, Vol. 17, pp. 47-56.

APPENDIX

Major Works of Wassily W. Leontief

- "The Use of Indifference Curves in the Analysis of Foreign Trade", 1933, *QJE.*
- "Delayed Adjustment of Supply and Partial Equilibrium", 1934, *ZfN.*
- "The Fundamental Assumption of Mr. Keynes's Monetary Theory of Unemployment", 1936, *QJE.*
- "Composite Commodities and the Problem of Index Numbers", 1936, *Econometrica.*
- "Implicit Theorizing: a methodological criticism of the Neo-Cambridge School", 1937, *QJE.*
- "The Significance of Marxian Economics for Present-Day Economic Theory", 1938, *AER.*
- *The Structure of the American Economy, 1919-39,* 1941.
- "The Pure Theory of the Guaranteed Annual Wage Contract", 1946, *JPE.*
- "Introduction to a Theory of the Internal Structure of Functional Relationships", 1947, *Econometrica.*
- "Wages, Profits, Prices and Taxes", 1947, *Dun's Review.*
- "Postulates: Keynes's General Theory and the Classicists", 1947, in Harris, editor, *The New Economics.*
- "Note on the Pluralistic Interpretation of History and the Problem of Interdisciplinary Co-operation", 1948, *J. of Philosophy.*
- "Input-Output Economics", 1951, *Scientific American.*
- "Machines and Man", 1952, *Scientific American.*
- *Studies in the Structure of the American Economy,* 1953.
- "Domestic Production and Foreign Trade: the American capital position re-examined", 1953, *Proceedings of American Philosophical Society.*
- "Mathematics in Economics", 1954, *Bulletin of the AMS.*
- "Factor Proportions and the Structure of American Trade: Further theoretical and empirical analysis", 1956, *REStat.*
- "Theoretical Note on the Time-Preference, Productivity of Capital, Stagnation and Economic Growth", 1958, *AER.*
- "The Problem of Quality and Quantity in Economics", 1959, *Daedalus.*

- "The Rise and Decline of Soviet Economic Science", 1960, *Foreign Affairs.*
- "The Economic Effects of Disarmament", with M. Hoffenberg, 1961, *Scientific American.*
- "The Rates of Long Run Growth and Capital Transfer from Developed to Underdeveloped Areas", 1963, *Proceedings of Conference on Role of Econometric Analysis.*
- "Modern Techniques for Economic Planning and Projection", 1963, *Scuola in Azione.*
- "Multiregional Input-Output Analysis", with A. Strout, 1963, in Barna, editor, *Structural Intedependence.*
- "The Structure of Development", 1963, *Scientific American.*
- "When Should History be written Backwards?", 1963, *Economic History Review.*
- "Proposal for Better Economic Forecasting", 1964, *Harvard Business Review.*
- "On Assignment of Patent Rights on Inventions Made under Government Research Contracts", 1964, *Harvard Law Review.*
- "Input-Output Analysis", 1965, *Scientific American.*
- *Input-Output Economics,* 1966.
- *Essays in Economics: Theories and Theorizing,* 1966.
- *Essays in Economics,* 1966.
- "Theoretical Assumptions and Non-Observed Facts", 1971, *AER.*
- "Structure of World Production: Outline of a Simple Input-Output Formulation", 1974, *AER.*
- *The Future of the World Economy,* with A.P. Carter and P. Petri, 1977.
- *Military Spending,* with F. Duchin, 1983.
- *The Future Impact of Automation on Workers,* with F. Duchin, 1986.
- "Money-Flow Computations", with A. Brody, 1993, *Econ Systems Research.*

On Demand and Supply Driven Input-Output Models

BISWAJIT CHATTERJEE AND RAM PRATAP SINHA

INTRODUCTION

The input-output method is an adaptation of the neoclassical theory of general equilibrium to the empirical study of the quantitative interdependence between interrelated economic activities. The method was originally developed to analyze and measure the connection between the various producing and consuming sectors within a national economy. However, it has also been applied in the study of smaller economic systems and thus the method has greatly facilitated the study of regions within a national economy.

In input-output models, the interdependence between the individual sectors of the given system is described by a set of linear equations. The specific structural characteristics of an input-output model are reflected in the numerical magnitude of the coefficients of these equations which are determined empirically. Further, one needs to distinguish between the technical coefficients and the physical quantities of outputs and prices as being magnitudes which are given by the technique of production and those which are subject of economic analysis, i.e., magnitudes which are considered as given and those which are the unknowns of the system.

DEMAND AND SUPPLY DRIVEN INPUT-OUTPUT MODELS

One can identify at least two variants of the input-output framework. The conventional model is due to Leontief (1941, 1953) who emphasized on the demand driven input-output models. In a demand driven input-output model, the output of any particular sector of the economy depends on the demand generated by all the interconnected sectors and this, in turn, depends on the input (requirement) coefficients. Ghosh (1958), however, provided an alternative framework where the emphasis is on the allocation of given output to different demanding sectors. The objective of the present paper is to make a comparative discussion of the two alternative approaches to input-output modeling. The paper is divided into three sections. Section I discusses the Leontief Input-Output Model; Section II discusses the Ghosh Input-Output Model; and finally, Section III makes the concluding observations.

I. THE LEONTIEF INPUT-OUTPUT MODEL

We now consider the static open input-output model where the final demand is considered exogenous to the system. The model is based on the following assumptions:

(i) The hypothetical economy is divided into two broad sectors—the business sector comprising of (n–1) industries and the household sector. The household sector consumes the final output generated by the business sector and supplies labour services to the various industries.

(ii) The production function for the ith sector (i = 1, 2, . . . , n–1) in our n sector model can be represented in the generalized form:

$$X_i = f(X_{1i}, X_{2i}, \ldots, X_{ni})$$

where X_i is the output of the I-th industry. The possibility of joint product is eliminated in our model. Further, it is quite clear that the factors of production are combined in fixed proportions in our model. The technology exhibits constant returns to scale.

The Leontief Input-Output (Quantity) Model

General equilibrium in the static open (quantity) model requires that demand and supply be equal to each other in each of the (n–1) industries and the household sector. Thus the commodity balance equations are as under:

$$X_1 = X_{11} + X_{12} + X_{13} + \ldots + X_{1,n-1} + C_1 \qquad (1a)$$
$$X_2 = X_{21} + X_{22} + X_{23} + \ldots + X_{2,n-1} + C_2 \qquad (1b)$$

$$\ldots\ldots\ldots\ldots\ldots\ldots\ldots\ldots\ldots\ldots$$

$$X_{n-1} = X_{n-1,1} + X_{n-1,2} + X_{n-1,3} + \ldots + X_{n-1,n-1} + C_{n-1} \qquad (1, n-1)$$
$$X_L = X_{L1} + X_{L2} + \ldots + X_{L,n-1} + 0 \qquad (1, n)$$

We now define the technical coefficients as: $a_{ij} = X_{ij}$, where X_{ij} = industry i's output used by industry j.

We can now rewrite the commodity balance equations as:

$$X_1 = a_{11} X_1 + a_{12} X_2 + a_{13} X_3 + \ldots + a_{1,n-1} X_{n-1} + C_1 \qquad (2a)$$
$$X_2 = a_{21} X_1 + a_{22} X_2 + a_{23} X_3 + \ldots + a_{2,n-1} X_{n-1} + C_2 \qquad (2b)$$

$$\ldots\ldots\ldots\ldots\ldots\ldots\ldots\ldots\ldots\ldots$$

$$X_{n-1} = a_{n-1,1} X_1 + a_{n-1,2} X_2 + a_{n-1,3} X_3 + \ldots + a_{n-1,n-1} X_{n-1} + C_{n-1} \qquad (2, n-1)$$
$$X_L = a_{L1} X_1 + a_{L2} X_2 + \ldots + a_{L,n-1} X_{n-1} + 0 \qquad (2, n)$$

In the matrix form, we can write

$$X = AX + C \qquad (2)$$

where X is an output vector, C is a final demand vector and A is a matrix of technological coefficients.

The output vector can be determined in the following manner:

$X\,(I\text{-}A)^{-1} = C$

Or, $X = (I\text{-}A)^{-1}\,C$ (3)

The Necessary and Sufficient Conditions for Solution

(a) The Necessary Condition

In respect of an open input-output system, given the final demands for the outputs of the (n–1) sectors, it is possible to determine the output quantities in absolute terms provided $(I–A)^{-1}$ exists. This necessitates that (I–A) is a non-singular matrix i.e. determinant $(I–A) \neq 0$. This is the necessary condition for a solution to exist.

(b) The Sufficient Condition

For our solution to be economically meaningful, it is essential that the outputs of the various sectors are non-negative. Since the vector C is necessarily non-negative, this, in turn, requires that all the elements of (I–A) are non-negative. This can be ensured by imposing restrictions on the matrix A: that the matrix $(I–A)^{-1}$ is the special case of the matrix $(\lambda I–A)^{-1}$ in which $\lambda = 1$. Invoking the Perron-Frobenius Theorems[1] we can infer that the necessary and sufficient conditions for the non-negativity of all the elements of the matrix $(I–A)^{-1}$, and hence of all the components of X is that the maximum eigen value of A, α_m should be less than unity i.e. $\alpha_m < 1$...(5). Condition (5) implies that the technical properties of the economic system must be such that the system produces some commodity in addition to those needed for the replacement of the means of production.

The Leontief Quantity Model: Interpretation of Inverse Matrices and Multipliers

From the quantity equation

$$X_i = a_{i1}X_1 + a_{i2}X_2 + a_{i3}X_3 + \ldots + a_{i,n-1}X_{n-1} + C_i \qquad (2i)$$

We find that when output in sector j is increased by 1 per cent (due to an increase in the final demand in that particular sector) the output in sector i is increased by a_{ij}. The jth column sum ($a_{1j} + a_{2j} + \ldots + a_{nj}$) represents the direct effect of demand pull in sector j on all the sectors. On the other hand, the jth column sum of $(I-A)^{-1}$ matrix represents both the direct and indirect effects of a demand pull occurring in sector j of the economy.

The Leontief Price Model

The Leontief price model may be considered as a dual of the quantity model. The determination of equilibrium prices is the same irrespective of whether the outputs and employment are found in quantity or value terms. The balance equations in the price system are presented below:

$$P_1 = a_{11}P_1 + a_{21}P_2 + a_{31}P_3 + \ldots + a_{n-1,1}P_{n-1} + W a_{L1} \qquad (7a)$$

$$P_2 = a_{12}P_1 + a_{22}P_2 + a_{32}P_3 + \ldots + a_{n-1,2}P_{n-1} + W a_{L2} \qquad (7b)$$

$$\ldots\ldots\ldots\ldots\ldots\ldots\ldots\ldots\ldots\ldots\ldots\ldots\ldots$$

$$P_{n-1} = a_{1,n-1}P_1 + a_{2,n-1}P_2 + a_{3,n-1}P_3 + \ldots + a_{n-1,n-1}P_{n-1} + Wa_{Ln-1} \qquad (7, n-1)$$

Each equation here describes the balance between the price received and the payments made by each endogenous sector per unit of its product. Wa_{Li} represents the payments made by sector i—per unit of its product—to all exogenous (i.e. the household) sectors. The internal consistency of the price and quantity relationships within an open input-output system is ensured by the following identity:

$$X_1Wa_{L1} + X_2Wa_{L2} + \ldots + X_{n-1}W a_{L,n-1} = P_1C_1 + P_2C_2 + \ldots + P_{n-1}C_{n-1} \qquad (8)$$

The left hand side of equation (8) represents the sum total of value-added paid out by the endogenous sectors to the exogenous sectors. The right hand side represents the combined values of the final demands made by the household sector in respect of the (n–1) producing sectors.

The Leontief Price Model: Interpretation of Inverse Matrices and Multipliers

From the price equation

$$P_j = \Sigma a_{ij} P_i + W a_{Lj} \quad (i = 1, 2, \ldots, n-1) \qquad (2i)$$

We find that when the price in sector i is increased by 1 per cent (due to an increase in the final demand in that particular sector) the output in sector j is increased by a_{ij} due to increase in value added. The jth column sum of the Leontief inverse matrix $(I-A)^{-1}$ represents the percentage increase in the output value of sector j due to an increase in value added in each sector, demand pull in sector j on all the sectors. This value added increase amounts to 1 per cent of each sector's original output value. The column sum of A $(a_{1j} + a_{2j} + \ldots + a_{nj})$ measure the direct backward linkages, i.e. if P_i is changed by 1 per cent for all i, P_j will change by $(a_{1j} + a_{2j} + \ldots + a_{nj})$ due to the backward linkage i.e. combined direct effect changes in all prices.

II. THE GHOSH INPUT-OUTPUT MODEL

An alternative for the traditional input-output model was presented by Ghosh (1958). As compared to the Leontief input-output model; the Ghosh model has the following distinguishing features:

(a) Fixed Output Coefficient

The Leontief model is based on the assumption that input coefficients are fixed, i.e. each additional unit of production in sector j requires the same fixed amount of input from sector i. In contrast, the Ghosh model assumes a fixed allocation of output over the sectors. The output coefficient describes the fixed part of each additional of output in sector i that flows to sector j. The output coefficients are also known as sales or allocative coefficients.

(b) Output Determined by Value Added

In the traditional Leontief model we derive the sectoral outputs from exogenously specified final demands. It is the final demand vector that drives the model. However, in the Ghosh model, one derives the sectoral outputs from the exogenously specified value added (comprising of payments to primary factors such as labour and capital). Thus while the Leontief input-output model is demand driven, the Ghosh model is supply driven.

The Ghosh Model

Let us continue with our hypothetical 'n' sector economy comprising of (n–1) industries and the household sector. We can write the allocation equations as:

$$X_1 = X_{11} + X_{21} + X_{31} + \dots + X_{n-1,1} + V_1 \qquad (9a)$$

$$X_2 = X_{12} + X_{22} + X_{32} + \dots + X_{n-1,2} + V_2 \qquad (9b)$$

$$\dots\dots\dots\dots\dots\dots\dots\dots\dots\dots$$

$$X_{n-1} = X_{1,n-1} + X_{2,n-1} + X_{3,n-1} + \dots + X_{n-1,n-1} + V_{n-1} \qquad (9, n–1)$$

$$X_L = X_{1L} + X_{2L} + \dots + X_{n-1,L} + 0 \qquad (9, n)$$

Where, X_{ji} is the supply of input from sector j to sector i. V_i refers to the value added in sector i (i = 1, 2, . . . , n). We now define output coefficient as: $b_{ij} = X_{ij}/X_i$. The output coefficient b_{ij} measures the input from sector i into sector j as a fraction of the seller's output.

Thus we can write the allocation equations in the matrix from as:

$$X = B'X + V \qquad (10)$$

Or, $X (I–B') = V$

Or, $X = V (I–B')^{-1}$ (11)

where, B is a matrix of output coefficients.

Problem with the Ghosh Model

In the context of a market driven economy, the Ghosh model is not tenable (as a quantity model). This becomes quite clear if we consider the following example: Starting from an equilibrium position, let us suppose that the value added in sector j is increased by one unit. In the Ghosh input-output framework, this induces an increase of output in each sector other than the jth Sector. Thus production in various sectors is increased without there being an increase in the value added (e.g. labour and capital).

The problem, however, is resolved if we consider the Ghosh model as a price (rather than a quantity) model. If the commodity price in sector j is increased due to an increase in value added in that sector, this will cause an all round price increase in other sectors through inter-industry price increases. Thus, in other sectors, although the output remains fixed, prices (and hence, the value added) will rise.

A comparison of the Ghosh model (as a price model) and the Leontief (price) model reveals the following:

(a) In response to a change in value added, the Leontief model gives us new prices. In comparison, the Ghosh model gives us new output values (price-times quantity)
(b) The Leontief model calculates price ratios for the goods from exogenous price indices for the sectoral value added. The Ghosh model computes output values on the basis of the value added information and the output coefficients. The jth column sum of the Leontief inverse matrix $(I-A)^{-1}$ represents the percentage increase in the output value of sector j due to an increase in value added in each sector. The ith row sum of the Ghosh $(I-B')^{-1}$ matrix expresses the amount of money by which the output value of all sectors together is to be increased, due to 1 unit increase in the value added of sector i.

The Ghosh Quantity Model

The Leontief price model is the dual of the Leontief quantity model. The Leontief price model takes quantities as fixed while the quantity model takes prices as fixed. In a similar fashion, it is possible to find out the Ghosh quantity model which is dual to the Ghosh price model. In matrix notation, the Ghosh quantity model can be written as:

$$Y = BY + C \tag{12}$$

where Y is the value of output vector; B and C have their usual meanings. The commodity balance equations can be written as:

$$Y_1 = b_{11} Y_1 + b_{12} X_2 + b_{13} X_3 + \ldots + b_{1,n-1} Y_{n-1} + C_1 \tag{12a}$$
$$Y_2 = b_{21} X_1 + b_{22} X_2 + b_{23} X_3 + \ldots + b_{2,n-1} Y_{n-1} + C_2 \tag{12b}$$

$$\ldots\ldots\ldots\ldots\ldots\ldots\ldots\ldots\ldots\ldots\ldots\ldots$$

$$Y_{n-1} = b_{n-1,1} X_1 + b_{n-1,2} X_2 + b_{n-1,3} X_3 + \ldots + b_{n-1,n-1} Y_{n-1} + C_{n-1} \tag{12, n–1}$$

The value of outputs can be determined from the following:

$$Y = (I-B)^{-1} C \tag{13}$$

The ith row sum of the Ghosh inverse matrix $(I-B)^{-1}$ gives the percentage increase in the output value of sector i, due to an increase of the final demand in each sector. This final demand increase amount to 1 per cent of the sector's original output value.

III. CONCLUDING OBSERVATIONS

In the present paper we have made a comparative discussion of the two complimentary approaches to the input-output framework. In both the approaches, the interdependence between the individual sectors of the given system is described by a set of linear equations. As mentioned earlier, the Leontief model derives the sectoral outputs from exogenously specified final demands. It is the final demand vector that drives the model. The Ghosh model derives the sectoral outputs from the exogenously specified value added (comprising of payments to primary factors such as labour and capital). Thus while the Leontief input-output model is demand driven, the Ghosh model is supply driven. However, both the approaches suffer from a number of limitations:

(a) The assumption of constant returns to scale does not hold well in real life circumstances. When the returns to scale are variable, the technical coefficients depend on the scale of operations. The usefulness of the Leontief-Ghosh type models, therefore, is inversely related to the non-linearity of the production process.

(b) In a modern market driven economy technological progress affect the production structures in a significant way. Thus an input-output framework developed in a particular point of time is likely to lose its relevance over a period of time and one need to check for the non-constancy of the technological coefficients at regular intervals. This diminishes the relevance of the input-output approach in the present day context considerably.

NOTES

Note 1: Perron-Frobenius Theorems

(a) The Concepts of Eigenvalue and Eigenvector

Let us consider a homogenous linear system of equations: $(\lambda\ I-A)\ X = 0$. The equation system has n solutions or roots, which are denoted by $\alpha_1, \alpha_2, \ldots, \alpha_n$ and these are called the eigenvalues of the matrix A. The maximum Eigenvalue may be denoted by α_m. The associated values of X are called eigenvectors.

(b) Frobenius Theorem I (For Indecomposable Matrices)

Let A be a non-negative indecomposable nxn matrix. Then,

(i) A has an eigenvalue $\alpha_m > 0$ such that an eigenvector $x_{ev} > 0$ can be associated with α_m.

(ii) If $AX = \mu X$ for some $\mu \geq 0$ and $X \geq 0$ then $\mu = \alpha_m$.

(iii) If α_i is an Eigenvalue of A then, $Mod(\alpha_i) \leq \alpha_m$.

(iv) The eigenvector x_{ev} is unique up to a scalar multiple, i.e. if y_{ev} is an eigenvector associated with ám, then $y_{ev} = \theta x_{ev}$ for some positive scalar θ.

(c) Frobenius Theorem II

Let A be a non-negative nxn matrix. Then,

(i) A has an eigenvalue $\alpha_m = 0$ such that an eigenvector $x_{ev} > 0$ can be associated with $á_{m.}$.

(ii) If $AX \geq \mu X$ for some $\geq \mu 0$ and $X \geq 0$ then $\alpha_m \geq \mu$.

(iii) If α_i is an Eigenvalue of A then, Mod $(\alpha_i) \leq \alpha_{m.}$.

In this case, we have the following differences:

(a) The root α_m can be zero.

(b) Some elements of x_{ev} can be zero.

(c) x_{ev} may not be unique.

REFERENCES

Leontief W.W. (1941): *The Structure of American Economy*, 1919-29. Cambridge (Mass): Harvard University (second edition: 1951, 1919-39, New York: Oxford University Press).

Leontief W.W. *et al.* (1953): *Studies in the Structure of the Indian Economy*, New York: Oxford University Press.

Ghosh, A.P. (1958): "Input-Output Approach in an Allocation System", *Economica*, Vol. 25, pp. 58-64.

Wassily Leontief's Life and Input-Output Analysis

V. ANBUMANI AND M. SARAVANAKUMAR

INTRODUCTION

The Swedish Academy has honoured Wassily Leontief by awarding him the Nobel Prize in Economics for the year 1973. Leontief is the seventh economist to be honoured, ever since the award was instituted in 1969. The Swedish Academy, while announcing the award, said that "Prof. Leontief is the sole and unchallenged creator of the input-output technique. This important innovation has given to economic science an empirically useful method to highlight the general interdependence in the production system of a society." The Academy further said that "one of the advantages of input-output analysis is its use in different types of economic systems, decentralized market economics with mainly private enterprise as well as centrally planned economies dominated by public ownership. In particular, it provides tools for a systematic analysis of the complicated inter-industry transactions in the economy" (Puttaswamaiah).

LEONTIEF'S LIFE

Leontief was born in St. Petersburg now Leningrad, Russia, on August 5, 1905, he obtained his Masters Degree in 1925 from Leningrad University. During 1928, he was awarded a Doctorate by Berlin University. He worked in Kiel between 1927 and 1930 as a member of the research staff. Then, he moved to the United States of America in 1931 as a Research Associate at the National Bureau of Economic Research.

In the same year, Leontief joined the Economics Faculty of the Harvard University, where he served as Henry Leo Professor of Economics from 1946. He was the Special Consultant to the Bureau of Statistics of the United States Department of Labour the Bureau undertook to build a large input-output table in connection with the war-time needs during the Second World War.

Leontief's contributions are mainly in the fields of general economic theory, economics and social accounting, economic planning—theory and policy. His main areas of research pertain to input-output system and multi-sectoral analysis of international trade. He has been conferred with several honorary degrees by several universities. The University of Brussels honoured him by conferring Dr. *Hon. Causa* in 1962. The York University in England conferred him the honorary Doctorate in 1967. He has been the member of the American Economic Association, American Philosophical Society and the Econometric Society. During 1953, Leontief was the Vice-President of the Econometric Society and in 1954 he was its President. In 1980, he joined the new Institute for Social Science Research in New York.

At the Institute of Economic Research Leontief continued to work on input-output models, devoting much of his time to a model of the world economy developed originally for the United Nations. He has also been deeply engaged in the recent debate over the desirability of some form of national economic planning in the United States (Cave, Martin).

Leontief's major publications are readily accessible. His first major study on input-output *The Structure of the American Economy, 1919-29* was republished in an amended version covering the years 1919-39 in 1951 and reissued in 1976 (Leontief, 1951). A larger collective work on the same theme, edited by Leontief was first published in 1953 (Leontief, 1953). Leontief published a set of later essays on input-output in 1966 (1966a), and his collected essays on economics were made available in two volumes in 1966 and 1977 (1966b, 1977a). His model of the world economy was also published in 1977 (1977b). These works have been extensively translated. In addition, Leontief has written widely on the development of economics, on economic policy, on the arts, and on his visits to Japan, China and Cuba.

INPUT-OUTPUT ANALYSIS

One of the advantages of the input-output analysis is that it ends itself to different types of economic systems. It assumes greater importance in view of the resource constraints, and, the need for optimal utilization of the available resources. It allows prediction of the economic consequences of change in one part with other sectors, invaluable in planning, which is an integral part of a modern industrial economy. The analysis describes the level of output of each sector of a given national economy in terms of its relationship to the corresponding levels of activities in all the other sectors. It divides the national economy into a number of sectors. Leontief himself explains the theory by giving a simple example of the inter-relationships; he says, "When you make bread, you need eggs, flour and milk. And if you want bread first you must get more eggs." There are similar cooking recipes for all the industries in the economy.

The application of input-output technique is relevant in any field of economic activity, the supply and demand side of the projects, identification of new industries, employment stability and in deriving input-output multiplier in planning application of input-output analysis in practice. The role of input-output analysis in defining the sectors of plan is important.

To emphasize its importance today in planning, it may be quoted: "The time has come, then, for the old question of whether it is feasible to construct a regional input-output table to be superseded by new questions of how such regional tables can be most usefully applied in operational planning. It is to be hoped that further parallel experiments in the academic sphere and in the practical planning situation will establish input-output analysis as an indispensable tool in urban and regional economic planning" (Morrison, and Smith).

Recognizing the depth of specialization of Leontief in the input-output analysis, the International Encyclopedia of the Social Sciences has published his invited paper on input-output analysis (David). While presenting the Alfred Memorial Nobel Prize to Leontief, Assar Lindbeck in his speech has said: "you have, by your input-output model, given economic science an important tool of analysis for studying the complicated interdependence within the production system in a modern economy. You have not only constructed the theoretical foundations of the input-output method; you have also by your painstaking work developed the empirical data that are necessary to utilize the method on important economic problems as well as test empirically various economic theories."

Leontief feels that "major efforts are presently underway to construct a data base for a systematic input-output study not of a single national economy but of the world economy viewed as a system composed of many interrelated parts. This global study, as described in the official document, is aimed at—'helping Member-States of the United Nations make their 1975 review of world progress in accelerating development and attacking mass poverty and unemployment—

(a) By studying the results that prospective environmental issues and policies would probably have for world development in the absence of changes in national and international development policies;
(b) By studying the effects of possible alternative policies to promote development while at the same time preserving and improving the environment; and
(c) By thus indicating alternative future paths which the world economy might follow, the study would help the world community to make decisions regarding future development and environmental policies in as rational a manner as possible'.

Input-output Analysis: Leontief's Open System

Leontief's open system because the final demand sector (or the consuming sector) is regarded as exogenous. Input-output is based on the use of certain simple operations in matrix algebra.

The basic equations of the static input-output model, set out in matrix form are:

$$X = AX + Y \qquad (1)$$

where X is an **n**-dimensional column vector of gross outputs of the **n** sectors; Y is an **n**-dimensional column vector of net outputs, or shipments to final demand, of the **n** sectors; and A is an **n × n** matrix of input coefficients a_{ij}. We can solve equation (1) for X, to yield

$$X = (I - A)^{-1} Y \qquad (2)$$

The matrix $\mathbf{(I - A)^{-1}}$ can now be interpreted as the matrix of total, direct and indirect, input coefficients. It can be computed directly by inversion, or by the expansion:

$$(I - A)^{-1} = (I + A + A^2 + A^3 \ldots) \qquad (3)$$
$$X = (I + A + A^2 + A^3 \ldots) Y$$

The expression shows how the total output of an economy is made of final output (Y), plus direct inputs into that final output (AY), plus inputs into those inputs etc. For the economy to be capable of producing net output, the matrix (I – A) must satisfy the so-called Hawkins-Simon condition that its principal minors are positive. This will ensure that the sequence in the expansion converges.

The dynamic model is formulated using the matrix **B** of capital coefficients. Element $\mathbf{b_{ij}}$ of matrix **B** expresses the amount of capital produced by sector **i** which must be accumulated to produce one extra unit of output in sector **j**. The basic equation (assuming full capacity utilization) becomes

$$X = AX + B\Delta X + C \qquad (4)$$

Where ΔX is an **n**-dimensional column vector or increases in output in the **n** sectors; and C is an **n**-dimensional column vector of net outputs of the **n** sectors, excluding investment demand. The system (4) determines the development of gross output in the economy for any sequence of values of **C.**

One of Leontief's innovations is the dynamic inverse. This is a dynamic equivalent of the static inverse matrix $(I - A)^{-1}$. Unlike the static inverse which is a single matrix, the dynamic inverse is a dated sequence of matrices showing the total inputs (direct and indirect) which must be produced prior to the delivery of a unit of final output in a given year. The dynamic inverse thus captures the time phasing of output required to produce a unit of final output in a given year. Leontief computed the dynamic inverse for a 52-sector model of the US economy based on 1947 and 1958 data. Other applications of this highly promising technique are however still fairly rare.

A simple price model in Leontief framework may be given as follows. We assume that labour is the only primary factor. The price of the output of sector **i** is given as:

$$p_i = a_{1i} P_1 + a_{2i}' P_2 .... + a_i P_1 + a_n{}^1 P_n + a_{oi}{}^w$$

where a_0 is the input of labour per unit of output **iw** is the wage rate.

In matrix form:

$$P = A'p + a_0 w$$

Where p is the column vector of prices; A' is the transpose of matrix A (found by converting the rows of A into columns); and a_0 is the column vector of labour-input coefficients. Solving for **p,**

$$P = (I - A')^{-1}\, a_{0w}$$

That is to say, prices are proportional to the total (direct and indirect) input of labour. More complicated relationships naturally apply when the number of primary inputs exceeds one. These relationships are explored theoretically in Sraffa (1960). Leontief's own framework enables him to compute directly the effect on prices of a 10 per cent change in wages or profits, either in all sectors or in one sector only.

The Hawkins-Simon Conditions

In the Leontief input-output system, it has been assumed

that the feasible gross-output vector must be a positive vector:

$$X > 0$$

In the vector Equation:

$$AX = Y$$

It is assumed that **A = I – A*** is non-singular. The net output **Y** will be positive, if the inverse of **A** or **I – A*** exists and is non-negative. The necessary and sufficient condition for this is that **A*** satisfies the Hawkins-Simon conditions that all the principal minors of **A** or **I – A*** are positive.

Consider the case of two industries (n = 2), where the first industry produces steel and the second, coal. The Leontief equations of output are:

$$X_1 = a_{11}X_1 + a_{12}X_2 + Y_1 \qquad (5)$$

$$X_2 = a_{21}X_1 + a_{22}X_2 + Y_2 \qquad (6)$$

Equations (5) and (6) may be rewritten as:

$$X_1 = \frac{a_{12}}{1-a_{11}}X_2 + \frac{1}{1-a_{11}}Y_1 \qquad (7)$$

$$X_2 = \frac{a_{21}}{1-a_{22}}X_1 + \frac{1}{1-a_{22}}Y_2 \qquad (8)$$

Substitute the coal demand Eq. (8) into the steel demand Eq. (7) to eliminate the coal output variable X_2 and obtain:

$$X_1 = \frac{a_{12}}{1-a_{11}}\left[\frac{a_{21}}{1-a_{22}}X_1 + \frac{1}{1-a_{22}}Y_2\right] + \frac{1}{1-a_{11}}Y_1$$

or

$$X_1\left[\frac{a_{12}a_{21}}{(1-a_{11})(1-a_{22})}X_1\right] = \frac{1}{1-a_{11}}\left[Y_1 + \frac{a_{12}Y_2}{1-a_{22}}\right] \qquad (9)$$

The net outputs $\mathbf{Y_1}$ and $\mathbf{Y_2}$ will be positive if:

$$1 - a_{11} > 0$$

$$\text{and } 1 - \frac{a_{12}a_{21}}{(1-a_{11})(1-a_{22})} > 0$$

so that $\mathbf{(1 - a_{11})(1 - a_{22}) > a_{12}a_{21}}$, that is

$$\begin{vmatrix} 1 - a_{11} & -a_{12} \\ -a_{21} & 1 - a_{22} \end{vmatrix} > 0$$

The left side of Eq. (9) tells us that if the steel output increases by ΔX_1 units, the amount of steel needed to produce steel and coal which will be used to produce the additional steel will be mn ΔX_1, where m = $\mathbf{a_{12}/1 - a_{11}}$ and n = $a_{21}/1 - a_{22}$.

The Hawkins-Simon conditions require that mn ≤ which implies that less than a ton of steel is used up in the course of producing an additional ton of steel:

$$\Delta X_1 - mn\Delta X_1 > 0$$

Solow has given a sufficient condition which is more stringent, but easier to use than the Hawkins-Simon conditions. The condition is that the column sum of the Leontief matrix **A** does not exceed one for all columns, and at least one column sum is less than one:

$$\sum_{i=1}^{n} a_{ij} < 1, \quad j = 1, \ldots, n$$

The Solow condition also satisfies the Hawkins-Simon condition.

THE WALRAS-LEONTIEF CLOSED SYSTEM

The closed Leontief system the equation system of physical quantities is linear and homogeneous. Mathematically, we have to solve the linear equation system. Since production cannot be negative, **X** is required to be non-negative for economic reason.

Being homogeneous, the system can have a non-trivial solution if and only if the matrix **(I – A*)** has a vanishing determinant, that is det (I – A*) = 0.

This implies that final demand is such as to require full employment of the existing resources and labour force. As the (n + 1)th column is linearly dependent on the others, there are **n** independent equations but (n + 1) unknowns, any one of which may be fixed arbitrarily. Then the solutions for the other **n** unknowns will be uniquely determined.

This means that the system of physical quantities determines the relative quantities or the proportions in which the various commodities are produced, but not the absolute levels of the outputs. In other words, it determines the structure of the economic system but not the scale of operations. Since the available labour force is assumed to be an exogenous quantity, the unknowns are reduced to **n** and they will be determined by the **n** independent equations of the system.

The closed system examined here is the simplest particular version of Walrasian general economic equilibrium. Leontief is associated with it because his assumption of fixed input coefficients is adopted. Leontief concentrated upon the distribution of inter-industrial transactions of different industries. By working out capital and current output matrices of these transactions his aim was to find out the direct and indirect input requirements per unit of say final output of a commodity. Leontief worked out both closed and open models. The input-output matrices require the assumption of fixed coefficients of production; the consumption demand mixed can be altered. This was the Walrasian procedure and Leontief followed it. Input-output tables can be extended to as many industries processes as one may require. Since these tables are deemed to correspond to the General Equilibrium profile of thė economy, as per Walras, we must assume that direct and indirect co-efficient requirements are fixed for each final commodity. Similarly, the prices, which are implicit in the table, must be equilibrium prices. The entire economy is viewed as one structure.

The input-output approach, because of its emphasis on the aggregate of direct and indirect effects, has been found useful in measures of, effective rate of protection, comprehensive effective real exchange rate, effective incidence of indirect taxes, gross forward and backward linkage effects, total effective incidence of indirect taxes, gross forward and backward linkage effects, total employment effects of alternative patterns of investments and so on. Even in respect of choice of techniques, when distribution mixed change or take different values, measures of capital intensity undergo a change. The hierarchical rankings also become different. The full implications of input-output do not warrant a general equilibrium solution to value, production and distribution.

INPUT-OUTPUT ANALYSIS AND LINEAR PROGRAMMING

In Leontief's open system, the final demand is the demand of consumers who provide the factors of production. In equilibrium, the value of final demand equals the cost of primary factors, so that factor income and expenditure balance:

$$pY = wBX$$

where the given data for the **n** industries (j = 1, 2, . . ., n) are: **Y,** the column vector of final demands for outputs of industries; **w,** the row vector of prices of factors (i = 1, 2, . . ., m); and $\mathbf{B} = [\mathbf{b}_{ij}]$, the **m × n** matrix of coefficients of production for the primary factors. The variables are: **X,** the column vector of total output of industries; and **p,** the row vector of prices of outputs $(p_1, p_2, \ldots, p_n)$.

The economy produces **n** commodities, using **m** primary (not produced) factor inputs. So that, summing over all outputs gives the economy-wide demand for the **ith** factor:

$$\sum_{j=1}^{n} v_{ij} = \sum_{j=1}^{n} b_{ij} X_j$$

But the demand for the **ith** factor cannot exceed the supply of that factor:

$$\sum_{i=1}^{n} b_{ij} X_j \leq v_i$$

where, v_i is the available supply of factor **i.** In matrix notation:

$$BX \leq v$$

where, **v** is the column vector of available primary factors.

PROBLEMS OF LEONTIEF'S INPUT-OUTPUT ANALYSIS

1. Primal Problem

This open form of Leontief's static model of inter-industry relations can be expressed in terms of a particular linear programme with its dual. The primal problem is that of maximizing the value of final demand by choice of non-negative values of outputs of all commodities, subject to the constraints of the Leontief equation and the conditions of factor supply and demand. The primal problem is therefore:

$$\max_{X} \mathbf{pY} \quad \text{subject to} \quad \mathbf{X = A^{*}X + Y}$$

$$\mathbf{BX \leq v}, \quad \mathbf{X \geq 0} \qquad (1)$$

Since $\mathbf{(I-A^{*})\,X = Y}$, the primal problem can be restated, in standard linear programming form, by eliminating **Y**, which yields

$$\max_{X} \mathbf{p\,(I - A^{*})\,X} \quad \text{subject to} \quad BX \leq \mathbf{v}\ \mathbf{X \geq 0} \qquad (2)$$

where, $\mathbf{pY = p\,(I - A^{*})\,X}$ is the value of final demand; $\mathbf{A^{*}} = [a_{ij}]$ is the $n \times n$ matrix of coefficients of production. Defining adjusted price $\hat{p}$ as $\mathbf{p\,(I - A^{*})}$, the primal problem is:

$$\max_{X} \hat{p}\ \mathbf{X = R} \quad \text{subject to} \quad \mathbf{BX \leq v, X \geq 0} \qquad (3)$$

In this problem the objective function is a value and the variables are quantities of outputs **X** given in terms of final demands **Y**.

2. Dual Problem

In competitive equilibrium, there can be no profits earned in any production process; this implies that the average cost of producing any commodity must be greater than or equal to the price of that commodity:

$$\sum_{k=1}^{n} p_k a_{kj} + \sum_{i=1}^{m} w_i b_{ij} \geq p_j \quad (j = 1, 2, \ldots, n) \tag{4}$$

The left-hand side of this expression is average cost, where $\mathbf{p_k a_{kj}}$ is the cost of the amount of commodity **k** required to produce one unit of commodity **j**, $\mathbf{w_i b_{ij}}$ is the cost of the amount of primary factor **I** required to produce one unit of commodity **j**. In matrix notation:

$$\mathbf{pA^* + wB \geq p} \tag{5}$$

Collecting terms:

$$\mathbf{P\ (I - A^*) \leq wB} \tag{6}$$

Defining adjusted prices $\mathbf{\hat{p} = p\ (I - A^*)}$:

$$\mathbf{wB} \geq \hat{p} \tag{7}$$

If the primal problem of a linear programme is the maximization of the value of final demand $\mathbf{\hat{p}X}$, its dual is the minimization of the cost of primary factors

$$\mathbf{wv} = \sum_{i=1}^{m} w_i v_i \tag{8}$$

by the choice of non-negative values of factor prices, subject to the constraint that the average cost of producing any good must not be less than the price of that good. In standard linear programming form, the dual problem is:

$$\min \mathbf{wv} = \text{subject to } \mathbf{wB} \geq \hat{p} \quad \mathbf{w \geq 0}$$

In this dual problem, the objective function is a value but the variables are prices **p**, given in terms of wage costs **wB**.

Recently, the emphasis of the input-output analysis has shifted towards the application of economic forecasting and planning. One of the most common uses of this analysis is the calculation of the quantity of each primary input absorbed directly and indirectly in the final delivery of one unit of output of a specified sector. Despite the difference which exists between centrally planned economics and market economics in institutional organization of their respective systems, the methods of application of input-output analysis to the future of these systems are quite familiar.

In centrally planned economics, emphasis is placed upon quantitative output objectives which it is hoped will be realized in the future and for the attainment of which the planning authority is ultimately responsible. In market economics, forecasts are simply expectations about the future course of events, the realization of which depends upon decisions taken by a large number of individuals, decisions which are un-coordinated except by price system. In centrally planned economics consumer decisions play an increasing part in determining output, while in market economics the role of government as a central coordinator of economic activity is growing.

CONCLUSION

Today input-output analysis is used by all the communist nations as a basis for planning. In capitalist countries, the tables are used extensively in market research by companies. Leontief's input-output analysis fuses theoretical clarity, mathematical manipulation and statistical fact into a tool of great beauty and practical power, one of the most impressive that economists have ever offered to the statesmen, and already in worldwide use. It is a paradigm of genuine and worthwhile econometrics. The aggregation problems, but input-output analysis brings their disturbing effects into the open.

Leontief describes the dynamic analysis and says that accumulation or deaccumulation becomes necessary where existing capital is not sufficient for the production of the quantities demanded or where the process of production of certain commodities is out of tune with existing economic conditions.

The use of input-output techniques in international comparisons can be extremely useful not only in the investigation of structure but also for studying primary factor content. The variants of the Leontief dynamic model are now implemented for a number of countries including Japan, India, Hungary and the United States.

REFERENCES

Dr. P.R. Brahmananda (1999), "Input-output, Economic and Social systems, Programming Leontief, Hayek, Myrdal, Kantarovich and Koopmans", *Nobel Economics (A Historical Commentary from the Classical Angle),* pp. 137-41.

Cave, Martin, "Wassily Leontief: Input-Output and Economic Planning", in Shackleton, J.R. and Locksley, Gareth, (ed.)), *Twelve Contemporary Economists,* John Wiley and Sons, 1981, pp. 160-61.

Dorfman, R., (1977), "Wassily Leontief's Contributions to Economics", *Swedish Journal of Economics,* Vol. 79, pp. 430-49.

Green, H.A.J., (1964), *Aggregation in Economic Analysis,* Princeton University Press.

Hawkins, and Simon, (1949), "Some Conditions of Macro-Economic Stability", *Econometrica,* Vol. 17, pp. 245-48.

Leontief, W., (1951), *The Structure of the American Economy,* Oxford University Press. (Reprinted by International Arts and Sciences Press, 1976).

—— (1953), "The Input-Output Approach in Economic Analysis", in *Input-Output Relations,* Netherlands Economic Institute, Leiden.

—— (1966a), *Input-output Economics,* Oxford University Press.

—— (1966b), *Essays in Economics: Theories and Theorizing,* Vol. 1, Oxford University Press. (Reprinted by Basil Blackwell 1977).

—— (1968), "Input-Output Analysis", in Sills, David L., (ed.), *International Encyclopedia of the Social Sciences,* Vol. 7, MacMillan and the Free Press, pp. 345-53.

—— (1969), "Notes on a Visit to Cuba", *New York Review of Books,* 21-August, pp. 15-20.

—— (1970), "Mysterious Japan—A Diary", *New York Review of Books,* 4, June, pp. 23-29.

—— (1977), *The Future of the World Economy,* Oxford University Press.

—— (1977a), *Essays in Economics,* Vol. 2, Basil Blackwell.

Morrison, W.I. and Smith (1977), P., "Input-output Methods in Urban and Regional Planning: A Practical Guide", in Diamond, D. and McLoughlin, J.B. (ed.), *Progress in Planning,* Part 2, Vol. 7, Pergamon Press, p. 131.

Nagpal, C.S., Mittal, A.C. (1993), "Wassily Leontief", *Economic Thought,* pp. 347-72.

Puttaswamaish, K. (2006), "Wassily Leontief Life and Contributions", *International Journal of Applied Economic & Econometrics,* Bangalore, India, Vol. 14, No. 1, pp. 1-14.

Roychowdhury, K.C. (1991), "Input-output Analysis and Linear Programming", *Micro-Economics,* pp. 369-89.

Sraffa, P. (1960), *The Production of Commodities by Means of Commodities,* (Cambridge University Press).

Solow, R., 1952, "On the Structure of Linear Models", *Econometrica,* pp. 29-46.

Xie Mei, Nie Guisheng, & Jin Xianglan (1991), Application of an Input-Output Model to the Beijing Urban Water-use System, in Karen R. Polenske and Chen Xikang (eds.), *Chinese Economic Planning and Input-output Analysis,* Hong Kong, Oxford University Press, pp. 239-57.

Indian Contribution to Leontief's Input-Output Economics

SHALINI SHARMA

Nobel Laureate Leontief enriched every branch of economics. His theory, method and empirics influenced economic thinking across the globe. This put him among the greatest economists of the century. India did not escape his influence. Mathur, Ghosh and Bharadwaj have been the main proponents of Leontief's economics in India. Mathur and Bharadwaj were associated with his 'Harvard Research Project', V.G. Bhatia completed Ph.D. under him and A.P. Ghosh was greatly influenced by him. Mathur himself is known as 'Leontief of India'. Mathur attracted scholars from India, UK, Latin America, Middle East, South and South East Asia. Pervasive Indian contribution to input output economics has been (i) theoretical; (ii) methodological; (iii) pedagogic; and (iv) empirical, widening scope, enriching theoretically and deepening knowledge base. This makes it practically impossible to evaluate individual contributions. This paper, therefore, undertakes thematic review of Indian contribution.

LEONTIEF'S MODEL AS THEORY AND METHODOLOGY OF ECONOMIC ANALYSIS

Mathur (1969) unrevelled multiple theoretical and methodological dimensions of Leontief's model with reference to Quesnay, Russian Economists, Veblen, German historical school, Pareto-Walras and post-first war empirical reality. He observes 'how the input output analysis provides with a framework which while being very well grounded in theory is also amenable to systematic and meaningful empirical work'. This is how Carter (1996) supports Mathur 'In the late fifties, . . . Mathur saw the potential of IO, not as a simplistic linear system but as Leontief's ingenious reformulation of general equilibrium theory to open the door to empirical implementation, to the essential step of testing economic theory'. Prakash (2006) later showed Leontief's economics as a 'confluence of all major streams and strands of economic theory' through the conversion of Quesnay-Pareto-Walras-Hicks Marxian–Keynesian models into General Equilibrium Model in Leontief's framework. Roots of input output economics in linear algebra might have made it appear unapproachable to non-mathematical economists. So, Marshallian tradition of presenting economic theory, through geometry, has been imported by Mathur into input output analysis. He developed graphics for two/three sector models and for self-sufficient closed economy and a surplus producing economy.

In certain areas of research, Mathur preceded not only Carter's contribution to technological transformation and Stone-Brown's maximal growth analysis but even Leontief's contribution to pricing, growth analysis and regional economics. Rendering of Philip's curve in I-O framework to analyze inflation-unemployment trade-off has been another area of Mathur's contribution.

DEMAND V/S SUPPLY SIDE INPUT-OUTPUT ECONOMICS

Input output economics was approached both from demand and supply sides. Leontief developed demand side input output economics, assuming input coefficients to be technologically fixed from outside. Single matrix equation with one degree of freedom determines gross output in terms of given final demand and input coefficient-matrix. A. Ghosh approached input output from supply side and assumed allocation coefficients and demands to be given exogenously to determine output.

CONSTRUCTION OF NATIONAL INPUT OUTPUT TABLES

I-O table is the elementary instrument of Leontief's economics. Initially, individual researchers constructed national tables. A.K. Chakravarti's 4X4 table for 1954 appeared first. Incidentally, the table appeared at a time when Mahalanobis 2/4 sector model was in an experimental stage. It was followed by 36×36 (ISI) table for 1962 and 32×32 table (Gokhale Institute) for 1963. Saluja made a more detailed table for 1965, the upgraded versions of which had appeared from time to time in the garb of new tables. Saluja's tables suffer from ambiguity of method, errors of specification, in-appropriate prices and up-gradation procedure.

STATES' INPUT-OUTPUT TABLES

Planning was decentralized in 1971, necessitating construction of state tables. M.P. (Prakash), Karnataka (V.R. Panchamukhi), Panjab (D.K. Rangnekar), Maharastra (Koti & Somayajulu), Gujarat (Alagh-Kashyap), West Bengal (Bhanwar Singh), Mizoram (K.K. Upadhyaya), Assam (Atul Sarma-M. Saluja), Rajasthan (Mehta) constructed state tables. Later, Venkatramaiha constructed tables (1965) of uniform size by application of one single method of compilation for all major states of India. Saluja has reviewed most of these tables in his book, 'State Input-Output Tables in India'.

AGGREGATION

Prasad (1969) analysed two aspects of sectoral aggregation: change in relative prices under the limitation of product homogeneity assumption and the effect of aggregation of elements of Leontief inverse. Prasad tested basic assumptions of aggregation. Aggregation is justified by Hicks-Leontief Theorem, which states that if prices/quantities of two commodities move together, these can be treated as one for analytical purpose. Prasad used disaggregated data of India's international trade from 1920 to 1956 for evaluating suitability of alternative aggregation schemes. His results were not very encouraging.

CHOICE OF TECHNOLOGY AND CHANGING COEFFICIENTS MATRIX

Choice of techniques and transition from old to new technology has been important problems of growth. Even before the problem was addressed by Carter (1963) for US economy. Mathur (1962) used a linear programming-IO model to simulate the transformation from less to more advance US technology in Indian economy in the shortest possible time. Subsequently, V.G. Bhatia (1968) used the same model to define the development distance between India and US.

Technological change and its incorporation in analysis is an important issue. Sarkar (1976) approximates unknown input coefficients by a new method. The method strikes a compromise between Stone-Brown method of coefficients correction for changes in accordance with an acceptable hypothesis and the method of correcting computed totals of output of inter-mediate demand, the impact of changes in coefficients of all sectors being aggregated. The method uses the hypothesis that quite a bit of "so called technological changes in a sector over years consist of changes in the product mix within each sector." The method is tested by using the Taiwan Table. In our opinion, change in product-mix, unless it is overlooked through aggregation, may generally involve a change in technology. Ghosh, Sarkar and Chakraborty (1976) tested nine models with known changes of input-output coefficients. Shanmukham and Shanthanam, using Chenery's technique, delineated technological change that occurred in almost all sectors in Indian economy from 1953-56 to 1964-65. But thereafter no technical change from 1960-61 to 1964-65 occurred. Their use of Saluja's table of 1964-65, based on 1960-61 data, adjusted somehow by Saluja, accounts for this result. Inconsequential adjustment by Saluja was brought out by the study. Rohit D. Desai decomposed the economy into clusters on the structural basis and suggests the incorporation of universal intermediaries into every cluster for successful decomposition.

DUAL PRICE MODEL

Mathur (1965) used classical theory to develop the price model as a dual of Leontief's quantity model. The model determines price vector in terms of value added that comprises of wages and interest. Classicals recognized labor and capital as the only factors of production. Prakash-Sharma (2005) modified Mathur–Morishima models to incorporate wages, interest and other cost of loan and equity capital, overall cost of equity capital to redefine value added as the sum of wages, overall cost of capital and profits (economic value-added). They used this model to determine (i) unknown price vector, and (ii) values of product and company brands. Later, Mathur (1973) used Hicksian flex-fix price theory to analyse the coexistence of recession in the midst of inflation. He also demarcated the flex and fix price sectors of Indian economy on the one hand, and determined price movements in British economy on the other.

R. Radhakrishna formulated an input-output model in general equilibrium framework for the analysis of cost based edible oil prices. Comparison of estimated cost-prices with the observed prices enabled him to draw inferences about market conditions in different phases of cycles.

Prakash modified the open into quasi open I-O model in order to work out interrelations between prices of flex and fix price sectors with a view to evaluate his twin theses of the convergence of demand pull into cost push inflation due to configuration of action-reaction chain of two sets of prices and convergence of flex (foodgrain) prices towards the publicly administered prices within the broadly defined ceilings and floors. In this context, he developed the concepts of Pipe-line, Buffer and Reserve Stocks of foodgrains. Prakash-Chowdhury-Sengupta endogenised the margins into I-O model to work out margins' interaction effect on prices. Prakash-Goel (1985) developed quasi-IO econometric model to empirically study the behaviour of 156 agro-based commodities over a period of 3 decades in flex-fix price framework. Prakash (1986) has also developed mathematical IO model of flex prices (1984). Shalini Sharma used a quasi econometric-input-output flex price model for empirically analyzing foodgrain prices in Indian economy with public and private stocks of foodgrains as the main determinants. She used procurement price as a floor with the ceiling being provided by market demand in excess of public distribution to examine the probable convergence of flex to fix price behaviour under the impact of public policy. Keya Sengupta (1993) used flex-fixprice I-O model to analyse the behaviour of prices of agro-linked industries, whereas Sumitra Chowdhury (1995) examined prices of manufactures in I-O model of fix-prices.

Samit Sharma examined the inter-relations between distributive margins and sectoral prices. Mohanty studied this problem for Jute and Mesta industries.

REGIONAL ECONOMICS

Regional Input-Output Economics deals with inter-regional-inter-sectoral-inter-dependence and balanced regional development which require both: (i) region wise commodity balances; and (ii) region wise development balance. It analyses industrial location, transport cost, and the pattern of trade and production, specially the terms, volume and number of goods involved in regional trade, relative to static comparative advantage. Regional Development is assessed relative to national/most/least developed regional economy. Development depends upon the level of investment and allocation of resources—natural and financial, and capital—physical and human. However, state tables were not the base of regional analysis in India.

Ranjit .Dhar (1968) was probably the first Indian to have worked out regional development in input output framework (ISI table). Mathur-Hashim analysed level and pattern of allocation of resources as balancing factors of regional development. Mathur-Hashim also developed a multi-regional-multi-sectoral programming—input-output model of optimum location and demonstrated its empirical efficacy. It was an improvement over Ghosh's programming model to evaluate: (i) efficiency of location and inter-regional flows of cement industry; (ii) multi-sector-multi-regional model of commodity production and transportation. V.G. Bhatia-Narain Das (1968) and Hashim (1969) estimated transport coefficients for different sectors of Indian economy.

Mathur has developed a detailed input output and inter-regional dynamic model for planning, which embodied the methodology of inter-regional resource allocation. The methodology is different from that of resource allocation based on static comparative advantage. Leontief-Strout Gravity model was modified by Mathur for analyzing Regional Trade and Cooperation which Deepa Saran also used for empirical study of SAARC.

INCOME DISTRIBUTION THEORY

Ghosh (1969) developed multi-sector input output models of income distribution on the basis of one sector models/theories of Keynes, Kaldor, Passiniti and Ozawa. Ghosh extended Kaldor-Passinitti one production-consumption sector Keynsian model into two production and one consumption sector model and multiple production consumption sector model in Leontief framework. Like Kaldor-Pasinitti, Ghosh related wages and profits to capital and investment and sectoral prices and wages are relatable either to sectoral final demand or sectoral investment. A new functional relation for determining the shares of consumers and producers in income has been evolved. Impact of sectoral output decisions on income distribution among groups, which is concealed in aggregative single sector models, has also been highlighted.

LEONTIEF DYNAMIC MODEL

Leontief (1968), introduced the stock matrix and dynamised the model. It is an essential element of both the economic dynamics and analysis of growth. India is one of the few countries, which constructed more than one complete capital coefficient matrix. Koti (1968) used company data for the first capital matrix of 1960. It was followed by (a) Mathur-Hashim's 65X65 (1969) matrix for 1963, (b) Mathur-Kulkarni-Baldota-Parkhi (1969) table for 1963, (c) Hashim-Dadi (1976) table for 1965 and Datt-Majumdar table for 1973. This is what Carter (1996) says about Mathur's tables "World Bank experts prepared a report on India only to find that Mathur had already constructed a capital coefficients matrix that was far more reliable than the one they used." Besides Leontief, 'Mathur may well be the only economist of this period with the courage and energy to construct a capital coefficients matrix rather than borrow the tired old one we improvised at Harvard in the early 1950s'.

Dynamic Inverse of Leontief's dynamic model is an extremely powerful instrument of economic analysis as well as capital theory. Mathur distinguished between two concepts of capital in terms of Leontief's dynamic inverse. He also highlighted the trade and growth gains of international trade. Bharadwaj (1969) resolved various problems of capital theory by the use of input-output technique. He further demonstrated input output to be a convergence of theory and empiricism. Koti used capital coefficients to articulate the Leontief's model and its dynamic inverse. Koti's contribution to capital theory is both theoretical and methodological and he differentiated the roles of various industries as raw material or capital goods suppliers. Hashim-Dadi computed capital-output ratios for Indian industries according to Leontief-Mathur conceptualization, taking into account both direct and indirect requirements of capital. They highlighted different results furnished by I-O and conventional methods of computation. Alagh-Shah (1976) estimated detailed row of capital co-efficient matrix of machine-tool industry to provide the building blocks of a comprehensive capital matrix. Koti-Somayajulu (1969) analysed the problems of estimation of replacement value of capital at sectoral level.

PLANNING AND GROWTH

Mathur highlighted three uses of input output analysis for planning: (i) ensuring mutual consistencency of targets for avoiding bottlenecks/surpluses; (ii) delineating dynamic inter-industry balance by combining it with linear-programming (Mathur,1968), (iii) derivation of Von-Neuman trajectory and Ponrgagin principle (Snirnov, 1969, Brody, 1969); and (iv) inter-regional analysis, including location and transport cost. Prakash-Buragohain (1993) worked out a balanced growth input output model for deriving empirical estimates of growth potential of Indian economy.

Growth Effect of Linkages has been an extensively studied phenomenon in India. Krishna Bharadwaj (1966) was first to estimate the linkage effect of growth for Indian economy. Alagh-Kashyap estimated linkages for Gujarat economy. Prasad used

Yatasomulous method for linkages to compare it with the Rasmussen's method. Prakash (1992) used both Leontief's inverse and dynamic inverse for (i) formulating and empirically illustrating the concept of Residentiary Linkages, (ii) developing formulae to estimate both direct and indirect linkage effects, and (iii) endogenising Multiplier-Acceleration processes into IO framework to show convergence of unbalanced towards balanced growth. His estimation method provides a better alternative to Rasmussen's linkage calculus to approximate real linkages in an economy. Superiority of his concept and method has been empirically illustrated by results of another scholar (Artha Vijnana, 2003). Kashyap-Pathak-Shah (1976) studied linkages of industrial estates of Gujarat both with neighbouring industrial centres and national economy. They showed that the smaller estates were not integrated properly. Hashim-Satyanarayan (2000) estimated sectoral input intensities of output and final demand in Indian economy over a period of time and changes that have taken place.

ECONOMICS OF UNDER-DEVELOPMENT

One view considers Dadabhai Naoroji as the founder of economics of under-development, who envisaged draining of resources of India under British rule as the prime cause of her poverty and under-development. He hypothesized under-development of developing countries and its perpetuation through time to be embodied in international economic order (1986). The developing economies have to pay for their technological inferiority in terms of low real wage rates, ranging from 2.9 per cent for Bangladesh, 4.5 per cent for India to 30.5 per cent for Israel, relative to US rate, in order to earn enough foreign exchange to pay for imports, since the developed countries transfer obsolete technology to the developing world. He (1992) validated the thesis empirically by applying the same to the data of numerous developing economies.

EXTERNAL TRADE

Bharadwaj evaluated Leontief Paradox and showed that India's pattern of trade conformed to her factor endowments.

Bharadwaj-Bhagwati also analysed human capital component in Indian exports and found the trade pattern in conformance to India's factor endowments. Prasad extended Bhardwaj's model further by incorporating natural resources as a part of resource endowments to evaluate Leontief Paradox. His results also conformed to the prediction of traditional theory. Panchamukhi (1968) developed a import substitution model for Indian economy for (1962, 1965), distinguishing technology matrix A into imported and domestically produced input coefficients matrix for 8 sectors. B. Hazari (1990) and Vidya Pitre (2000) analyzed import dependence of the Indian economy as a whole. Atul Sarma estimated import dependence of Indian exports for a later period.

S.P. Gupta developed an experimental model synthesizing cost-benefit approach into inter-industry programming model for planning foreign trade on the basis of foreign aid. His results suggested top priority to agro-based industries and reduction of cost of tied aid through rational planning. He also concluded that sourcing time has greater influence than project time.

Debesh Chakravarti with Thijs Ten Raa (2005) investigated the pattern of production and trade of India and Bangladesh. They have come out with interesting results. Sastry estimated direct and indirect income benefits accruing to the economy from automobile industry as an import substitute in India and inferred that income accruing to the economy far exceeded the resource cost.

HUMAN CAPITAL AND MANPOWER PLANNING

Rabindranath (1968) estimated labour coefficients for 32 sectors of Indian economy to bring manpower planning within the domain of input-output economics. Prakash worked out education-occupation-wise labour coefficients for HMT, Hindustan Steel Ltd., Bharat Heavy Electrical Ltd. for (i) forecasting manpower requirements at the industry/firm level, and (ii) examining stability of labour coefficients under constant technology but changing: (a) output levels, and (b) product-mix.

Prakash imported input output modeling into demography for forecasting human resource development as a fully blown up and nicely integrated area of input-output modeling. He (1971a, 1971b, 1976) pioneered input-output modeling of human resource development in India. He endogenised demographic forecasting in input output models to predict age and gender-wise population, which he fused into education processes to work out class-wise enrolments, dropouts, repetition and passouts. For this, he developed three specialized matrices. He combined input output model into econometrics for determining inter-temporal variations of human capital formation in an innovative way. Reviewers classified his work in the same category as that of Smith, Blaugh, Tinbergen, Stone and Dalvi (ICSSR, First Survey of Research in Economics). Prakash-Dutta (1994) developed a supply side human resource allocation model, endogenising household sector into IO model to determine education-employment trade-off. Besides, he developed social accounting matrix to workout flows of men, money and materials into different activities, including education and sectoral employment. Prakash-Nain and Prakash-Inderjit Singh also endogenised education-employment vectors into a dynamic model of balanced growth. Human development index has been endogenised in IO model by Prakash (2005). This paper also offers an alternative to Kendall's method of principal component analysis on the basis of variables measured in ordinal terms.

A Parikh used an input output model to estimate employment and import requirements per unit of final demand from Leontief Inverse. But the Leontief inverse was modified to distinguish technology matrix A from domestic input coefficients matrix A.

GOVERNMENT EXPENDITURE

R.G. Paithankar (1969, 1978) estimated commodity composition of government expenditure. He used input-output model to analyse the growth of commodity expenditure of government, an element of final demand, by a sort of partial approach to widen the scope of multiplier analysis. He developed and used a functional regional input-output coefficient table (not full table) for Marathwada Region of Maharastra to derive significant conclusions about the disaggregative regional multiplier. Atul Sarma subsequently worked it out at the regional level for Assam.

DISTRIBUTIVE MARGINS AND SECTORAL STUDIES

Venkatramaiha studied the implications of choice of Purchasers' (Market) and Producers' prices to estimate input coefficients matrix. He also highlighted the sector-wise effect of distributive margins on prices. As regards sectoral input coefficients, there is an interesting study to compare inter-firm input structure of some dye industry groups. Naik brings out an important point that there is a limit to a meaningful disaggregation. Beyond that point, disaggregation becomes counter-productive.

POLICY AND OTHER IMPACT ANALYSIS

Policy Impact has also been an area of research in input-output framework. Jayant Kumar Malik (2000) has developed an IO model to analyse the impact of import liberalization on output growth. Sharma-Saxena and Latika Argade also analysed the impact of trade liberalization on growth, economic structure and employment.

MISCELLANEOUS

G.S. Bhalla used IO model to estimate Income-Employment Multipliers for Panjab. Mathur developed input output models for studying: (i) resource mobilization for defense, and (ii) environmental effects of economic operations. Prakash Chowdhury developed an I-O model of deforestation. Debesh Chakravarti also studied environmental problems in IO framework.

P.N. Mathur, Shri Prakash, and H.S. Sarkar developed macro-models of Indian economy in input-output framework. S. Prakash and S. Chowdhary and Prakash Inderjeet Singh also used IO models to analyse inventory investment. R. Subramanian (2005) mixed company level data into national table to examine micro-effects of macro-operations and macro-effects of micro (Company) operations. Bharadwaj (2005) analyzed Dabba business in Bangalore in I-O framework. R.G. Parkar has based his study of factor productivity in Indian economy on IO framework not only to take into account factor inputs but also intermediate inputs.

Prakash-Balakrishnan developed decomposition model of growth of: (a) employment, and (b) productivity, which they fused into input output model to examine technology-human capital effect on productivity. Prakash-Singh (1985) used an I-O model for estimating electricity intensity of Indian economy. Dash-Saxena (2000) used an I-O model to estimate sectoral energy intensity. Prakash-Inderjeet Singh, Prakash-Chowduri developed programming-input-output models for determining optimum inventory holdings, showing: (i) private sector to pay for public policy inefficiency, and (ii) lower growth rate. Financial sector modeling has attracted research efforts of R.S. Ramchandra Rao (2000) and D.K. Bhatia (1973). Prakash (1986) used an IO model to estimate impact of indirect taxation.

CONCLUSION

The above review, focused as it is on studies that I am familiar with, amply demonstrates the range, reach, quality and vivacity of Indian contribution to I-O analysis. To the best of my knowledge, the Indian contribution to input output economics is comparable to that of American and Dutch scholars' contribution to this branch of knowledge.

REFERENCES

Bhardwaj, Krishna (1966), "A Note on Structural Interdependence and the Concept of Key Sector", *Kyklos*.

Bhardwaj, Rangnath, B. (1962), *Structural Basis of India's Foreign Trade*, Bombay University.

Bhardwaj, Rangnath, B. (2005), "Economics of Meal Service Sector in Growing Cities: The Case of Bangalore—A study suggested by Input-Output Analysis", Fifteenth International Conference on Input-Output Techniques, Beijing, China.

Chenery, H.B. and Watanbe, T. (1958), "International Comparison of the Structure of Production", *Econometrica*, October.

Carter, Anne P. (1996), "Scholarship and Recognition: Reflections on the contributions of P.N. Mathur", *Economic Systems Research*, Vol. 8, No. 3.

Chakravarti, A.K. (1968), *The Structure of the Indian Economy: 1953-54*, ISI, Kolkata.

Ghosh, Ambika (1958), "Input Output Approach in an Allocation System", *Economics*, 25, No. 97.

Ghosh, Ambika (1964), *Experiments with Input-Output Models*, Combridge University Press, Massachusetts.

Ghosh, Ambika (1968), *Planning Programming and Input-Output Models*, Cambridge University, Cambridge (U.K.).

Mathur, P.N. (1962), "Two Concepts of Capital Output Ratios and Their Relevance for Development", *Artha Vijyana*, Vol. 4, Dec.

Mathur, P.N. and Bhardwaj, R. (Editors, 1968), *Economic Analysis in Input-Output Framework with Indian Empirical Explorations*, Vol. 1, Input-Output Research Association, India.

Mathur, P.N. and Vekatramaiha, P. (Editors, 1969), *Economic Analysis in Input-Output Framework*, Vol. II, Input-Output Research Association.

Mathur, P.N. (1976, Editor), *Economic Analysis in Input-Output Framework*, Vol. III, Input-Output Research Association.

Mathur P.N. (1976, Editor), *Economic Analysis in Input-Output Framework*, Vol. IV, Input-Output Research Association.

Mathur, P.N. (1986), *Schism in Indian Polity and Gandhi*, NEHU Publications, Shillong.

Mathur, P.N. (1992), *Why Developing Countries Fail to Develop?*, Macmillan, London.

Mathur, P.N. (2000), "Embodied Technical Change and Technological Transfer to Developing Countries", In Somayajulu, V.V.N. and Prasad, K.N. (Eds.), *Indian Economy in Input Output Framework*, Allied.

Panchamukhi, V.R. (1991), "Linkage in Industrialization: A Study of Selected Developing Countries", *Journal of Development Planning*, United Nation, New York.

Prakash, Shri (1971), "Projection of Occupational-Educational Structure of Manpower—A Study of two Indian Public Sector Industries: Machine Tools and Heavy Electrical Equipment", *Artha Vijnana*, Vol. XIII, No. 1.

Prakash, S. (1971), "An Input-Output Model for Educational Planning", *Artha Vijnana*, Vol. XIII, No. 2.

Prakash, S. (1974), "Level of Output, Product-Mix and Stability of Labour Coefficient—A Study of Hindustan Steel Ltd"., *Southern Economic Journal*, Vol. 3, No. 2.

Prakash, S. (1975), "Input-Output Models of Education with Applications to Indian Data", *Anvesak*, Vol. 3, Reprinted in Mathur, Vol. III.

Prakash, S. (1981), "Cost-Based Prices in Indian Economy", *Malayan Economic Review*, Vol. II.

Prakash, S. (1991), "Generalised Dynamic Linkage Pattern as a Base of Convergence of Unbalanced to Balanced Growth Theory: Some Methodological and Theoretical Issues with Application to Indian Economy", *International Journal of Development Planning Literature*, Vol. 6, No. 3-4.

Prakash, S. and Chowdhury, Sumitra (1993), "Consumption of Forest Produce and Deforestation in India", *Journal of Quantitative Economics*.

Prakash, S. and Dutta, Ranita (1994), "Human Resource Allocation and Education-Employment Trade Offs", *Macro Models*, 1994, University of Lodz/Polish Academy of Sciences, Lodz.

Prakash, Shri (1999), "Obitury: W.W. Leontief", *Indian Economic Journal*, Vol. 47, No. 1.

Prakash, S. (2005), "Human Development Index in Input-Output Framework—An Alternative Approach", Fifteenth International Conference on Input Output Techniques, Beijing, China.

Prakash, S. and Balakrishnan, B. (2005), "Input-Output Modelling of Employment and Productivity as Base of Growth", Fifteenth International Conference on Input-Output Techniques, Beijing, China.

Prakash S. and Sharma, Shalini (2005), "Determining Values of Product and Company Brands in Input-Output Framework As Outcomes of Intellectual Property Rights", Fifteenth International Conference on Input-Output Techniques, Beijing, China.

Prasad, K.N. (1983), "Strategy for Developing Inter-Sectoral Linkages in North-East Region Based on their Input-Output Table—A Critique of Hirschman's Approach and an Application of Yau Amnes Index of Interrelatedness", Seminar on Strategies of Development for North-East India, Department of Economics, North-Eastern Hill University, Shillong.

Ramasubramanian, A. (2005), "Macro Contribution of a Micro Level Company: A Study through Input-Output Framework, Fifteenth International Conference on Input-Output Techniques", Beijing, China.

Sarma, A. and Kewal, R. (1989), "Income, Output and Employment Linkages and Import Intensities of Manufacturing Industries in India", *Journal of Development Studies*, Vol. 25, No. 2.

Sharma, Shalini (2004), "An Empirical Study of Food-grain Prices in Indian Economy", Ph.D. Thesis in Economics, Aligarh Muslim University.

Somayajulu, V.V.N. and Prasad, K.N. (2000, Editors), *Indian Economy in Input-Output Framework*, Allied Publishers.

Yotopaules, P.A. and Nugent, J.B. (1973), "The Balanced Growth Version of the Linkage Hypothesis: A Test", *The Quarterly Journal of Economics*.

---

* Such Contributions as are mentioned in the text but for which explicit references are not given above are published in 4 volumes of IORA or Somajulu-Prasad.

SECTION II

HUMAN DEVELOPMENT

Human Development Index in Input-Output Framework: An Alternative Approach

SHRI PRAKASH

I. INTRODUCTION

This paper seeks to develop an Input-Output Model for Estimating Human Development Index to capture both direct and indirect, and instantaneous and medium run effects of processes/sources of human resource development. Some of these processes/sources and variables involved in HD have been overlooked in UNDP's and Planning Commission's estimates of HDI. The Commission's approach is a replica of UNDP's concept, method and approach, except that it incorporates spatial variation of educational development in Educational Development Index (EDI). Besides, the Commission developed this index at sub-national levels also (For details see, Mohanty, 2003). The author of this paper and his associates at NIEPA has developed a Comprehensive Index of Educational Development both at the level of states and India in 1995. The Educational Development index has been based on as many as 31 variables, including the qualitative ones (Prakash *et. al.*, 1995). Planning Commission, probably in its eagerness to conform to UNDP framework, has overlooked that study. UNDPs and Commission's indexes have mostly the same concepts and share a common method of estimation. Errors of commission and omission are also the same.

Three basic dimensions, covered by UNDP and imitated by the Planning Commission are: (i) Healthy long life as measured by life expectancy at birth; (ii) Knowledge as measured by literacy and enrolments in primary, secondary and tertiary education; and (iii) A decent standard of living, as measured by per capita GDP.

II. LIMITATIONS OF CONVENTIONAL INDEX

Numerous variables, which affect human development are overlooked e.g. expected life depends on adequate consumption of food, nutrition, child and mother care, specially maternity child bearing, health, sanitation, potable water supply, hygiene. Moreover, per capita GDP as a measure of standard of living is not appropriate because increase in GDP need not necessarily reflect a higher standard of living. Personal distribution of income and wealth, besides the level of GDP, level and structure of taxation, the determinant of disposable income, number and quality of goods available for inclusion in consumption basket, and level and structure of prices are important determinants of the standards of living. Per capita income is only a crude proxy. Compilation of human poverty index (HPI) offers to extent some corrective to this proxy. But poverty focuses on (i) relative lower level of living, and (ii) the relative extent of deprivation. It overlooks the level of fulfilment and prosperity, the counterpart of deprivation as reflected by the general consumption standard of living. Incorporation of consumption explicitly will meet the requirements of adequacy and representativeness as a measure of welfare of the population as a whole. The poor may derive relatively less benefit as the trickle down effect of development may not operate. A proportion of GDP, is saved, while the rich may spend a lot on luxuries or foreign tours, etc. Then income does not take public provision of the social services into account, which have an important bearing on the standard of living.

The basic idea of the study is to (i) include additional variables to have a wider coverage in HDI, and (ii) integrate alternative to principal component analysis in commodity production model. An attempt has been made to include the following facets of life which have a direct bearing upon human resource development:

I. the following variables relating to expected life and health have been considered: (i) birth rate; (ii) death rate; (iii) number of doctors; (iv) population served per doctor; (v) number of PHC's and CHC's and sub-centres; (vi) average rural population served; (vii) auxiliary health workers; (viii) number of hospitals; (ix) number of beds. Output of pharmaceutical industry and proportion of population covered by preventive and promotive measures of health also need inclusion;

II. numerous variables pertaining to education and training; and

III. variables related to the mitigation of poverty and promotion of welfare such as public distribution of goods of basic needs, measure of inequality of income distribution, and range and quantity of consumer goods.

Planning Commission, Government of India, has developed Human Development Index, including education index, to supplement rather than supplant UNDP index. Both these indexes suffer from numerous infirmities due to: (i) exclusion of some processes and sources of human resource development, (ii) arbitrarily determined weights, and (iii) exclusion of important variables from the index. Limitations and shortcomings of these indices are both conceptual and methodological. UNDP's HDI neglects (a) certain elements of competence and competency acquired through (i) heritage and nature's gifts to man, (ii) formal training, and (iii) non-formal systems of training and learning, specially learning by doing and on the job experience; (b) qualitative capabilities of human resources. All these are the recognized sources of human capital formation. UNDP's approach is not consistent in so far as it takes account of outcome(s) of some process/source and some determinants, e.g. determinants say of expected age. It also overlooks variables of vocational, higher and professional education, the dominant determinant of human capital, (c) finally, level and pattern of utilization of available human resources is totally neglected. Thus, it focuses only on the most rudimentary elements of human resource development, compromising the representative character of the index. The study first explains the importance of the omitted variables in human resource development.

Accumulation of human resources involves the transformation of population into resource, which needs investment. Transformation mitigates supply constraints: (a) Rising incomes with economic growth loosens financial constraint both at macro and micro-levels, accelerating private demand and promoting public investment in health and education; (b) Increased supply eliminates the need for qualificational down gradation to overcome shortages; and (c) Rising stock and diversification of manpower with the growth of education encompass the changes in level, kind, content and quality of learning. These changes reflect higher capability profile of younger manpower, affecting both flows and stock of human resources (Prakash, 1995, 2000, Cf. Schultz, 1966). As the supply constraints are mitigated, twin processes of upgradation of the base of human capital comes into operation: (i) practitioners, personnel without formal education and/or training, are not recruited any more at the entry level; (ii) qualifications at entry as well as higher levels are upgraded, (a) raising the minimum level of education required; and (b) substitution of general by vocational or professional education. Taking only enrolements in different levels of education along with literacy into account for HDI misses the core element of aspect of educational processes, and hence, human capital accumulation in the dynamic state. The wastage, as represented by dropouts and failure lowers both the quantity and quality of human resource development (For details, See Prakash, 1995, Prakash and Chowdhury, 1994). Variables like pass and leavers' ratios, attendance rates, minimum level of learning acquired are important determinants of human capital accumulation rates and their quality.

III. HUMAN RESOURCE DEVELOPMENT

Human resource development depends upon (a) the quantity and quality of inputs used in building human capability, (b) process(es) of capability building and its quality dimension, and (c) outcome/output. UNDP and Planning Commission neglect some elements of all the above three factors and variables associated with these. This study addresses some of these issues and highlights some variables overlooked in the conventional indexes.

Conventional indexes fail to (i) distinguish human resources from population, and (ii) differentiate between human resource and human capital. Despite the widespread networking of institutions of technical and professional education, colleges and universities, imparting general education, polytechnics and other institutions of vocational studies, non-formal system still remains an important source of supply of lower and lower middle technical and professional manpower. Non-formal sector institutions impart training and build knowledge base of a large segment of population, especially in areas relating to emerging occupations/professions relating to emerging areas of knowledge. De-skilling and un-learning effect of non-utilisation and/or under-utilisation, or mis-matched use of knowledge and skills are also overlooked (for Conceptualization and Estimation, See Prakash, 2000, for Deskilling Effect, See M. Jain, 2003). For example, one estimate shows that a minimum of 3-4 years' continuous primary schooling is needed for literacy. But prolonged non-use of the ability to read, write and/or numeracy pushes the person back into illiteracy (Prakash *et. al.*, 1994). This applies to other skills and levels of knowledge/education also. Then, past stock of human resources, brought forward into the current year, requires adjustment for wastage due to ageing, death and retirement and non or under-utilization of acquired capability.

The current index of HRD also overlooks the difference between (i) autonomous process of development of man's capabilities, which materialize even if minimal subsistence for physical survival is available; and (ii) non-autonomous process of human development based on investment in man. The latter process supplements, reinforces and accelerates the outcome of autonomous process on the one hand, and it magnifies and diversifies the effect on autonomous development of human resources on the other. Autonomous process and some components of non-autonomous process, such as investment in food, potable water supply, nutrition, clothing, housing, hygiene, sanitation, health and health care, focus largely on protective, preventive and curative measures of health on the one hand, and the building of physical strength, stamina and endurance on the other. None of these enters into UNDP's index of HD. This study has, therefore, explored several variables pertaing to health and health care on the one hand, and component of sectoral output catering to the consumption needs of human resources employed in various production sectors of living conditions. As against per capita income as a proxy the consumption variable (determined by IO model on the basis of private final consumption expenditure directly affect the building of strength, stamina, endurance and other components of physical capability directly and intellectual capability indirectly on the one hand, it also relates to welfare on the other.

Variables like birth and death rates and expected age which UNDP assigns high importance, need supplementation by variables pertaining to control over maternity-related deaths, infant mortality, morbidy, fecundity, and child and mother care measures. These variables affect status of health. Investment in family welfare, including control over population growth, is the important means of HRD. Effect of all these factors either on population growth or human resource development are not captured by expected age at birth, notwithstanding the inclusion of birth and death rates in UNDPs HDI. Variables like expected age do not reveal the quality of life. Living a long life does not necessarily mean living a healthy or productive or happy life. Frequency of sickness and its duration affect both regularity/ punctuality and productivity at the work place.

Age and gender structure, upon which impinges the dependency ratios, are equally important from the view point of growth of both intellectual and physical capability on the one hand, and participation rates in economic and educational activities on the other. Matrimony and child birth affect female participation in workforce and after a particular age, one has to withdraw from the workforce, when a productive asset becomes a non-resource. These two factors affect the stock of human resources and their availability for utilization. Gender and age structure of population directly affect participation in productive activities, whereas unemployment affects utilization of available resources. Similarly, one becomes eligible to partake in education, while after crossing a specific age; most participants go out of education. Then, empirical evidence suggests that younger workers are better educated and more qualified than the older ones (Prakash, 1995). This is an outcome of the following factors: As an economy moves from lower to maturer stages of development (a) Educational development occurs concurrently; (b) Investment in nutrition, hygiene, sanitation, health and health care, both in absolute and relative terms, rises; and (c) Qualitative improvement gets greater attention as a part of the consolidation of gains of quantitative expansion. Still girls and children belonging to SC and ST mainly suffer from various handicaps such as dropping out of school prematurely and/or remaining totally out of school (Prakash *et. al.,* 1996). Gender inequality becomes important from this view point. Some estimate of the degree of gender and spatial inequalities needs incorporation in the index. In my view, GDI of UNDP needs to be supplemented, if not substituted by GII, and SII, the gender and spatial inequality index. Net rather than gross enrolments take care of some facets. Why are these variables not used in HDI/EDI by UNDP? A comprehensive composite index needs incorporation of all the pivotal factors of supply and demand. This study has incorporated as many as 37 variables relating to education, 9 variables relating to health and 9 related to output and consumption of basic consumer goods.

Learning by Doing Professionals

The products of non-formal system of learning and training acquired by actually doing the job also end up as professionals. Such professionals are defined as Practioners in Manpower Accounts of India. Manpower Accounts show their occupation profile according to sector of their employment. Number of such professionals and positions they occupy in occupational hierarchy reflect the past degree and direction of down-gradation of qualifications to overcome shortages of specific high and middle level manpower for particular occupations/sectors. This process also highlights the importance of non-formal learning, training and job experience. This also manifests the level and structure of educational development and its flexibility and responsiveness to the emerging need for new knowledge.

Change in the proportion of practicing professionals in total may highlight the coverage of demand-supply gap, while productivity may highlight the contribution of this source and mechanism of HRD to economic growth. Incidentally, Guilds and Professional Associations used to impart training for skill building in a non-formalised system not very long ago. Even today, the large army of mechanics, even those of high priced machines and such high priced and white goods as cars and domestic gadgets, are either self-employed or employed in big organizations, learn their trades and acquire skills through non-formal streams of human resource building. Lower and lower middle manpower is mostly accumulated by this process of HRD. Vertical mobility takes many of them very high up in occupational hierarchy.

Formal system of education and training focuses only on high and middle/lower middle level manpower and it is extremely slow to respond to emerging changes in manpower needs of the economy in the wake of technological upgradation of production base, which necessitates new skills, occupations and knowledge. Private initiatives of non-formal system(s) are not only flexible but these also fill up the gaps in formal system timely. In fact, a very large proportion of software operators and average level computer operators/experts in the wake of information technology revolution have emerged largely from non-formal system of learning/training initially. Success of NIIT is just one example. This source of HRD is totally missing in UNDP's accounting. Due to paucity of time, I have not been able to access these data. The updated version of the paper shall use these data.

Training for Filling Precept-Practice Gaps

In-house training focuses on the (a) induction of chosen personnel into the culture and work environment of employer organizations; (b) filling up of gaps in the knowledge, skills and training received and that required for particular jobs to be assigned to the employed professionals; and (c) there is in-service training imparted to human resources of a company or organization from time to time to update their knowledge and skill base. University Grants Commission has established a wide spread net work of Academic Staff Colleges, which organize a number of orientation and subject-based refresher courses each years for college and university teachers. AICTE also sponsors Faculty Development Programmes. Such training constitutes an important instrument of human resource development to meet the changing knowledge and skill needs of manpower employed by corporates and other organizations. Both these facets of training involve huge investment in augmenting human capability. The number of training institutes, training programmes conducted, persons trained thereof and their annual budgets may highlight the importance of training needs of human resources and its cost. Sizeable investment is made in such sources of human resource development both in the developed and developing countries. How does one then overlook these in estimating HRD index? All this investment is totally overlooked by UNDP's HDI. Updating exercise of this study is expected to take care of this aspect.

Both conceptually and empirically, distinguishing the means and mechanisms of HRD from their outcomes and differentiating actual from potential outcome/gain is needed. Students, human resource in the making, and labour force participation rates, preferably age and gender-wise, are also important indicators of human resource development. These two variables together manifest accumulation/flow and stock components of human resource development. Besides, incidence of unemployment, casual and marginal employment, level and pattern of optimum, under and over utilization of available resources facilitate assessment of actual use and possible deskilling effect of non-utilization. Then experience also contributes to development of skill, knowledge and understanding of professional needs of the jobs. In this illustrative and experimental exercise, time constraint has forced the neglect of some of these variables as a factor of HD.

Alternative Principal Component Analysis

The study proposes to use evolve an alternative method of factor/principal component analysis for estimating HDI, which takes into account both the quantitative and qualitative aspects.

It also determines weights objectively. Alternative method of component analysis had been developed in the context of quality of education on behalf of Regional Office of UNESCO, Bangkok, Thailand (Prakash *et. al.*, 1995). This study extends that method to cover non-educational components of human resource development also. Synthesis of this model into input output model of the economy has also been attempted. Thus, the study incorporates HDI into input-output analysis to push forward the threshold of IO models and endow the compilation of HDI with a highly sophisticated methodological base.

IV. DATA BASE

Data of Indian economy have been used for empirical illustration of the conceptual and methodological base of the alternative approach. Input-Output Table of Indian Economy, 1993-94, the last table compiled and made available by Planning Commission, constitutes the base of empirical prognostication of the input-output model. Information about health, education and employment has been gathered from such other sources as Census 1991, Economic Survey, Fact Book of Manpower, IAMR and Reports of NSSO.

V. METHOD AND MODEL

Complementary sub-models have been developed:

(i) A partially decomposable input-output model of production;
(ii) A model, designed for identifying and clustering of both ordinally and cardinally measured variables into different factors of human resource development; and
(iii) A model to determine weights of different factors/sub-indices to be used in composite HDI.

Results of application of all three models are synthesized and integrated to determine state-wise one single composite index of human development.

I. Model of Production System

Want of universal mutuality of inter-relations or inter-dependencies in developing economies make a decomposable model suit the analysis better. Education and health, in so far as supply of material goods is concerned, have only unidirectional relationships with commodity production. Similarly, commodity production sectors of the economy draw their human capital from education but supply the material inputs to education and training. This also makes decomposable model appropriate for this study. It will also simplify the estimation of Leontief inverse.

Economy has been classified into 2 groups of sectors:

(i) sectors pertaining to factors of human resource development; and

(ii) commodity production sectors, producing goods and services.

The triangularised decomposable input-output model is given below:

$$\begin{bmatrix} X^1 \\ X^2 \end{bmatrix} = \begin{bmatrix} A_{11}X^1 & A_{12}X^2 \\ 0 & A_{22}X^2 \end{bmatrix} + \begin{bmatrix} F^1 \\ F^2 \end{bmatrix} \quad (1)$$

The following solutions hold

$$X^2 = (I-A_{22})^{-1} F^2 \quad (2)$$

$$X^1 = (I-A_{11})^{-1} A_{12} (I-A_{22})^{-1} F^2 + (I-A_{11})^{-1} F^1 \quad (3)$$

where X^1 is a column vector of output $(X^1_1\ X^1_2 . X^1_3 \ldots X^1 m)$;

$F^1 = F^1_{1,}\ F^1_{2,}\ (F^1_3 \ldots F^1 m)$;

F^2 are column vectors w of final use, $(F^2_{m+1}\ F^2_{m+2}\ F^2_{m+3} \ldots F^2 n)$;

and

A is input coefficients matrix, partitioned into 3 sub-matrices.

Employment

Solution values of X^1 and X^2 from relations 2 and 3 are used in order to determine employment in terms of F^1 and F^2. Employment involved in the production of given output is given by

$$\hat{N}^1 = L^1 \hat{X}^1 \qquad (4)$$

$$\hat{N}^2 = L^2 \hat{X}^2 \qquad (5)$$

where $\hat{N}^1$ and $\hat{N}^2$ are row vectors of estimates of sectoral employment. L^1 and L^2 are row vectors of sectoral employment coefficients, a_{0i} where $a^1_{0i} = N^1_{0i}/X^1_i$, that is, labour required per unit of output, $X^1_{i;}$ $\hat{N}^1 = \sum_i^m N^1_{oi}$ is total employment in the first sub-group of sectors. Substituting for X^1 and X^2, we get

$$\hat{N}^1 = L^1 (I - A_{11})^{-1} [A_{12} (I - A_{22})^{-1} F^2 + F^1] \qquad (6)$$

$$\hat{N}^2 = L^2 (I - A_{22})^{-1} F^2 \qquad (7)$$

Vectors of labour coefficients of relations 4 and 5 have also been decomposed into three sub-vectors according to level/type of education: L^{11}, L^{12}, L^{13}, and L^{21}, L^{22}, L^{23}. Equations 6 and 7 may be replaced by similar equations to furnish estimates of N^{11}, N^{12}, N^{13}, N^{21}, N^{22} and N^{23} that correspond to L^{1k}, L^{2p}, k, p = 1, 2, 3.

Productivity

Contribution of human capital to output and its growth can be derived from factor productivity. So the productivity has to be estimated. But three different concepts of productivity are distinguished: productivity for growth; productivity for welfare, and productivity for competition (Cf. Juan & Febrero). The gross factor productivity[1], $\hat{P}$ is given by **

$$\hat{P}^1 = (N^1)^{-1} X^1 \qquad (8)$$

$$\hat{P}^2 = (N^2)^{-1} X^2 \qquad (9)$$

where $\hat{P}^1$ and $\hat{P}^2$ are sector-wise column vectors of productivity for two groups of sectors, $p^1_j = \hat{X}^1_j/N^1_{0j}$, where $l^1 = L^1(I-A_{11})^{-1}$, $l^2 = L^2(I-A_{22})^{-1}$, and $l^1 = (l^1_{01}, l^1_{02}, \ldots l^1_{0m})$, $l^2 = (l^2_{0m+1}, \ldots l^2_{0n})$.

Use of solution rather than observed values of X in the estimation of employment and productivity focuses on consideration of both (i) direct and indirect requirement of labour for production, (ii) direct and indirect requirement of capital, (iii) inclusion of both direct indirect components of net output in productivity. But the aversion of double counting warrants that either (i) $\hat{X}^1$ and $\hat{X}^2$ are used to estimate the elements of the vector L of labour coefficients, or alternatively (ii) $l^1 = L^1 (I-A_{11})^{-1}$ and $l^2 = L^2 (I-A_{22})^{-1}$ are used. It shall still be better to use RHS of relations 8 and 9 for estimating productivity. Capital requirements are embodied in final demand from which solution values of X are derived; capital comprises of Gross Fixed Capital Formation (GFCF) and Change in Stocks, and (iii) requirements of growth that are met out of surplus. Matrix A takes into account what Sraffa calls "Requirement of Self-Replacement of Commodity Production by Commodities in the Economy" at a given level, whereas capital coefficients take care of growth.

Growth Concept of Productivity may be used to evaluate the growth effect of human capital, which relates surplus of output over inputs used in production to human and physical capital requirements. The surplus output constitutes the supply pool for allocation among consumption, investment and exports. The consumption component of productivity relates both to human capital accumulation and welfare.

VI. MODEL OF CLUSTERING/FACTORING VARIABLES

Thurstone introduced the concept of factor analysis in 1931. Factor is defined as a linear combination of two or more variables. Principal component/factor analysis may, therefore, be defined as the method of compressing or combining two or more variables to define a new variable, called factor/component. Factors/components reduce the number of variables involved in the system. Since linear combinations are based on the structure of relationships, the factor analysis may also be defined as the method of detection of structure of relationships to facilitate classification and clustering of variables according to twin principles of maximizing (i) homogeneity/inter-relatedness within the cluster/factor, and (ii) heterogeneity between clusters/factors. Naturally, correlation/association and/or regression analysis may be used as the base of factor analysis. Since indexing, including the human resource index, involves the further combining of numerous variables/factors into one single value, factor/component analysis comes as a handy tool for indexing. This study has, therefore, chosen to use an innovative model of factoring/clustering.

The New Model of Identification and Clustering of variables into factors is an extension and modification of the Kendall's method of ranking rank sums and then combining these clusters with Kendall's Coefficient of Concordance with a view to further reduce the number of variables within each brad cluster to form factors, and extract weights scientifically rather than arbitrarily. Rank correlation coefficient has been calculated according to Spearman's rather than Kendall's formulation (1975):

$$\rho_{sj} = 1-[6\sum\{d^2(i)\}/\{n(n^2-1)\}] \quad (10)$$

where ρ is rank correlation coefficient, d(i) is difference between two ranks allotted according to criteria s and j to i^{th} unit, n denotes units ranked, and s/j = 1 . . . m are variables/ranking criteria.

The coefficient of concordance, W, is estimated as follows:

$$W = [12S]/(m^2 (n^3 - n)] \quad (11)$$

where S is the sum of squares of deviations of the sum of ranks of an individual unit from the mean of rank sums according to all m criteria used for ranking n units/entities; mean of ranks is given by

$$M= (1/2)(n+1)\ m$$

where, M denotes mean of ranks of rank sums.

χ^2, used to test the statistical significance of W, is calculated as follows:

$$\chi^2 = m\ (n - 1)\ W \quad (12)$$

Factoring Model

Identification and Clustering of variables into distinct factors is the first step. Rank correlation coefficients are the base of this step. Rank correlation coefficients between all possible pairs of variables of n units/entities, ranked according to m criteria, taken two at a time, say ${}^{m}c_{2}$, have to be worked out for clustering variables into homogenous clusters. One pair of two most closely related variables is identified as the core variables of first factor. Further scrutiny is done for identifying variables for inclusion in the core group of first factor. First factor will have only such variables as are positively correlated significantly with either variable of the core pair. Second group, having variables negatively correlated significantly with either variable of the core pair, is kept apart. Third group will have all other variables, having no correlation with variables of first two groups.

Variables, correlated with either variable of the first core pair, are added to the group one by one successively. Coefficients of Concordance are calculated for successive groups of 3, 4 . . . variables of this group. The significance of observed value of W, Chi-square, χ^2 with (N–1) degrees of freedom will be used as the test, where N denotes total observations; $N < mn$. Results are then used for grouping variables into first cluster. If the coefficient of concordance indicates statistical significance the additional variable(s) is included in the first cluster. If the concordance coefficient indicates non-significant agreement, the additional variable(s) is excluded from the core pair. Change in concordance as a result of addition of a new variable to the core group is thus used to decide whether additional variable(s) is retained in the cluster. If a third variable is retained in the group, then another variable, showing high correlation with any of these three core variables, is brought into this cluster of 3 variables. The coefficient of concordance for this augmented cluster of 4 variables is again evaluated. The process is repeated till all variables, having significant positive correlation with any variable(s) of the core group, have been exhausted. In all probability, some variables initially included in the first cluster will be left out. Once the first cluster has been finalized, the process is repeated on the second most closely correlated pair of another two variables till all such variables, that show a very high degree of concordance with second group, have been identified and clubbed together in the second cluster. We end up with say, k clusters of m variables; n-m variable having been excluded from all the clusters, $1 < k < {}^{m}c_2$. Each cluster constitutes one factor or component. First core set of variables furnishes one cluster of variables, defined as first factor. Each of the subsequent sets will furnish one cluster/factor each. The coefficients of concordance and rank correlation are thus used jointly as discriminants for clustering given variables into a limited number of factors.

All unrelated variables are excluded from the given cluster one by one. The coefficient of correlation and coefficient of concordance rather than rank sums are used to eliminate subjective judgment involved in Kendall's method of arriving at appropriate components/factors, each factor having 2 or more variables showing maximum degree of inter-relatedness and concordance.

VII. DETERMINING OPTIMUM NUMBER OF VARIABLES AND FACTORS

Different factors are formed according to the principles of (i) minimizing variables in a factor, (ii) maximizing inter-relationship between variables within the cluster, and (iii) minimizing relationship between variables constituting different factors. Variables excluded from factor show independence. Each consecutive factor captures the maximum joint variability of the variables excluded from preceding factor. These selected factors will then constitute the base of composite index. In some cases, criterion of significance of correlation and/or concordance may lead to an ambiguity regarding inclusion of a variable(s) in one or other factor, if the variable(s) qualifies for inclusion in more than one factor. Besides, initially formed clusters on the basis of significance of correlation and concordance coefficients may not minimize the number of variables within a cluster. A supplementary condition, over and above the above criteria, is imposed. Some value of significant correlation coefficient is specified as the minimum for inclusion of the variables in a factor. The minimum critical value, taken as the cut-off, will thus represent cases where at least the specified percentage of total change in one variable is explained by the other. Explained proportion of variation of lesser magnitude than the cut-off, will leave too wide a margin for residuals to be more dominant than the chosen determinants. The process of factoring should stop at a point where only little relatedness/joint variability remains for exploration. This is a point beyond which random variation can not be reduced and systematic variation can not be raised.

Maximum Number of Factors

There arises the question of number of factors to be included in an index. As more and more factors are formed, less and less joint variability remains to be explored. Extraction of more and more systematically related variables through factoring also tends to lower random variance. But the factors formed should neither be far too many nor far too few. There exist criteria to guide the determination of the optimal number of factors to be extracted from the given variables. Kaiser (1960) criterion, widely used in conventional principal component analysis, suggests the retention of factors having an Eigen value larger than one. It is based on the assumption that the factor should explain variance at least equal to that of one original constituent variable, variances of all variables having been standardized to unity. Cattel suggests the point where the decrease of Eigen values tapers off. To the right of this point, one finds only what is defined as Factorial Scree. Scree, in geology, refers to debris at the lower part of a rocky slope. Kaiser criterion may at times suggest the retention of too many factors, while Cattel criterion may lead to the retention of too few factors. This may suggest the combined use of two criteria.

Can we formulate similar guidelines for determining optimum number of factors for the new method? For the given number of observations, there is a minimum critical value of the coefficient of concordance among the variables of a factor, which varies according to the number of variables included in the factor. The number of variables included in a factor may lie between the minimum 2 and maximum m. Maximum of these minimum values/variables may be taken to determine the point below which the debris of the scree will lie. Besides, average of rank correlations among the variables of first and last clusters may be taken to set-up the average degree of variability as acceptable for the formation of a factor. These two parameters may be supplemented by the interpretability of the results furnished by differentiating the number of factors to be finally included in the index.

Generally, 4-5 factors exhaust 95 to 100 per cent of total variation. Besides, first 2-3 factors normally exhaust 65-85 per cent of tótal variation. Peripheral factors are generally excluded and a rule of thumb and nail is employed to pick up only such factors as explain at least 65-75 per cent of total variation. This generally requires the inclusion of 2-3 factors/components (Prakash and Mohapatra, 1981, Kendall, 1975). This technique may be adopted for the formation of composite index as efficiently as Principal Component/Factor Analysis or Kenall's method of ranking successive rank sums.

A common facet of multi-criteria of ranking is that larger the number of variables, lower tends to be the degree of inter-relation, and hence, concordance among them. It implies that any factor should not have too many variables to jeopardize the homogeneity and coherence, and it should not be too small to make factoring redundant.

VIII. DETERMINATION OF WEIGHTS OF FACTORS

The composite index may be estimated from the chosen factors. But the factors have to be weighted. Eigen values of principal components furnish the weights. But Kendall's method does not use weighting. This method derives weights to be attached to each factor as follows: Sum of ranks of each spatial unit, according to variables of each factor is divided by the number of variables constituting a factor for each ranked unit separately. Average of all units for all criteria, taken together, is also determined. Let $\overline{X}$ (1i) be the average rank sum of ith unit, based on variables of first factor, and let $\overline{X}$ be the average of all ranks according to all criteria of all units taken together. The product of the proportion of divergence of $\overline{X}$ (1i) from this overall average, $\overline{X}$, and the ratio of concordance coefficients of the factor and its difference from unity is defined as w (1i) as the weight of first factor in indexing:

$$w(1i) = \left[\frac{\overline{X}(1i) - \overline{X}}{\overline{X}}\right] \cdot \left[\frac{W(1)}{1 - W(1)}\right] \tag{13}$$

Where w (1i) is the weight assigned to first factor for i[th] unit for estimating composite index and W(1) is the coefficient of concordance of first factor. Sum of all weighted values of all factors for each unit will determine its composite index of human resource development.

IX. DATA MASSAGING

First, 40 of the 115 sectors of the economy have been identified as the base of human resource development. These sectors pertain to (i) health, health care and health service, (ii) education and training, and (iii) production of consumer goods, specially the goods satisfying basic needs, and commodities/services satisfying professional needs. Remaining 75 sectors constitute the group of other commodity production. Both groups of sectors have been aggregated into 45 sectors. Data difficulties, pertaining to employment and its education-occupation composition, led us to aggregate 115 into 45 broad sectors of the economy. Nature and level of aggregation are data rather than concept or method-related.

In all, 10 out of 45 aggregated sectors pertain to the provision of goods needed as investment in physical strength and stamina of human resources. Number of sectors in these groups is listed below:

TABLE 1

Sectors Producing Provision For	*Number of Sectors*
Food	7
Personal Effects/Necessities	3
Education	5
Health	3
Total	18

Sectors, considered as the base of HRD, pertain to food and food processing, clothing, other necessities such as gas, electricity and water supply, transport, education, training and health. Sectors needed to sustain education and health such as printing and publishing, health care services and pharmaceutical industry also constitute a part of this group.

X. EMPLOYMENT AND PRODUCTIVITY

Productivity is the manifestation of economic contribution of human capital to output and its growth. For its estimation, employment involved in the production of given output has to be determined first. In order to relate productivity to human resource capability, labour coefficients a^1_{0i} and a^2_{0j} have been decomposed into sub-coefficients according to educational qualifications. But the level and type of education required in relation to actual education possessed by employees are considered in relation to (i) sector, (ii) occupation, and (iii) position in the hierarchy: (i) workers having below average general education and training, including illiterates; (ii) workers having below average professional/technical/vocational education and training; and (iii) workers having professional/technical, vocational education required for occupations of their employment (Cf. Parnes, 1959, Tinbergen and Correa, 1963). Estimates have been derived on the basis of Education-Occupation-Industry matrix, based on information culled from Census data, 1991 and Annual DGET reports.

Sectoral profits have been used to decompose sectoral value added to yield estimates of wage and salary component. These two components have facilitated the estimation of contribution of human and physical capital to value added. Whereas wages and salaries reflect the productivity of human capital, profits manifest the productivity of physical capital. Manpower is the carrier of human capital; while machinery, equipment, and tools are the carriers of physical capital and technology. As a first approximation, it is assumed that expenses on food, clothing, hygiene, sanitation, potable water, medicines and health care reflect the physical component of human capital, whereas investment in education and training reflect intellectual component of human capital. Three fold classification of sectoral employment according to education is used to estimate the contribution of human capital to output in terms of productivity differentials.

Thus, we have 3 distinct groups of variables that relate to (i) (a) consumption designed for the building of physical strength and stamina of manpower, (b) health and health care services that service the needs of preservation of health, and cure and prevention of disease, and (ii) education and training. Since a certain level of both direct and indirect inter-relatedness has already been exhausted through the use of matrix multiplier, these variables are kept as clusters. But within the group, interrelatedness and variability are detected by the use of clustering model in order to extract distinct factors within each group. All above parameters and variables have been used to rank in ascending or descending order of values according to the nature of the variable. For example, lowest death and birth rates command first rank, whereas the highest expected age at birth is ranked first.

On the basis of sectoral employment and average private per person consumption of specified goods, output for final consumption for the sustenance of human capital deployed on productive activities is estimated. Estimated output of such goods is then allocated among the states according to their SDP. It furnishes estimates of output produced for the sustenance of human capital in the commodity production sectors. Same procedure is applied to estimate the component of output of education and health to estimate their contribution to the physical and intellectual capabilities of human capital. Population is not included in human capital.

XI. EMPIRICAL RESULTS

Experiment shows that the statistical significance of either rank correlation or concordance coefficients is a necessary but not sufficient condition of high degree of inter-relatedness and/or high degree of concordance. Inclusion of too many variables in a cluster leads to a decline in the (i) average value of rank correlation coefficients, and (ii) degree of concordance.

Therefore, a critical minimum value for significant correlation has been determined. The variables within a cluster, having inter-correlation lower than the critical minimum, are dropped to maximize inter-relatedness and degree of concordance. This facilitates the formation of factors having optimum degree of homogeneity, as determined by inter-correlations and concordance. This explains the exclusion of as many as 25 educational variables from the finally chosen four rather than five factors.

Concordance tends to increase with a decline in the number of variables in a cluster upto a point. The acceptable degree of inter-relatedness and agreement in our empirical exercises is .388 for concordance, and average of 0.56 for rank correlation coefficients. These values have been chosen as the minimum of the cut-off point for inclusion of variables in factors. On the whole, average of rank correlations and corresponding value of chi-square for concordance increase with the increasing degree of concordance.

As many as 37 variables relating to education have been analysed. The following table shows the factors formed, variables they comprise of, average of rank correlation among the variables of each factor, and their corresponding coefficients of concordance:

TABLE 2

Sector	*Factor*	*Factor Variables*	*Average rank*	*Coefficient of Concordance*
Health	Factor – I	7	49.0	0.388
	Factor – II	2	27.0	0.693
Education	Factor – I	3	49.5	0.893
	Factor – II	2	0.33	0.821
	Factor – III	4	66.0	0.579
	Factor – IV	3	49.5	0.67
Consumption	Factor - I	9	38.0	1.00

Initial analysis leads to the identification of 15, 8, 8, 3 and 2 variables constituting 5 factors. After the identification of final clusters and their constituent variables, the variate values have been normalized by the national average corresponding to a given variables so as to make them scale free. The normalized value has then been used to estimate each factor and the associated sub-index separately. These have then been used to estimate three indexes, one each corresponding to health, education and consumption. These indexes, in turn, have been converted into a single composite index of human resource development. Results reported in Table 2 facilitate the formation of three crude indexes of three factors of human development. The crude indexes have been merged to furnish an estimate of one single composite index of human development, which is expected to differ significantly from UNDP's index in (i) magnitude, (ii) range of variation among spatial units, and (iii) number of variables considered, and hence, the coverage.

National index serves as the reference point for the relative position of individual states. But this index does not have any base year for reference. Results are reported in Tables 1 and 2.

The results show that (i) average human development index has a value of 232.39; (ii) the human development index varies sharply among the states; (iii) the coefficient of variation has as high a value as 190 per cent; and (iv) the range of variation is from the minimum 161.43 for Rajasthan to a maximum of 307.38 for Andhra Pradesh.

A perusal of the three constituent factors of human development index reveals that (i) education, the dominant determinant of intellectual profile of human resource, is the pivot of human development index: on an average, contribution of EDI to composite HD index ranges from approximately two-thirds to nine-tenths of the total, though, like the composite HDI, EDI and its contribution to HDI varies sharply among the variables; (ii) education is followed by health, though its relative contribution to HDI is much lower than that of education; (iii) surprisingly, investment in physical component of HD occupies the last position, its relative and absolute contribution being very low; (iv) these results, however, may act as the sign posts and delineate the road map for future research. Since the study is highly experimental and illustrative of concepts and methodology, the author expects to come forward with more precise empirical estimates with comparable values of UNDP's HDI in near future.

XII. MAIN FINDINGS

The results highlight that :

(i) Contribution of both human and physical capital vary sharply between sectors;

(ii) Technology and physical capital dominates sectors where processing of materials are pivotal, whereas knowledge-based sectors are dominated by human capital;

(iii) Intellectual component of human capital dominates such sectors where high proportion of professional and technical workers are employed;

(iv) Effect of technical and professional education and skills thereof is reflected in the contribution of human capital component of productivity;

(v) Practitioners constitute non-negligible proportion of professional and technical workers (approximately 13%) across the sectors, though the proportion varies greatly between sectors. Naturally, contribution of such constituents of human capital, overlooked by conventional indexes is substantive. So long as on the job learning and non-formal training remain important sources of human capital accumulation and means of filling up the supply-demand gaps, it is not rational to leave it out of reckoning in HDI as is done by UNDP and Planning Commission. *A priori* reasoning and thesis proposed in this study are thus supported by empirical evidence. UNDP has to have a look at such results; and

(vi) For sectors having low capital and technology base such as primary sectors, physical component of human capital emerges as dominant.

NOTES

1. Entire Output is attributed to labour, implying as if it were the only factor used in production. Besides primary factor labour, capital is an important factor of production. The grossness arises from two sources (i) total output is attributed to labour; and (ii) gross rather than net output is used as denominator.
   Net productivity may be estimated by working out the ratio of factors used in production and net output. Net output may itself be conceptualized in two alternative ways: (i) Output of a given good net of its inter-industry use/demand for sectoral output, which is defined as surplus output; and (ii) value added, which is defined as excess of output over and above the value of intermediate inputs used up in production.
2. Marshall, in a different context, describes the experience of mining industry in 1870's in similar terms. See Principles of Economics, Macmillan.

REFERENCES

Correa, H. and Tinbergen, J. (1962), "Quantitative Adaptation of Education to Accelerated Growth", *Kyklos*, Vol. 15.

Jain, Manish (2001), "Managing Deskilling Effect of IT Enabled Services (ITES) in Electronics Engineering Industry—A Study of Competence Profiles of Design Engineers", Synopsis of Ph.D. Thesis, BIMTECH.

Kaiser (1960), Quoted from *Principal Components and Factor Analysis,* File:///c:/Documents %20Settings/Administrator/My %20Document

Kendall, M.G. (1975), *Multi-Variate Analysis,* Charles Griffin and Co., London.

Kendall, M.G. (1962), *Rank Correlation Methods,* Hazuer Publishing Co., New York.

Mohanty, N.K. (2003), "A Comparative Study of Education Indices of UNDP's Human Development Report and National Human Development Report of India", *Business Perspectives,* Vol. 5, No. 2.

Oscar de Juan & Eladio Febrero (2000), "Measuring Productivity from Vertically Integrated Sectors", *Economic Systems Research,* Journal of the International Input-Output Research Association, Vol. 12, No. 1.

Prakash, S. and Chowdhury, S. (1994), *Expenditure on Education—Theory Models and Growth,* NIEPA, New Delhi.

Parnes, Herbert, S. (1956), "Manpower Analysis in Educational Planning", in *Parnes, Ibid.*

Prakash, S. (2000), "Utilization of Human Resources," *Business Perspectives,* Vol. 2, No. 2.

Prakash, S. (1995), *Cost of Education,* Anamika, Delhi.

Prakash, S., Mehta, A.C. and Zaidi, S.M.A. (1995), "Indicators of Quality of Education," National Status Paper, UNESCO Regional Office, Bangkok and NIEPA, New Delhi.

Prakash, S. and Mohapatra, A.C. (1980), "Development of the State of M.P.—A Study of Intra State and Inter-Temporal Variations", *Third World Planning Review,* Vol. 2, No. 2, Liverpool, U.K.

Prakash, S., Srivastava, R., Mehta, A.C. and Zaidi, S.M.I.A. (1994), "Use of Sample Survey Techniques for Educational Statistics", UNESCO, Paris.

Principal Components and Factor Analysis, File:///c:/Documents %20Settings/Administrator/My %20Document

Thurstone Quoted from Principal Components and Factor Analysis, File:///c:/Documents %20Settings/Administrator/My %20Document

Education in Human Development Index of India

R. HEMALATHA

INTRODUCTION

No system in the world can be static. Systems undergo both desirable and undesirable changes. The desirable changes in an economic system will bring about progress, leading to growth and development that refer to the positive changes in the various economic variables of an economy, (Prakash, 1994). Hence development may mean industrial and technological growth, competitive edge, increase in per capita income and net national product; it needs coupling with improvement in the quality of life in the form of reduction in negative indicators. Hence, development in any society should be viewed by what it does to the average individuals.

ROLE OF HUMAN CAPITAL FORMATION IN GROWTH AND DEVELOPMENT

Human capital can be conceived as the stock of knowledge,

information, skills, health, strength and stamina, vigor, initiatives and motivation accumulated by the people in a country for employment in production of goods and services, defense, and machinery to carry country forward (Prakash,1996). The quantity and quality of human resource depends a great deal on the size, age and gender profile of population, which is the supply pool for human resource development. Other resources of an economy will be under-utilized, mal-utilized and un-utilized without proper development and deployment of human element. It becomes essential therefore, to have a framework and evolve strategies that forge and strengthen the link between economic growth, with social well through investment.

EDUCATION IN THE DEVELOPMENT OF HUMAN CAPITAL

Investment in education is central to investment in all other areas needed for human resource development, as it creates a store-house of knowledge and skills that can be used and developed by generations to come. Knowledge created through education is useful and is essential for creating awareness on proper utilization of investment in all areas of human development. Role of education in the development of an economy can never be overemphasized. Education may not rank first in the order of priority for an individual and the society in comparison to food, shelter, clothing and health but the provision and utilization of these is itself dependent on education of the people.

Education is a labor intensive, knowledge based industry, characterized by four-fold inter-sectoral linkage. It is a universal supplier of knowledge and know-how to all sectors of the economy. The contribution of education to economy is not in material terms alone in the form of manpower inputs but is also in the imperceptible forms of:

- Providing consultancy and advice to the industry;
- Providing scientific research output to industries for innovation;
- Social science research output plays a key role in management of organizations in the form of managerial

techniques, organizational behaviour, formulation, implementation and evaluation of policies and strategies; and

- Education supplies and absorbs educated manpower endowed with the required skills, knowledge and aptitude.

It is the universal intermediary providing, technological knowhow, managerial reasoning and advice to each and every sector of the economy. Besides, creation of awareness about the products produced advertisement and publicity, which lead to increased efficiency and value added in the economy. It also supplies manpower endowed with inherent abilities as well as knowledge acquired from education industry.

INPUT-OUTPUT FRAMEWORK

Theories of growth have measured growth in economies and the contribution of various sectors towards growth through linkage effects in input-output framework. Two contradictory development theories have been propounded, the balanced theory of growth and the Hirschmanian theory of unbalanced growth. The Rostow hypothesized that investment in 'key' sectors propels an economy towards the stage of take-off. Leontief hypothesizes that input-output tables of different countries may serve as a basis of comparison on their respective internal structure of economic development. He brings out that triangularisation of the matrix of an economy reveals the hidden ordering embedded in the input output table. Chenery and Watanbe have estimated inter-sectoral linkages from matrices of input-output coefficients for analyzing development.

These analyses also guide economies in identifying 'key sectors' or leading regions which need to be induced so that the growth process gets transmitted through inter-sectoral and inter-regional linkages. The proponents of the theories—both balanced and unbalanced, emphasize that ranking countries on the basis of "proportion of inter sectoral transactions to total output" will show "a close correlation between per capita income and percentage of population occupied in manufacturing", and hence, the position of the country at the international level.

MODEL OF PRODUCTION SYSTEM AND LINKAGES

This central role of education can be studied using input-output framework. A model has been developed and tested using input-output table of 1993-94 to show that the contribution of education to the various sectors may not be reflected in the linkage indices but will be understood from the increases caused to individual incomes of educated population and effects on their capabilities. So the current HDI, both national and international suffer from infirmities:

Sector	C_1	C_2	HH	E	FD
C_1	X_{11}	X_{12}	X_{13}	X_{14}	F_1
C_2	X_{21}	X_{22}	X_{23}	X_{24}	F_2
HH	0	0	X_{33}	X_{34}	F_3
E	X_{41}	X_{42}	X_{43}	X_{44}	F_4

A partially decomposable block triangular input output model has been used in this study for analytical purposes:

$$\begin{bmatrix} X_1 \\ X_2 \end{bmatrix} = \begin{bmatrix} A_{11}X_1 & A_{12}X_2 \\ \cdots\cdots & \cdots\cdots\cdots \\ 0 & A_{22}X_2 \end{bmatrix} + \begin{bmatrix} F_1 \\ \cdots\cdots \\ F_2 \end{bmatrix} \tag{1}$$

Relation 1 furnishes the following two solutions of the system which, taken together, determine output vector in terms of final use:

$$X_2 = (I-A_{22})^{-1} F_2 \tag{2}$$

$$X_1 = (I-A_{11})^{-1} A_{12} (I-A_{22})^{-1} F_2 + (I-A_{11})^{-1} F_1$$

$$X_1 = (I-A_{11})^{-1} [A_{12} (I-A_{22})^{-1} F_2+F_1] \tag{3}$$

where X is a column vector of output $X_1=(x_{11,} x_{21} \ldots x_{k1})$; F is also a column vector of final use: $F_1=(f_{11,} f_{12} \ldots f_{1k})$ and A's are input coefficients' matrices, $A_{11} = (a_{1ij})$, i, j = 1, 2 . . . k. X_2, A_{22} and F_2 are defined analogously. Since the developing economies are characterized by the want of universal mutuality of inter-relations or inter-dependencies, a decomposable triangularised model suits the analysis better.

This tendency is further strengthened by relatively low capital and low commodity but high employment and knowledge base of production of education industry's output. The knowledge and technology, and hence, capital intensity of education industry has, however, been substantially raised recently by the process of slow but steady privatization. The contribution of education industry to this conventional thesis is that the forward linkage of education to the other sectors of the economy is universal, as it provides knowledge and research output to the whole of the economy and hence has an extremely high level of 'Residentiary Linkages' with the rest of the economy (For Conceptualization of the non-Hirschmanian Residentiary Linkage and the Method of its Estimation, Shri Prakash, 1986, 1991).

This paper attempts to identify the inter-sectoral linkages that education has with the rest of the economy with the help of input output matrix, and the contribution made by education in leading the developmental process.

Linkages

The Hirschmanian Theory (1957) of unbalanced growth combines the Rostowian concept of the leading/key sector of the economy with his concepts of backward and forward linkages. The concepts of linkages and key sectors have been operationalised empirically through Leontief's Static Input-Output Model. Extension of Leontief Model by Chenery and Watanbe (1958) facilitated empirical testing of the theory extensively in numerous national economies.

Prakash (1991) highlighted the following limitations of these studies: (i) Growth pertain to dynamic rather than static model used in such studies. Negligence of investment/capital matrix jeopardized the relevance of the findings of these studies, since static linkages were not only a gross underestimate of the real linkage effect but these concealed more than what they revealed; (ii) the formulae used for estimating the linkages focused on accelerator rather than the multiplier process of growth; (iii) use of the elements of coefficients matrix to estimate indices of linkages captured only direct and neglected indirect effects. In several cases, indirect effects are even more important than the direct effects. Prakash, therefore, propounded the use of (i) Leontief Inverse in place of input coefficients' matrix to capture both direct and indirect effects; (ii) Leontief's Dynamic rather than Static Inverse to capture fully the impact of accelerator on growth; and (iii) formulated and operationalised the concept of Residentiary Linkage to capture the multiplier effect on growth.

A recent study of information technology based sectors of Indian economy, published in *Artha Vijnana*, 2000, has shown that Prakash method yields better estimates of linkage indices than Rasmussen and other conventional methods. Education being a service industry, having high knowledge intensity, this paper has chosen Prakash Model for analyzing education-economy inter-relations.

There are conventional formulae for estimating linkages from the above input output model are given hereunder. But the paper uses the revised formulae of Prakash (1991)

$$I_j^{BS} = \sum_{i=1}^{n} A_{ij} \quad (4)$$

$$I_j^{FS} = \sum_{i=1}^{n} A_{ji} \quad (5)$$

where A_{ij} are the elements of Leontief Static Inverse.

$$I_j^{TDS} = \frac{1}{2n}(I_j^{BS} + I_j^{FS}) = \frac{1}{2n}\left(\sum_{i=1}^{n} A_{ij} + \sum_{i=1}^{n} A_{ji}\right) \quad (6)$$

Indices of Dynamic Linkages may be derived from Leontief Dynamic Inverse (Prakash, 1991) analogously.

The Leontief Dynamic Inverse is as given below:

$$(I-A-GB)^{-1} = [I-GB\ (I-A)^{-1}]^{-1}\ (I-A)^{-1} \quad (7)$$

The reciprocal of the smallest positive Frobinius root, defining the existence of solution to the above model (Mathur, 1967), will furnish technically feasible and economically maximal growth rate, if all sectors of the economy grow at the same constant rate,

$g_i = g_j = G$ for all i and j.

As the B matrix, corresponding to A matrix of 1993-94, is not available, the direct and indirect sectoral investment requirements have been estimated from the information about the sectoral gross fixed capital formation and change in stock, contained in I-O Table of 1993-94:

$$b_j = c_j + \Delta s_j \tag{8}$$

$b_j = \sum_i b_{ij}$ is output of all sectors used up for capital formation in sector j, $s_j = \sum_i s_{ij}$, s_{ij} is the output of sector i held as capital/stock in sector j, and Δ is the change operator. Thus, b_j denotes total investment in capital inputs of all producer goods in sector j. This furnishes the Sector-wise Investment Vector $b = (b_j)$, $j = 1, \ldots n$ for the economy as a whole. Sum/total of investment, comprising of both direct and indirect investment requirement per unit of final demand, will be given by

$$B = (I - A)^{-1} b \tag{9}$$

The dynamic linkages may then be estimated as follows:

$$I^{BD} = \sum_i a_{ij} + b_{.j} \tag{10}$$

and

$$I^{FD} = \sum_i a_{ji} + b_{j} \tag{11}$$

where $b_{j.}$ will show the supply of investment funds from education sector to all other industries and $b_{.j}$ will display the investment made in the education industry, as estimated from relation 9.

We develop a criterion to identify those sectors of the economy whose residentiary linkages are stronger than the Hirschmanian linkage effects. First linkage index of this type is given by

$$V_j^{RBS} = V_j / I_j^{DBS} \le 1 \tag{12}$$

where superscripts RBS denote residentiary static linkage relative to direct backward linkage effect and $V_j = 1 - \sum_{i=1}^{n} a_{ij}$ Obviously V_j is value added per unit of good j.

Similarly another index has been developed which is given by

$$V_j'^{RFS} = f_j / \sum_{i=1}^{n} a_{ji} \leq 1 \tag{13}$$

where superscripts RFS denote residentiary relative to direct static forward linkage effect. Here f_j is the final demand for good j per unit of its output.

Then, we consider residentiary linkage effect in relation to overall Hirchamanian linkage effects by means of the following index:

$$L_j^{RDS} = V_j / I_j^{TDS} \lesseqgtr 1 \tag{14}$$

where superscripts RDS denote residentiary relative to direct Hirschmanian static linkage effect. As against this, both direct and indirect requirements are taken into account in estimating residentiary linkage if relation is formulated as follows:

$$I_j^{TS} = \left(\sum_{i=1}^{n} V_i A_{ij} + \sum_{i=1}^{n} V_j A_{ji} \right) \bigg/ I_j^{TS} \lesseqgtr 1 \tag{15}$$

where superscripts RDS denote residentiary relative to direct Hirschmanian static linkage effect.

The dynamic total residentiary relative to total dynamic linkage effect is given by the following:

$$I_j^{TD} = \left(\sum_{i=1}^{n} V_j B_{ji} + \sum_{i=1}^{n} V_i B_{ij} \right) \bigg/ I_j^{DD} \lesseqgtr 1 \tag{16}$$

where superscripts RTD denote residentiary relative to total dynamic linkage effect.

DATABASE AND ADJUSTMENTS

The data used in the calculations are from the Input-Output Transactions Table of 1993-94, published in the year 2000 by the Central Statistical Organization of the Government of India. The data relating to 115 sectors have been compiled to make a 44 × 44 matrix suitable for calculation. The sectors have been grouped on the basis of the nature of industry. The sector under study, the education sector, has not undergone any reclassification.

EMPIRICAL RESULTS

The estimates based on relations are reported below:

Linkage Type	*Backward*	*Forward*
Direct	0.830789	0.051106
Both Direct and Indirect	2.438300	1.314700

These results show that the 'education and research' industry, unlike other service providers, has extremely low forward linkages. But this inference is based on the result furnished by the conventional approach, which overlooks the indirect effects of linkages. The overall backward linkage effect, calculated from relation 7, is as high as 2.43. It is 2.93 times higher than the direct backward linkage effect. This lends credence to the thesis that the indirect effect, like in several other cases, is more important in education industry than the direct effect. In case of education and research industry, the index of indirect effect is as high as 1.6075 (2.4383 – 0.830789). Indirect effect itself is three times the direct backward linkage effect. Moreover, the indirect backward linkage effect is 25 times the direct forward linkage and the indirect component, 1.2629 (1.314 – 0.0511) itself is 24 times more than the direct linkage (0.0511).

The direct forward linkage effect of education is much less pronounced than its direct backward linkage effect. In fact, backward linkage is 16.26 times higher than the direct forward linkage index. The total forward linkage (both direct and indirect) is 1.3147, which is again less than the overall backward linkage effect.

Total linkage effect cannot be identified through either the static or dynamic linkages. Only the residentiary linkages can capture the residentiary linkage as it represents the pure employment effect. Besides, education utilizes a major portion of its own output in its production process.

Dynamic and Residentiary Linkages

The results of the application of residentiary linkages are reported below:

Linkage Type	*Backward*	*Forward*
Dynamic	1.084289	0.304606
Residentiary	0.203675	0.052334

Here again, the backward linkage is more than the forward linkage. And in fact it is 3.559 times the forward linkage effect.

Role of Institutional Expenditure on Education

School education is the most important stage as it receives more entrants than any other stage in the total education process. Investment made by parents and individuals at this stage which culminates into education at higher stages. It was felt essential to analyse the role of school in the total education sector. Data on institutional consumption and capital expenditure during the year 20001-02 was collected from a few schools in and around Delhi. Total number of students covered in the experiment is 4,000. This was replaced in the input-output transaction matrix. Calculations of all the linkages were repeated. The results are as follows:

Linkage Type	*Backward*		*Forward*	
	Table data	*Experimental data*	*Table data*	*Experimental data*
Direct	0.8307	0.8307	0.0511	0.0475
Both Direct and Indirect	2.4383	1.1841	1.3147	1.2269

Linkage Type	*Backward*		*Forward*	
	Table data	*Experimental data*	*Table data*	*Experimental data*
Dynamic	1.084	1.073	0.300	0.290
Residentiary	0.203	0.203	0.052	0.0487

The following points need to be noted:

- The backward linkages have not shown any change at all.
- The changes in the forward linkages are due to scalar effect.
- The experiment will affect a number of sectors whose outputs are used by the education sector. The effects of these changes may not remain confined to these sectors alone.
- The overall effect will be estimated from the inverse. The direct impact of this change can be gauged from the difference in the technology matrix X and X′. But the overall effect may be spread over many more sectors.

The direct impact of this change can be gauged from the difference in the technology matrix A and A′ but the overall impact may be spread over a number of sectors which may be estimated from the inverse of the two matrices. Two alternative solutions worked out are derived from the standard Leontief model:

$$X = (I - A)^{-1} . F \qquad (17)$$

$$X' = I - A')^{-1} . F \qquad (18)$$

where A is the technology matrix of the economy as given in the 1993-94 Table published by Central Statistical Organization, Ministry of Statistics and Program Implementation, Govt of India; 'A' is the modified technology matrix of the economy in which the coefficients of 18 rows and columns were regrouped suitably in order to synthesize the company technology matrix into the 'technology matrix of the economy'; and F is the final demand vector.

The vector D of differences in the two sets of output is given by:

$$D = (X - X') \qquad (19)$$

where X and X′ represent the two solutions respectively as mentioned above.

Transaction matrix has been regrouped into 44 sectors. Corresponding outputs and final demand for 115 sectors have been aggregated for this aggregated schemata. And the coefficient matrices A and A′ have been derived. The vector D was derived from these solutions. A comparison of original solution of input output with experimental school data shows that 42 sectors were impacted by the substitution of the initial output coefficients by the school's coefficients (Table 2).

The maximum impact of 20% has been in the drugs and cosmetics sector. The maximum positive impact has in the two sectors: (a) Paper and paper products, printing and publishing; and (b) Furniture, wooden and steel. The macro-impact, namely that of the national economy on the individual institutions is reflected by the negative change in outputs in three sectors.

Human Development Index by UNDP

Economic growth and development is intended to bring about the well-being of the people of a society. However, industrial, democratic, technologically advanced an economy, if the quality of life of the people is not comparable with the best in the world, efforts made in all the spheres will become a colossal waste. Hence economic development is 'by' the people and 'for' the people.

This central role of human resources made UNDP develop the concept of human development index, which is a summary measure of human development. It measures the average achievement in a country in three basic dimensions: (a) A long and healthy life indicated by life expectancy at birth; (b) Knowledge as measured by education; and (c) A decent standard of living measured by GDP per capita. This index has been developed by a number of countries of the world, based on their data availability. Following the UNDP's initiative on human development framework, India has developed its Human development index on a comparable basis.

The HDI developed by India on the basis of the example of UNDP considers age specific enrolment for calculating the index. The efficiency of the main workforce as decided by their qualifications and knowhow decidedly has a direct impact on the developmental process of the economy. Enrolments are not the correct indicator of the education level of the population as there may be many drop outs, failures and dropouts mid-session. The average number of school years of the workforce will be a better indicator of the contribution made by education and its linkage effects. An index has been calculated using the average school years of the workforce employed in various industries.

Moreover, education expenditure unlike other investments is not made at one go, it becomes a compulsory part of the family budget. Investment in education starts bearing fruit only after a period of time once the person gets employed and earns an income. Hence the immediate impact of education is felt in the earnings of workers. Human capital is the main carrier of knowledge and skill and these are the products of the research and educational investment made by institutions and industries. Therefore, the true forward linkages of education can be captured by means of relating differential earnings in various sectors in relation to the school years completed by employees of those sectors.

Data on earnings per day of salaried employees and casual workers was collected from the Manpower Profile India collected and presented by Institute Of Applied Manpower Research. The supply of educated manpower has been taken from the census of India 1991 from the "B-3 (F) Main workers other than cultivators and agricultural labourers classified by industrial category, educational level and sex" and the number of school years completed by them is taken to give the index of growth of the economy through employment in the various sectors. These results were correlated and the coefficients are as follows:

	Male salaried employee	*Female salaried employee*	*Casual labour male*	*Casual labour female*	*Combined for salaried employees*	*Combined for casual labourers*
Correlation Coefficient	0.391	0.815	0.1614	0.5179	0.5585	.0172

The results show that there is a high positive correlation between the school years and the wages of female salaried employees. There exists a positive correlation between education and wages of all employees although it is not very high.

INFERENCE

1. Education sector contributes to the other sectors in a positive manner.

2. The input-output framework provides a glimpse of the impact but cannot explain it completely because of the nature of the sector.

3. When the inputs of the country were substituted by the figures of a few institutions, the results showed impacts in some important sector.

REFERENCES

Census of India 1991, Office of the Registrar General of India.

Chenery, H.B. and Watanbe, T. (1958), "International Comparison of the Structure of Production", *Econometrica*, Octorber, 1958.

Clark, Colin (1953), *Conditions of Economic Growth*, Macmilan.

Hirschman, A.O. (1957), *The Strategy of Economic Development*, Yale University Press, New Haven.

CSO (2000), *Input-Output Transaction Table 1993-94*, Central Statistical Organisation, Ministry of Statistics and Programme Implementation, Government of India.

Leontief, W.W. (1966), "The Structure of Development", In Leontief (ed.), *Input-Output Economics*, Oxford University Press.

Lewis, Arthur (1958), *Economic Growth*, Macmilan.

IAMR (2003), *Manpower Profile India 2003*, Institute of Applied Manpower Research.

Mathur, P.N. (1967), "Neumann-Leontief Growth Trajectories". In Mathur, P.N. and Bhardwaj, R. (Ed.), *Economic Growth, Economic Analysis in Input Output Framework with Indian Empirical Explorations*, Vol. 1, Input Output Research Association, India.

National Human Development Report 2001 to 2004. Planning Commission of India.

Prakash, S. (1996), *Cost of Education*, Anamika Publishers.

Prakash, S. (1977), *Educational System of India—An Econometric Study*, Concept, New Delhi.

Prakash, S. and Mohapatra, A.C. (1981), "Economic Development of the State of M.P.—Analysis of Inter-Temporal and Intra-Regional Variations", *Third World Planning Review*, Vol. 2, No. 1, Liverpool University.

Appendices Tables

Table 1

Code of industry	*Industry*	*Average number of school years*
III	Livestock	3.1232804
IV	Mining and quarrying	3.8296475
VA	Manufacturing and processing and repairs of goods for household purposes	2.638155
VB	Manufacturing and processing and repairs of goods for other than for household purposes	5.8684905
VI	Constructions	5.8684905
VII	Trade and commerce	7.0036943
VIII	Transport and communications	6.3459602
IX	Other services	8.4956734

Table 2

No.	*Sector/industry*	*1.0e+007 X*	*1.0e+007 X′*	*Percent Difference*
1	*2*	*3*	*4*	*5*
1.	Paddy, etc.	1.2793	1.2759	0.27
2.	Sugarcane, etc.	0.4165	0.4132	0.79
3.	Tea, etc.	0.3121	0.3116	0.16
4.	Rubber, etc.	0.0534	0.0511	4.31
5.	Tobacco	0.090	0.0899	0.11
6.	Other crops, milk, livestock products, etc.	1.780	1.7723	0.43
7.	Forestry and logging, fishing	0.202	0.1999	1.04
8.	Coal and lignite, petroleum	0.6567	0.6294	4.16
9.	Iron ore, manganese, bauxite, etc.	0.1946	0.1811	6.94
10.	Limestone, non-metallic minerals	0.1145	0.1041	9.08
11.	Sugar	0.1955	0.1918	1.89
12.	Hydrogenated oil (Vanaspati)	0.1182	0.1180	0.17
13.	Miscellaneous food products	0.2629	0.2626	0.11
14.	Khadi, miscellaneous textile products	0.5355	0.5316	0.73
15.	Jute, hemp, mesta textiles	0.1883	0.1824	3.13
16.	Furniture and fixtures-wooden	0.1171	0.1051	10.25
17.	Paper, paper products & Newsprint	0.5523	0.4656	15.70

1	2	3	4	5
18.	Leather footwear	0.2397	0.2362	1.46
19.	Petroleum products	0.3974	0.3843	3.30
20.	Coal tar products	0.0289	0.0281	2.77
21.	Inorganic heavy chemicals, others	0.8024	0.7540	6.03
22.	Drugs and medicines	0.0724	0.0871	(20.30)
23.	Soaps, cosmetics & glycerin	0.0810	0.0818	(0.99)
24.	Structural clay products, others	0.2660	0.2579	3.05
25.	Cement	0.16890	0.1614	4.44
26.	Iron, steel and ferro alloys	1.1262	1.0421	7.47
27.	Non-ferrous basic metals	0.5988	0.5771	3.62
28.	Hand tools, hardware	0.1439	0.1379	4.17
29.	Tractors and agricultural implements	0.0464	0.0457	1.51
30.	Industrial machinery (f & t)	0.2912	0.2865	1.61
31.	Office computing machines	0.0056	0.0055	1.79
32.	Electrical industrial machinery	0.1030	0.0999	3.01
33.	Electrical wires & cables	0.1690	0.1626	3.79
34.	Electronic & communication equipments	0.1315	0.1289	1.98
35.	Ships and boats	0.0123	0.0123	—
36.	Rail equipments	0.8121	0.8890	(9.47)
37.	Motor vehicles	1.4068	1.4033	0.25
38.	Bicycles, cycle-rickshaw	0.0837	0.0824	1.55
39.	Miscellaneous manufacturing	0.3378	0.3340	1.12
40.	Construction, Electricity, railways	4.2552	4.2066	1.14
41.	Communication, trade, banking	3.3292	3.2771	1.56
42.	Education and research	0.9672	0.9543	1.33
43.	Medical and health	0.7385	0.732	0.88
44.	Other services	1.977	1.977	—

Input-Output Modelling of Employment and Productivity as a Base of Growth

SHRI PRAKASH AND BRINDA BALAKRISHNAN

INTRODUCTION

India has concertedly endeavored to upgrade the technological base of production from 1956 to the mid-1970's. Thereafter, the process somehow appears to have slowed down resulting in technological stagnation, which extended right upto the late eighties. The nineties were an era of improvement in technology and managerial practices that bore results in the period of globalisation and liberalization. New technology tends to be more Knowledge and Capital-intensive and Labour Displacing. The movement of the national economy from lower to higher stages of techno-centric development requires a transformed production from Material Processing to Knowledge and Information Processing. The modern age Industrial Revolution is manifested as Knowledge Revolution. Hence, highly knowledgeable persons alone can mange new technology. Competencies need to be broadened as production requires greater expertise in terms of knowledge and skills. A shift from general to professional/technical/vocational streams of education becomes an essential requirement of this transformation process. Labour displacement processes result in Labour Extension and Augmentation in so far as production capacity of human capital gets increased. As against this, greater capital-intensity leads to augmentation of capital, both in quantity and quality through enhancement of capital's productivity. The resultant effect of both these is reduction in costs. The theories of growth, propounded by Clark and Lewis, also come into operation at this mature stage in so far as tertiary sector emerges in the center stage of development at the cost of primary and secondary sectors. Tertiary sectors are more human than physical capital intensive. This process of growth may be designated as, using Barewald's terminology, Factor Transformation Process.

The factor transformation process through technological improvement may be envisaged to have three different impacts on Employment; (i) Employment Less Growth; (ii) Employment Loss Growth; and (iii) Employment Gain Growth. The use of technology of different vintages in developing countries implies the simultaneous operation of Factor Multiplication and Factor Transformation processes of growth. It is, therefore, probable that all three types of employment effect of growth are manifested as the economy moves from lower to higher stages of growth. Within each broad sectoral category, some sub-sectors tend to stagnate and even decline, while some others emerge as fast growing/leading/key sectors of development within the given category; growth may carry different employment implications for different sectors.

Some more knowledge and human capital intensive leading/key sectors, may register employment gain, whereas the employment loss of other sectors may swamp this gain. Therefore, the thesis that Liberalization, Privatization and Globalization has resulted in Employment less growth may be empirically and logical valid in a macro sense. But the evaluation of the validity of the theses of Employment Less, Employment Loss and Employment Gain process of growth needs a structural approach. Employment, defined as the deployment of labour, undergoes a structural change both in terms of demand and supply as a result of Quantitative and Technological transformation of production; such changes impact upon education and knowledge intensity, embodying skills, quantity, quality, and hence, competencies of human capital. The changes in level and Structure of Knowledge are both demand and supply centric. Then, there are variations between different sectors of the economy and occupations between and within sectors—Primary, Secondary and Tertiary. The structural differences result in differential competency level of human capital in terms of knowledge and skills.

The dominant view of economic and social change assumes that the developed economies are in the midst of a knowledge revolution, driven by the application of new technologies. It is argued that innovation holds the key to the competitive advantage of countries and the welfare of individuals. Consequently, in a global economy, the prosperity of a country depends on the skills, knowledge and intellectual capital of those capable of creating and fostering innovations. In this scenario, education becomes central to economic policy because it is through education that knowledge revolution can take place. This exercises direct effect on employment.

Employment has always been in the centre stage of both economic analysis and policy ever since the inception of economics as a modern science. Employment and income have both tended to rise in the process of growth. But growth can occur through factor multiplication process or factor transformation process (Barewald, 1970). Factor multiplication involves increase in the quantity of the same factor inputs of the given quality to be transformed into highest output of the same type and quality through the use of the same production function. But the factor transformation process involves a different production function resulting in more and different quality output per unit of factor inputs. New production function generally embodies different technology. Technology affects the nature, direction and magnitude of relationship between employment and income. Development of technology has generally been capital-intensive and labours displacing, and hence, labours augmenting. Besides, new technology is often more knowledge and skill intensive. Knowledge and skill requirements are not only greater in magnitude and superior in quality but these are also very different from earlier ones. This makes some occupations and types of knowledge/skills redundant and obsolete, while some new occupations and types of education emerge (Cf. Prakash, 1977). Knowledge and skill upgradation is also facilitated by the concurrent and even prior development of education and training in order to avert the growth lowering supply constraints of human capital (Prakash, 1995, 1996). Consequently, new generation manpower is healthier, more, better and differently educated. Human capital, which is the human resource deployed on productive work, embody different knowledge profiles to match the changing industry-occupation structure as the economy moves from lower to higher stages of growth. Therefore, transformation of both: the economy and human resources. Hence, the replacement of the old by new technological transformation of production may involve knowledge, skills, industry and occupational production function through the change in technology may adversely impact employment in the process of growth of income. Factor transformation seems to be the basis of the growth of income in India.

The Indian economy today instills optimism and inspires confidence for the future. Foreign exchange reserves have been bulging, inflation has been slowing down and factor productivity has improved. Intensification of competition and new policy paradigm have reduced labour militancy and made the product quality and consumercare emerge in the centre stage. Range of consumer choices has been raised significantly. The technology and capital base have been consolidated. The emergence of consumerism makes the country appear more prosperous than ever before. But employment has become an increasing concern. The concept of 'jobless growth' has emerged as the focus of debate both among analysts and policy-makers. We, however, postulate that the employment income-growth interrelation can not be a homogenous phenomenon across the sectors, over space and through time; nature and degree of this relationship is bound to vary among sectors. Probably the nature of employment, specially its knowledge and skills profile, has undergone radical transformation. *A priori* reasoning suggests the tertiary activities to have emerged as the dominant generator of job opportunities. The traditional 'bricks and mortar economy' seems to have faded away into background. Conceptual categories, such as casual and marginal employment, knowledge, skilled, technical and professional workers have now acquired greater importance in the knowledge economy. The transitional phase is characterised by continuously decreasing craze for government jobs, which have, in any case, been dwindling fast. Emerging competition among the corporates for recruiting technical, medical, engineering, managerial and other professionals even through campus interviews, corporates' rising level of manpower turnover and the resulting concern for the retention of the capable hands, job satisfaction and corporate performance are becoming increasingly important.

INCOME EFFECT ON EMPLOYMENT

The income effect of technological transformation arises from its impact on: (i) Factor productivity; and (ii) Knowledge, skills and occupational structure of employment (Prakash, 1977, 1995, 1996). Rise in productivity, induced by technological and knowledge up-gradation of the production base is labour augmenting, since it raises the productive capacity of manpower, reducing overall human capital requirements per unit of output. Growth of output beyond the threshold level of labour displacing effect of factor transformation involves quantitative expansion of employment. The overall income effect may, therefore, be decomposed into its constituent effects:

- Substitution of capital for labour in production displays labour displacement effect of technology;
- Labour augmentation effect manifests through productivity growth, that is, more output per unit of labour, where labour coefficient, employment per unit of output, is the reciprocal of productivity; and
- The scale effect of production may still raise employment in the process of growth. As the nature and degree of factor transformation may vary between sectors and even companies within sectors, employment effect of growth of income may also differ between sectors.

All the sectors of the economy do not undergo technological

transformation at the same time, technology of different vintages remain operative (Mathur, 1959). This makes it difficult to predict employment effect of growth. Whether the impact of growth is employment-neutral, employment-enhancing, or employment-reducing, needs to be investigated. Employment has acquired a sharper edge in the context of globalization and liberalization of Indian economy. For investigating employment-economic growth inter-relations, two complementary models have been developed.

The propositions outlined above may warrant the decomposition of overall effect into component parts in order to assess and evaluate the countervailing nature of the positive and negative effects of technological transformation and growth of income on employment. The decomposition model will separate (i) labour displacement effect of growth from productivity augmenting effect; and (ii) scale effect on employment to determine employment neutrality, enhancing, or displacing nature of growth.

But the overall employment effect of growth of income comprises of both direct and indirect repercussions, the capturing of which requires an Input-Output model. An Input-Output model has, therefore, been formulated to endogenise employment and growth within the system. Income and employment estimates, derived from this model, have then furnished the data base for prognosticating the decomposition model. Empirical results will furnish estimates of overall, productivity and employment effects of growth of income, facilitating verification of the empirical validity of the theses stated above. The results will also highlight the relative contribution of growth of productivity and employment to the growth of income. The models are outlined below.

DECOMPOSITION MODEL

It is postulated that total output, X equals the product of total employment, N and average productivity, P:

$$X = P \,.\, N \tag{1}$$

where X is GDP at factor cost in 1993-94 prices. Differencing the equation partially, we get

$$\Delta X = \Delta P.N + \Delta N.P + \Delta P.\ \Delta N \qquad (2)$$

First term of this equation measures the effect of income growth due to change in productivity, when employment is constant, second term determines employment effect of income growth with constant productivity, and the last term determines the interaction effect of change in employment and productivity in response to the given change in output. Interaction effect may be distributed between employment and productivity effect exactly in proportion to the shares of first and second terms in overall growth. Division of equation 2 by X yields

$$\Delta X / X = (\Delta P / P + (\Delta N / N) + \{\Delta P / P\}.\ \{\Delta N / N\} \qquad (3)$$

which can be also expressed as:

$$G_x = G_p + G_n + G_p .\ G_n \qquad (4)$$

where G_x is the rate of growth of income, G_p is the rate of growth of productivity and G_n is the rate of growth of employment.

The model can also be modified as follows in order to estimate the relative shares/contribution of productivity and employment growth in the growth of income.

$$\{G_p/G_x\} + \{G_n/G_x\} + \{(Gp .\ G_n)/G_x\} = 1 \qquad (5)$$

INPUT OUTPUT MODEL

In order to capture both the direct and indirect repercussions of growth of income on employment and productivity, Input-Output model has been used to determine output, X:

$$X = (I-A)^{-1} f \qquad (6)$$

where X is the column vector of gross output, $(I\text{-}A)^{-1}$ is Leontief Inverse, and f is final demand. Employment involved in the production of this output may be given by

$$\hat{N} = LX \qquad (7)$$

where N is a column vector of sectoral employment. This will also furnish an idea about the sectoral composition of total employment. L is a diagonal matrix of employment coefficients, a_{oi} where $a_{oi} = L_{oi}/Xi$, that is, labour required per unit of output, $\sum_i L_{oi}$ is total employment in the economy. Substituting for X from 5 into 6, we get

$$\hat{N} = L\,(I\text{-}A)^{-1}.f \tag{8}$$

The gross factor productivity[1], $\hat{P}$ is given by

$$\hat{P} = L^{-1}X \tag{9}$$

where P is sector wise column vector of productivity, $p_j = X_j/L_{oj}$;

Use of solution rather than observed value of X in the above formula is an attempt to: (i) consider both direct and indirect requirement of labour for production; (ii) direct and indirect requirement of capital; and (iii) requirements of growth, since growth is financed out of surplus. Matrix A discussed above takes this into account; which Sraffa calls "requirements for Self-Replacement of Economy" at a given level. This surplus feeds the multiplier process through consumption while accelerator is taken care of through change in stock reflecting working capital requirements and fixed capital formation part of final demand. The consumption component of productivity estimates relate to welfare. There is another concept of productivity which is used to evaluate the competitiveness of a firm or industry in the market given by X_j/L_{oj}, which is the conventional measure of productivity (Cf Juan & Febrero). Thus we can distinguish three different concepts of productivity—productivity for growth; productivity for welfare and productivity for competition;

The growth rates of sectoral productivity are given by

$$G_p = \Delta\hat{P}.\bar{P}^{-1} \tag{10}$$

where $\Delta\hat{P}$ is the row vector of change in sectoral productivity, G_p is the vector of productivity growth rates, and $\hat{P}^{-1}$ is a diagonal matrix of initial levels of sectoral productivity. Following equation yields the estimate of sectoral employment growth:

$$G_n = \Delta\hat{N}.\bar{N}^{-1} \qquad (11)$$

where ΔN is the row vector of change in employment, G_n is the vector of sectoral employment growth rates and $\hat{N}^{-1}$ is the diagonal matrix of sectoral employment levels. Growth rates of sectoral output may be derived analogously:

$$G_x = \Delta\hat{X}.\ \hat{X}^{-1} \qquad (12)$$

where ΔX is the row vector of change in output and $\hat{X}^{-1}$ is the diagonal matrix of initial output. Since the capital coefficients matrix B, corresponding to input coefficients matrices of 1989 and 1994, is not available, solution values of X determined by relation 5 for these two years have been used to derive the rates of growth of sectoral output. It is implicitly assumed that the change in output $\Delta\hat{X}$ embodies the effect of change in (i) technology, (ii) human capital, (iii) policy regime, from the base to the terminal year. An attempt has been made to isolate the effect of change in technology from other components of change:

$$X_t = (I - A_{t-1})^{-1}\ f_t \qquad (13)$$

where t refers to the current period. The use of the preceding period's I-O table to estimate X_t from relation 5 nullifies at least a part, if not the whole, of the change in technology. Similarly, the effect of change in final demand may also be worked out:

$$X_t = (I - A_t)^{-1}\ f_{t-1} \qquad (14)$$

Differential output of 5 and 12 will furnish estimates of differential employment and productivity levels due to the difference of technology. As against this, differential of output of 5 and 13 will reflect the effect of change in final demand that may manifest the human capital effect on employment.

The above models will be empirically worked out on the basis of Input-Output Tables of Indian economy for 1988-89 and 1993-94, the latest available table.

DATABASE

Data relating to employment has been the real constraint since sector-wise employment is available only for nine highly aggregated sectors, 115×115 IO tables of 1988-89 and 1993-94 have been accordingly aggregated into 9×9 tables. Empirical results related to those aggregative data.

1. Evaluation of the hypotheses pertaining to Employment-Output interrelations. Output elasticity of employment on the one hand, and productivity elasticity of employment on the other have been used as analytical tools both at macro-level of the economy, taken as a whole, and micro-sectoral level;
2. Prognostication of Decomposition Model through inter-relations of employment, productivity and output;
3. Analysis of the results at sectoral level to deduce inter-sectoral variation; and
4. Empirical prognostication of Input-Output Model.

ANALYSIS OF THE RESULTS

Output has grown at the rate of 30.53% over a period of five years from 1988-89 to 1993-94. These are the two years for which Input-Output tables are available and have been used for the prognostication of the models in this study. Output estimates have been derived from equation 5 (Table 2.2), which indicates that the real GDP at factor cost in 1980-81 prices has, on an average, grown by 6.10% per annum. Employment, estimated from equation 6 (Table 2.3), indicates a much lower growth of 3.31% during the same period, yielding an average annual growth rate of 0.662%. Employment has grown at a rate hardly one-tenth of the growth of output. Thus, the growth of employment has substantially lagged behind the growth of income/output. Measely growth of employment suggests its stagnancy, implying employment neutrality of output growth.

Lead of output over employment growth indicates that Factor Productivity must have grown much faster than employment. Productivity has, in fact, increased at the rate of 26.35% over the five-year period; it approximates 5.27% per annum growth rate. Output has grown 1.16 times faster than even productivity and 10 times faster than employment. But productivity has grown 8 times faster than employment. Thus, employment expansion accounts only for 11 per cent, while productivity growth explains 79.61 per cent of the growth of income. The growth rates of employment and output embody as low employment elasticity with respect to output as 0.108. Output elasticity of employment is, in fact, practically zero. Employment is almost perfectly inelastic with respect to output. As against this, output elasticity of productivity, that is, growth of productivity with respect to output is 0.863. Thus, productivity elasticity with respect to output is also substantially less than unity. Therefore, productivity may be dubbed as output inelastic. These results lend credence to the hypothesis of employment neutral growth, which however, is not the same as 'Jobless Growth'.

Jobless Growth would have occurred if the factor productivity increased faster than output. These results furnish no empirical evidence to support the thesis of Job Displacing Growth also. But these results lend credence to the thesis that the technological upgradation and improvement of human capital base of production have promoted the growth of income in India. Scale effect of output growth on employment has been extremely limited.

The nature and degree of interrelations among these three variables have been examined by means of rank correlation analysis also. Rank correlation coefficients between the 3 paired rates of growth are listed below:

ρ^{12}	ρ^{13}	ρ^{23}
.164	.382	-0.661

Notes: 1. Output/income; 2. Employment; 3. Factor Productivity.

Employment neutrality of growth of the Indian economy is reflected by as low a value of rank correlation coefficient as 0.134 between the sectoral rates of growth of (i) output, and (ii) employment. The coefficient is not only statistically non-significant but its magnitude is also negligible. But the positive sign of the coefficient refutes the thesis that the growth of Indian economy has been employment displacing. The coefficient of rank correlation between output and productivity growth is positive, but statistically not significant, t value being only 1.17. However, the coefficient of rank correlation between employment and productivity is negative but statistically significant, value of t is (t=2.5). These results imply that with the growth of output productivity grows and employment declines.

Sectoral Variation

Estimates of growth of sectoral output, employment and productivity are reported below: The results highlight the reduction of employment in 3 sectors, 'Manufacturing', 'Electricity, Gas and Water', and 'Construction'. (See Table on next page)

These 3 sectors have recorded negative growth of employment, giving credence to job displacing growth. The traditionally labour-intensive sectors like Agriculture and Community and Social Services have displayed near stagnancy in employment, implying that these sectors have registered jobless growth. Transport, Storage and Communication, and Finance, Insurance and Real Estate are two sectors, which have registered phenomenal growth in employment. But Transport is the only sector where employment has led the output growth. For rest of the sectors, output has rather dominated employment growth. Thus, the growth of employment in most of the sectors has lagged behind the output growth. Employment in Mining and Trade has also expanded quite rapidly. But the growth of employment has lagged behind the growth of output in all sectors except transport, storage and communication. Naturally, the factor productivity has registered substantial decline in transport sector. But the growth of output of all other 8 sectors has substantially led the growth of employment. Six of 9 sectors have registered dramatic gains in productivity, growth of productivity ranging from 17.78 per cent for trade to 76.28 per cent for construction. Finance and Mining have registered the improvement in productivity at high to modest rates of 7 to 3 per cent. Mining, Transport, Storage/Communication and Finance are three sectors in which employment growth dominates the growth of productivity. These three sectors appear to have been under factor multiplication process of growth. As against this, productivity growth has almost matched employment growth in agriculture, where both green revolution and traditional technology coexist.

	Agriculture	*Mining*	*Manufacturing*	*Construction*	*Electricity, Gas & Water*	*Transport, Storage & Communication*	*Trade*	*Finance, Insurance & Real Estate*	*Community, Social & Personal Service*
Gx	30.86	9.68	36.16	29.29	8.87	29.45	26.79	37.93	59.87
Gn	0.73	6.09	-5.62	-26.66	-6.23	37.91	7.64	28.80	1.10
Gp	29.90	3.38	44.27	76.28	16.11	-6.13	17.78	7.09	58.13

This leaves five of the nine sectors, where Factor Transformation process triggered and sustained the process of growth of output.

Had the growth process been purely factor multiplication process, employment growth alone would have accounted for output growth. Employment would have expanded at the same rate as output growth rather than lagging behind it. Obviously, the growth process has been based on factor transformation process in some sectors. Had the growth process been factor transformation process, productivity growth alone would have accounted for output growth. But actual results embody a mixture of growth of both employment and productivity in all but one sector. Probably the high level of aggregation has shadowed a part of factor transformation process. Besides, the coexistence of vintages of technology also explains this facet. Factor transformation process is associated with advances in technology and/or improvement in quality of factor inputs like human resources' capability, managerial techniques and organizational decision-making. These parameters are reflected in the growth of productivity. All the above inferences are well supported by estimated elasticity. The sectoral employment elasticity given below indicates a significant positive elasticity in Transport, Storage and communication. This sector is also plagued with low productivity growth.

Employment and Productivity Elasticities with Respect to Output

Sectors	*Employment Elasticity*	*Productivity Elasticity*
Agriculture	0.024	0.969
Mining	0.63	0.349
Manufacturing	-0.155	1.224
Construction	-0.910	2.60
Electricity, Gas and Water	-0.702	1.82
Transport, Storage and Comm.	1.290	-0.208
Trade	0.285	0.664
Finance, Insurance and Real Estate	0.759	0.187
Commun., Soc. and Personal Serv.	0.018	0.971
Aggregate	0.108	0.863

Impounding Technology and Human Capital Effects on Productivity

The traditional theory explained growth in terms of growth of labour and capital but studies by Abramowitz, Kendrick, Dennison and Solow found a big residual in the growth of economy of the US. Technological change was hypothesized to be the primary mover of economic growth. Technological transformation is reflected by the changes in input-output coefficients (S. Prakash, 1976). Within limits, technology explains partly the changes in productivity. Productivity is greatly affected also by techniques of organization, administration and management, which relate to human resource capability. (For details see, Prakash, S., 1976, Layard and Saigal, 1966)

Productivity is basically a function of technology, managerial techniques and the operational organizational efficiency/ performance. Last two factors reflect the human capital capability. Technological and Human capital effects on productivity are assumed to be additive. This facilitates the decomposition of productivity growth into technology and human capital effects. Pure Technology Effect, the leading factor of Factor Transformation, and Human Capital Effect may then relate to Change in Productivity as follows:

$$\Delta P = \Delta T + \Delta H \qquad (15)$$

where ΔT reflects the contribution of technological advances and $\Delta(HC)$ manifests Human Capital effect on the change in productivity. Relation 14 then gives:

$$\Delta H = \Delta P - \Delta T \qquad (16)$$

where

$$\Delta T = L_t (I\text{-}A_t)^{-1} - L_{t\text{-}1} (I\text{-}A_{t\text{-}1})^{-1} \qquad (17)$$

The change in productivity has been deduced from the results yielded by the application of equations 5, 6 and 8 to 1988-89 and 1993-94 I-O tables. Technology effect on productivity has then been deduced from relation 16. Substitution of these values of ΔP and ΔT in relation 15 furnishes the estimate of ΔH.

The table below gives the sectoral variation in the changes in productivity comprising of technology effect and human capital effect:

Sectoral Variations in Productivity

Sectors	*Productivity Differential*	*Productivity differential due to tech. change*	*Percentage of technology effect in total*	*Productivity differential due to human factors*	*Percentage of human capital effect in total*
Agriculture	407190.38	155238.62	38.12	251951.77	61.88
Mining	27276.11	19338.82	70.90	7937.29	29.10
Manufacturing	190181.42	125162.48	65.81	65018.93	34.19
Construction	373628.36	80269.54	21.48	293358.82	78.52
Electricity	173412.74	89603.85	51.67	83808.89	48.32
Transport	-15003.26	-4990.77	-33.27	-10012.48	-66.73
Trade	280419.26	125363.60	44.71	155055.66	55.29
Finance	26531.35	25459.28	95.96	1072.07	4.04
Community, Social & Personal Services	46060.83	7387.95	16.04	38672.88	83.96

Productivity in manufacturing, mining and in the generation and distribution of electricity improved substantially during the post-reform period but employment growth in these sectors was low. The productivity growth in 4 sectors, namely, Mining, Manufacturing, Electricity, Gas and Water and Finance, Insurance and Real Estate sectors has been dominated by technology effect. The productivity growth in finance is almost totally accounted by technology effect, the share of human capital effect being hardly 4 per cent of the total. The Information Technology Revolution has brought about radical transformation in technological base of tertiary activities including Finance, Insurance and Real estate. The technology effect on productivity growth of mining is 2.4 times greater than the human capital effect, while it is almost twice as large as human capital effect for manufacturing. It is pertinent to note that mining has been brought in Public Sector under 1956 policy resolution and its later day modification. Public Sector has been the abode of disguised unemployment as a result of which the wage rates and marginal productivity have remained in dissonance. However, with the emphasis on privatization and technological up gradation, technology has now emerged as the dominant factor. But for Electricity & Gas sector, the share of two effects is almost balanced, technology effect being only 1.07 times the human capital effect. Though it is also under the focus of privatization and technological up gradation. Thus, productivity growth of 44 per cent of all the sectors of the Indian economy has been accounted largely by the technological upgradation of the production base, while the human capital base of these sectors seems to have lagged behind.

As against this, productivity growth of 56 per cent of the total sectors is accounted mainly by the upgradation of human capital base of production. The domination of productivity growth by human capital effect on productivity is not surprising. Several studies have shown investment in education and hence human capital to be the major force behind Green Revolution in India. [Chaudhary, D.P., Prakash, S. (1995)]. Though Construction is labour intensive, during the last two decades; technological upgradadtion has taken place in mega projects like barrages, bridges, flyovers and more land intensive multistoried buildings. This has led to the upgradation of knowledge and skill base of human resources associated with the sector. With the growth of industry and agriculture trading has emerged as the fast growing sectors and there is a consistent movement from traditional ways of trading to see commerce, and retail trading and merchandising where augmented human resource capabilities have been in the centre stage. The emerging trend is towards employment of more qualified and professionally trained personnel being employed in Community, Social and Personal services sector. But one of these sectors, namely, transport, registered decline in productivity and the negative human capital effect is twice as large as the negative technology effect on productivity. This leaves the technology and human capital dominated sectors exactly equal in number. Community and Social Service and Construction are two sectors the productivity growth of which has been dominated largely by human capital effect, it being 5.23 and 3.7 times greater than the technology effect. Impact of human capital on productivity in trade and agriculture has been 1.24 and 1.62 times greater than the technology effect. Estimate of human capital effect on the productivity growth of agriculture is in consonance with the findings relating to the role of education in green revolution (For example, See Prakash, 1995, Chaudhary, D.P., 1969).

MAIN FINDINGS OF THE STUDY

The input output model of production seems to have performed well in so far as the output and employment estimates, furnished by the model, are extremely close to the actual figures. The results yielded by the model of decomposition of growth of output highlight the employment neutrality of growth. But there is no evidence to support the thesis of, either jobless or the job displacing growth. Both output elasticity of employment and correlation coefficient between output and employment growth support the thesis of employment neutrality of growth. Domination of the growth of output by productivity suggests the growth of Indian economy being factor transformation rather than factor multiplication based. Results also lend credence to the thesis that productivity and employment growth are inversely related.

As expected, the model results support inter sectoral variation in interrelations between employment, productivity and output growth. Growth of output is employment dominated in mining, transport and finance, whereas output growth of agriculture, manufacturing, construction, electricity, trade and social services is productivity dominated.

The decomposition of productivity growth into technology and human capital effects highlight that (i) human capital explains the major share of productivity growth of 4 sectors; (ii) technology accounts for the major proportion of productivity growth of another 4 sectors; and (iii) transport is the only sector showing negative change in productivity, which is accounted both by negative technology and negative human capital effects. The sector seems to have grown through factor multiplication process, where disguising unemployment might have led to the negative growth of productivity.

NOTES

1. Entire Output is attributed to labour implying as if it were the only factor used in production. Besides, primary factor labour, capital is an important factor of production. The grossness arises from two factors: Total output is attributed to labour (i) and (ii) Gross rather than net output is used as denominator. Net productivity may be estimated by working out the ratio of factors used in production and net output, i.e value added which is given by V_j/l_j, where $l_j = a_{oj} \times \Sigma A_{ij}$ and V_j is the value added per unit of output.
2. Marshall, in a different context, describes the experience of mining industry in 1870's in similar terms. See Principles of Economics.

REFERENCES

Abramowitz, N. (1956), "Resources & Output Trends in the United States since 1870's", *American Economic Review*, Papers and Proceedings, page 6.

Barewald, F. (1969), *History and Structure of Economic Development*, India Book House.

Bowen, W.G. (1968), "Assessing the Economic Contribution of Education" in Blaug Mark, (ed.), *Economics of Education*, Volume 1, Penguin.

Clark, Colin (1957), *The Conditions of Economic Progress*, Macmilan, London.

Dennison, E.F. (1966), "The Sources of Economic Growth in the US and the alternatives before US", National Bureau of Economic Research, Paper 13.

Lewis, Arthur (1959), *Economic Growth*, Oxford.

Layard, P.R.G. and Saigal, J.C. (1960), "Educational and Occupational Characteristics of Manpower: An International Comparison", *British Journal of Industrial Relations*, Vol. 4, No. 2.

Mathur, P.N. (1963), "An Efficient Path of Technological Transformation of an Economy", in Barna, Tibor (Ed.), *Structural Interdependence and Economic Development*, Macmillan.

Oscar de Juan & Eladio Febrero (2000), "Measuring Productivity from Vertically Integrated Sectors", *Economic Systems Research*, Journal of the International Input- Output Association, Vol. 12, No. 1.

Prakash, Shri (1977), *Educational System of India—An Econometric Study*, Concept, N. Delhi.

Prakash, Shri (1995), *Cost of Education*, Anamika, N. Delhi.

Solow, R.M. (1962), "Technical Progress, Capital Formation and Economic Growth", *American Economic Review*, Volume 52.

TABLE 1

Aggregation of Input-Output Transaction Matrix, 1988-89

Input Coefficient Matrix

Agriculture	0.197097	0.000003	0.063134	0.042662	0.000696	0.319560	0.000000	0.0000000	0.057295
Mining	0.295974	0.004960	0 11917	0.058455	0.162385	0.016375	0.000000	0.0000000	0.079531
Manufacturing	0.067997	0.124789	0.34532	0.320677	0.037528	0.221650	0.033905	0.0086995	0.085647
Construction	0.011899	0.003151	0.00093	0.003417	0.024884	0.021049	0.007413	0 0769823	0.004374
Electricity, Gas & Water	0.018447	0.037589	0.34532	0.007383	0.254556	0.040143	0.021169	0.0847894	0.015572
Transport, Storage, Communication	0.010303	0.013658	0.04139	0.049187	0.073885	0.046096	0.113960	0.0192441	0.013316
Trade Finance, Insurance	0.033551	0.017467	0.06308	0.063984	0.041164	0.030268	0.003866	0.0010808	0.024031
Real Estate Community	0.008046	0.013616	0.02596	0.021785	0.027461	0.030789	0.025177	0.0351868	0.023312
Social & Personal Service	0.010632	0.015273	0.04139	0.050937	0.076990	0.050829	0.119170	0.0282575	0.016216

TABLE 2

Aggregation of Input-Output Transaction Matrix, 1993-94

Input Coefficient Matrix, 1993-94

Agriculture, Hunting, etc.	0.25071	0.0000	0.06251956	0.0245669	0.00134	0.041139	0.00294015	0	0.0464807
Mining & Quarrying	0.25071	0.0046	0.052600955	0.0492702	0.078262	0	0.00151717	0	0.0016174
Manufacturing	0.08487	0.0349	0.311790157	0.3346345	0.015905	0.0072203	0.01323626	0.0064579	0.1144201
Construction	0.00773	0.0031	0.004535204	0.0078684	0.004312	0.0017972	0.0005732	0.0002808	0.0042667
Electricity, Gas & Water	0.01665	0.0129	0.035029613	0.0154745	0.096618	0.0130537	0.00165057	0.0116753	0.0516931
Transport, Storage & Comm.	0.03869	0.0143	0.063433256	0	0.035943	0.0055294	0.00744101	0.0049456	0.0414725
Trade	0.17350	0.0041	0.135855887	0.0170539	0.014917	0.0252997	0.01297929	0.0226283	0.0131954
Finance, Insurance, Real Estate	0.00970	0 0048	0.024164664	0	0 007797	0.0024027	0.00030043	0.002149	0.0531963
Community, Social & Personnel Service	0.00275	0.0044	0.026923232	0.0171258	0.003484	0.0095597	0.0001329	0.0085502	0.0382368
Labour Coefficient	5.6534E-07	1.19972E-06	1.297E-06	1.158E-06	8E-07	4.355E-06	3.2256E-07	1.915E-06	7.981E-06
Gross Value of Output	26143431	9110437	49313991	10594200	12111670	7141259	13920024	7984346	13692013

SECTION III

STRUCTURE AND STRUCTURAL CHANGE

A Simulation Exercise on the Sri Lankan Economy in the Keynes-Leontief-Klein Framework

PARTHA PRATIM GHOSH, ARPITA DHAR AND DEBESH CHAKRABORTY

INTRODUCTION

The small island economy of Sri Lanka is a well-known outlier among developing economies. Its human and social indicators such as Average Life Expectancy, Adult Literacy Rates, Infant Mortality Rates and similar indices of development compare favorably with those of the fastest growing and most prosperous nations. However, Sri Lanka's per capita income during the year 2000 has been no more than USD 860, reflecting low productivity of capital and labor (World Bank, 2001). For quite some time, the country's internal political unrest and its economic performance have had negative feedbacks on each other. Economic growth, sustained employment generation, reasonable price stability, balance in the external sector, and reduction in income inequality have not been adequate enough to propel the economy into the league of Developed Nations.. As such, the search for a proper framework to analyze the working of this economy is warranted.

SALIENT GROWTH-FEATURES OF THE ECONOMY

Let us look at the overall growth performance of this economy during the period 1975-2001. The average annual cumulative growth rate during this period is 4.91% as computed from the National Income Accounts Statistics for the country. Economic theory teaches that saving creates capacity for growth. OLS Regression of the growth rate on the national saving rate shows that variations in the growth rate are not explained by variations in the saving rate. An economy grows by utilizing its capacity as also by expanding it. It appears that the economy has not, on the whole, used its existing resources adequately during the period 1975-2001. This could be one of the major reasons for the observed growth pattern of the economy. With these preliminary conjectures we may take a look at the policy orientation of the economy before turning to the proposed framework of analysis.

ECONOMIC POLICY ORIENTATION OF SRI LANKA SINCE 1948

In our study of the Sri Lanka Economy, we aim at understanding how this small island economy actually operates. Specifically, we want to identify the major driving forces in the county's economic framework. To obtain a clear picture of the economy we start by discussing the evolution of economic policy in the country since its independence in 1948. For almost a decade after political independence, Sri Lanka carried on the legacy of Liberal Trade Regime which it inherited from its colonial rulers. After that, on account of growing BOP problems, there was a shift in the policy-stance and a move towards protectionist and Import-Substituting-Industrialization (ISI) policies that continued till the middle of the 1970's. The ISI policy was again replaced by Economic Liberalization policies from 1977 onwards. Private domestic and foreign investment was identified as the harbinger of capital accumulation in the economy. The limited size of the domestic market size led to the special importance of overseas markets and coupled with import dependence, it forced an open-door policy upon the economy. Concomitants of these were Macro-economic policies that had to be adapted to suit the requirements of a highly open economy.

In this paper, we intend to analyze the impacts of such policies on the economy and also assess the likely outcomes of policy changes in historical time. Before that we briefly mention the theoretical framework for the economy keeping in mind the saline features of the economy as also its structural features discussed above.

THE THEORETICAL FRAMEWORK

Leontief developed a methodology known as the Input-Output Framework, which is very useful for the detailed quantitative and qualitative analysis of the structure of an economy, involving its inter-sector linkages and associated multipliers. The Keynesian framework helps to analyze the Macro-economic performance of the economy, through appropriate Macro-Econometric Modeling. These two approaches are suitable and hence widely used for quantitative economic modeling and for generating policy prescriptions. This paper argues that by combining both these mainstream methodologies, we would obtain a more suitable theoretical framework for analyzing a developing economy like Sri Lanka. The methodology draws from the works of Klein (1965, 1978, 1986) as also from applications on the economy of Bangladesh by Dr. A. Choudhury (1986).

The Input-Output component of this model capture of details of the production structures of the various sectors of the economy working as a highly disaggregated production function and providing the much needed supply content to the model. The Econometric Model serves the purpose of modeling the aggregative expenditure components on the demand side as also the GDP using these components. With this type of a model, it would be possible to determine the sector-wise investments required to free the individual sectors from their respective bottlenecks (from the Input-Output Sub-model), and also, to arrive at the necessary policy adjustments to ensure that the required policy stimulus comes forth (from the Macro-Econometric Sub-model), such that there is a proper co-ordination between the sets of policies at the two levels.

DATA BASE

The Input-Output Tables from Sri Lanka for 1986, 1994 and 2000 have been sourced from The Department of National Planning and The Institute for Policy Studies of Sri Lanka. Other macroeconomic data have been collected from the following sources:

(1) National Income Accounts Statistics: Main Aggregates and Detailed Tables, Parts I and II, Published by the United Nations.
(2) Statistical Yearbook for Asia and the Pacific, UN Publications.
(3) International Trade Statistics Yearbook, Published by the United Nations.
(4) Foreign Trade Statistics Yearbook of Asia and the Pacific, UN Publications.
(5) Handbook of International Trade Statistics, Published by The United Nations.
(6) Commodity Trade Statistics, UN Publications.
(7) Direction of International Trade Statistics Yearbook, IMF Publications.
(8) Government Finance Statistics Yearbook, Published by the IMF.
(9) International Financial Statistics, IMF Publications.
(10) Trade Policy Review, Sri Lanka, 1995, Published by the IMF.

SIMULATION FOR THE PERIOD 1976-2000

We want to investigate whether the performance of the Sri Lanka economy could have been better during the period 1975-2000. Our Macro-Model identified four major exogenous variables that could possibly affect the growth performance of the economy. These are:

- BCP (Bank Credit to the Private Sector).
- BCG (Bank Credit to the Government),
- FA (Foreign Assets), and
- EXCH (Exchange Rate between Sri Lanka Rupees and USD).

The model was solved for GDP in terms of the purely exogenous and predetermined (lagged) variables. Repeated substitutions of the functional forms of the variables lead to a convergence of the GDP values that are very close to the actual figures. The figures are recorded in Table 1 and the accompanying diagram below.

TABLE 1

YEAR	*GDPACT*	*GDPESTNW3*	*GDPESTNW2*	*GDPESTNW1*	*GDPESTNW*
1976	397056	367722	355066	385458	312473
1977	412226	393596	393858	408729	335791
1978	442764	464589	468595	474998	402158
1979	469674	487202	491501	493259	420380
1980	496415	505652	509246	508255	435578
1981	523944	539261	541912	539390	466741
1982	551121	566171	568015	564573	491932
1983	577314	599731	600951	596951	524276
1984	606473	610617	611360	607066	534191
1985	636898	627961	628424	623826	550982
1986	664118	650330	650575	645778	572965
1987	674887	669509	669588	664662	591874
1988	693643	692282	692264	687190	614570
1989	707337	722714	722594	717462	644933
1990	751470	772699	772501	767346	694868
1991	787698	791289	7914011	785904	713320
1992	822191	827548	847241	722142	749477
1993	879050	884842	884530	879402	806724
1994	928709	923006	922669	917558	844782
1995	980061	956886	956539	951433	878558
1996	1016885	999604	999287	994098	921321
1997	1082431	1048442	1048108	1042911	970144
1998	1133840	1110423	1110090	1104857	1032176
1999	1183140	1198629	1198267	1193064	1120353
2000	1253624	1261964	1261622	1256363	1183792

In simulating the performance of the economy, we have altered the values of the policy variables BCP, BCG, EXCH and FA at selected points of times as far as permissible within the board limits of historical data and checked on the sensitivity of GDP to such changes.

A method similar to the iterative convergence-based estimation procedure has been used for simulating the GDP of the economy during the period 1975-2000. Starting from the estimated GDP for 1976, estimates of CP, CG, TI EX and IM were obtained. These formed the predetermined variables for the next year. Using those and the exogenous variables as per proposed alterations, the same procedure was repeated to arrive at the GDP of 1977. In this manner a simulated series was obtained for the entire time period 1976-2000. The proposed values of the exogenous variables were experimentally determined after closely observing their actual behaviour.

The first series to be considered was BCP. It is seen that this variable recorded negative growth rates during the years 1980, 1988, 1989 and 1996. The value of BCP for 1980 was considered to be a 3% increase over the previous year, instead of a decrease of 18.7%. To revive the economy, the value of BCP for the next year (1981) was also considered to increase at the same rate of 3%. After that for each of the years 1988 to 1992, it has been proposed that BCP grows annually at 1%. Finally for the years 1996, 1997 and 1998 it has been considered that BCP grows annually at 2%. The proposed changes are well within the limits set by the actual growth rates experienced by the variable during the entire period 1975-2000.

Next we turned our attention to the second variable BCG. Historically, this series shows nine years with negative growth rats. These years are 1978, 1983, 1984, 1990 to 1994 and 1997. It has been proposed that there be an annual growth rate of 1% in BCG during 1978 and 1984 to 1986 while the tempo should be maintained though a 0.5% annual growth rate of BCG for 1990 through 2000. If these changes alone were possible to have been implemented then too, it would raise the time-path of GDP above the actual figures for the entire time span 1975-2000. In addition, we have included some minor proposed changes in the series for FA. We have considered a very mild annual growth rate of 0.25% p.a. from 1980 onwards, except for 1998 and 1999 when the actual growth rates were a shade higher. Finally we have considered changes in the exchange-rate depreciation for the years 1979, 1986, 1991 and 1995.

Together, all these proposed changes mentioned above cause the simulated time-path of GDP to be substantially higher than the actual time-path as shown in Table 2 below and its accompanying diagram. The average compounded annual growth rate of GDP would have been 5.42% instead of 4.91% for the entire time-period if it were possible to implement these modest proposed changes.

TABLE 2

Simulation Results for the Period 1976-2000

Year	*GDP Actual*	*GDP After Simulation*
1976	397056	362452
1977	412226	396393
1978	442764	469687
1979	469674	493973
1980	496415	526720
1981	523944	554587
1982	551121	575618
1983	577314	613600
1984	606473	648247
1985	636898	665071
1986	664118	692217
1987	674887	711471
1988	693643	745464
1989	707337	782700
1990	751470	827640
1991	787698	848625
1992	822191	874758
1993	879050	923798
1994	928709	954535
1995	980061	991785
1996	1016885	1039247
1997	1082431	1080200
1998	1133840	1139039
1999	1183140	1218428
2000	1253624	1286520
Growth Rate P.A.	4.91%	5.42%

FURTHER DISCUSSION ON THE RESULTS OF SIMULATION

I. Prospects of Growth in the Initial Years of Liberalization

During the early years 1976-83, in spite of periodic declines, the actual average annual growth rates of BCP, BCG and FA were 13.74%, 13.11% and 19.65% respectively. The corresponding growth rate in GDP was 5.49%. It has been observed that the economy is most sensitive to change in FA. Instead of the drastic fall in the FA figures during 1980 and 1983, if it were possible to maintain even a slightly positive growth rate of 0.25%, the economy would have been on a higher time-path of GDP, recording an impressive 7.81% annual growth on the average.

TABLE 3

Year	*GDP NEW*	*GDPACT*
1976	362452	397056
1977	396393	412226
1978	469687	442764
1979	493973	469674
1980	526720	496415
1981	554587	523944
1982	575618	551121
1983	613600	577314

II. Effect of Government Intervention during the War

The actual average annual growth rate of GDP during the period 1984-90 was 3.64%. It would have been possible to set-up the growth rate of 4.16% under an alternative moderately improved scenario provided that the growth rate of foreign assets had been maintained even as low as 0.25% p.a., the growth rate of BCG had been maintained at 1% p.a. during 1984-87 and the historical figures for BCG had been maintained thereafter. An alternative optimistic scenario would consist of maintaining the 0.25% growth rate in FA while going for a 15% growth rate in BCG. The results are shown in the Table and diagrams below. The average growth rate of GDP now becomes 5.09% p.a.

TABLE 4

Year	GDP (1)	GDP (2)	GDP (3)
1984	653118	648247	606473
1985	675593	665071	636898
1986	709287	692217	664118
1987	736120	711471	674887
1988	775109	745464	693643
1989	822720	782700	707337
1990	879530	827640	751470

In the Table 5 we compare the actual GDP with two alternative scenarios during the period 1991-2000. In the moderate-improvement scenario corresponding to the GDP (2) column, changes in the BCG and FA figures has been considered. Stronger government intervention in this third phase raises the growth rate from 5.3% to 6.55% p.a. on the average.

TABLE 5

Growth Possibilities in the Post-war Period

Year	GDP (1)	GDP (2)	GDP (3)
1991	854521	848625	787698
1992	887466	874758	822191
1993	944367	923798	879050
1994	984175	954535	928709
1995	1031887	991785	980061
1996	1091409	1039247	1016885
1997	1146262	1080200	1082431
1998	1221116	1139039	1133840
1999	1318953	1218428	1183140
2000	1408291	1286520	1253624

CONCLUDING REMARKS

The Sri Lankan economy is a very open economy. As such its fortunes are closely linked with the global economic scenario due to the high degree of openness. Nevertheless the government can play an important role in the economic arena not just as a facilitator but in a more direct manner, as borne out by the impact of changes in BCG and BCP on the GDP of the country. As mentioned earlier, a higher time-path of GDP is possible through changes in these two variables alone. In addition, a very modest but steady increase in Foreign Assets acts as a highly effective stimulator for investment in the economy. Investment expenditure being the fountainhead for economic growth, these policies lead to a higher projected GDP for almost all the years between 1976 and 2000. Finally, attempts at making the Sri Lankan exportable goods more price-competitive and raising the relative price of importable goods through proposed changes in the exchange rate adds further to the stimulatory effect on GDP. The next area of investigation would be the detailed impacts of the proposed changes in the above-mentioned variables on the value addition of each of the nineteen sectors of the economy.

REFERENCES

Athukorala, P.C. (2000), "Market Oriented Reforms & Industrial Restructuring in Sri Lanka", in Dilip Dutta (Ed.), *Economic Liberalization and Institutional Reforms in South Asia*, (Atlantic Publishers, 2000)

Choudhury, A. (1986), "Integrating Macro-Econometric and Input-Output Models: A Study of the Bangladesh Economy," *Singapore Economic Review*.

Klein, L.K. (1986), "An Outline of the Keynes-Leontief Macro-Model", *The Handbook of Econometrics*.

Klein, L.K. (1978), "The Supply Side", *AER*.

Klein, L.K. (1965), "What Kind of Macro-Econometric Models For Developing Economies?", *Indian Economic Journal*.

Structural Analysis of the Indian Economy in the Conventional and Augmented Input-Output Frameworks

PARAMITA DASGUPTA AND DEBESH CHAKRABORTY

INTRODUCTION

Input-Output methodology developed by Leontief (1951) offers important insights into the structure of an economy. The concept of inter-industry linkages based on this methodology is often used for assessing the impact associated with the growth of a particular sector. Conventionally, the sectoral linkages are measured within the Leontief Input-Output Open framework, where the final demand comprising household expenditure, government expenditure, capital formation and net export are treated as exogenous. The exogenous character of the final demand in the Open model implies that all of the components of demand have to be given from outside of the input-output system in order to derive the gross output levels of the sectors. On the other hand, the intermediate input requirements are determined endogenously. As a result, the inter-industry linkages measured by the Conventional Open model are entirely based on the inter-industry technological relationship.

However, in the underdeveloped and developing economies the inter-industry relations are usually lacking on a substantial scale while a large extent of the outputs are determined by the final demand components (final consumption demand in particular) leaving a small portion to be determined by inter-industry transactions of outputs. Therefore, it may be argued that the linkage measures based on the Conventional Open model do not provide a better picture of the structural interdependence as far as the underdeveloped and developing economies are concerned. The exogenous character of the final demand reduces the usefulness of the Open model in predicting the structural relationship.

Ghosh (1964) proposed an alternative approach where the Input-Output structure was modified by regarding Household as a production sector, which was supposed to consume the outputs of the sectors producing the non-durable goods endogenously in fixed proportion of its output. The wage income of the Household sector is considered as the output of the sector. In the modified version the vector of final consumption expenditures on the non-durable goods and services, which are simple direct function of the Household income, are endogenised into the Input-Output matrix and thereby the model is made partially closed. This process results in an Augmented Input-Output matrix, increasing the number of rows and columns by one each. While the additional column consists of final consumption expenditures on non-durable consumer goods and services, the value added by these sectors are the elements of the additional row. With the inclusion of the Household sector as a production sector in the input-output system, the behavioral elements are incorporated into the model and therefore the Augmented model is expected to be a better predicting mechanism than the Conventional one. The linkages measured within the augmented framework may be more reliable and better suited, particularly for the underdeveloped and developing economies.

Over the years, several studies were conducted on the Indian economy to explore its structure. Some pioneering studies include those by Bharadwaj (1966), Hashim (1970) and Hazari (1970). The other researches in this field were conducted by Mehta (1977), Venkatramaiah and Argade (1979), Saxena and Bhatnagar (1987), Saxena and Dhawan (1992), Sastry, Singh, Bhattacharya and Unnikrishnan (2003). However, most of these studies are based on the Conventional Model while very little attempt has been made to use the Augmented Model to explore the structure of the Indian economy, which is a developing one. The current paper aims at studying India's production structure within both the Conventional and the Augmented frameworks using the Input-Output Tables for 1983-84, 1993-94 and 1998-99 and makes a comparison of the inter-industry linkages, as measured by the two models. In this paper we will first estimate the sectoral linkages and identify the key sectors using the Conventional model and then see how far the results are changed when the same measures are applied in the augmented model.

In this study, we have used the Input-Output Transaction Tables for 1983-84, 1993-94 and 1998-99 prepared by Central Statistical Organization. The commodities of the original (115 × 115) transaction matrix have been aggregated and reduced into a (72 × 72) matrix. The tables are converted into 1993-94 constant prices to make them comparable. All the subsequent analyses have been in terms of aggregated transaction matrix.

The subsequent three sections of this paper are arranged as follows: In section 2, the Methodology is discussed. Section 3 explains the empirical results. Finally, Section 4 presents the conclusions of the study.

2. METHODOLOGY

2.1 Conventional Input-Output Model

Input-Output model depicts the monetary flow of goods and services throughout the economy. All the sectors in the economy purchase goods from one another and use these goods as intermediate input in the production of the final products. In the Conventional Input-Output model the production of output of each sector is just sufficient to meet the input requirements of all sectors including itself as well as the final demand of the open sector. In matrix notation the relationship can be presented as,

$$x = X\,e + D, \qquad \text{(i)}$$

where X is the transaction matrix of order (n × n), e is the unit vector of order (n × 1) and D and x are the (n × 1) order final demand vector and (n × 1) order gross output vector respectively. The components of final demand are private consumption demand, Government consumption demand, gross capital formation and net export. Each sector is assumed to require the intermediate inputs in fixed proportion to its own output, i.e.

$$A = \hat{X} x^{-1}, \qquad \text{(ii)}$$

where A is the Input-Output Technical Coefficient matrix of order (n × n) and x is the diagonal matrix of gross output. Therefore, two interacting forces originated from the supply and demand sides can be represented by the following input-output balance equation

$$x = A\,x + D$$

or,

$$x = (I - A)^{-1} D \qquad \text{(iii)}$$

This is the fundamental equation of the Input-Output Open model. $(I - A)^{-1}$ is the Leontief Inverse, an element of which gives the direct and indirect requirements of intermediate inputs per unit of final output.

In Input-Output framework, inter-industry linkages, which mean the interconnection between a sector and the other sectors, are of two types—backward linkage and forward linkage. While the backward linkage reflects the relation between the total output of a sector and its purchases of other sector's output as intermediate input, the forward linkage shows the relation between the output of a sector and its sale of output as intermediate input to other sectors. As far as the measures of the backward and forward linkages are concerned, Rasmussen's (1956) approach is most widely used which relies on the Leontief Inverse. Let us now define Rasmussen's backward and forward linkages.

(a) Backward Linkage in the Conventional Model

Backward linkage is the increase in the gross output of an economy resulting from a unit increase in the final demand of a particular sector. For sector j, it is defined as,

$$I_1 = (\sum_i p_{ij}/n) \,/\, (\sum_{i,j} p_{ij}/n^2), \qquad \text{(iv)}$$

where, p_{ij} is an element of the Leontief inverse which is the amount of the ith sector's output required directly and indirectly as an intermediate input for a unit increase in the demand for the jth commodity; and Sp_{ij} is the column sum for the jth sector which gives the total direct and indirect requirement of the intermediate input for a unit increase in the final demand of the jth sector. $(\Sigma\ p_{ij}/n)$ is the mean of the jth column sum where n is the number of the sectors. The denominator gives the grand mean of the column sums, i.e. $(\Sigma\ p_{ij}/n^2)$ which is the average backward linkage.

Therefore, I_1 is an index, which measures the extent of expansion of the output as a whole by an expansion of the jth sector. If $I_1 > 1$, it implies the backward linkage of the jth sector is greater than the average backward linkage.

(b) Forward Linkage in the Conventional Model

The forward linkage gives the direct and indirect expansion in the ith sector for a unit increase in the final demand of any sector which utilizes the output of the ith sector as input. For sector i, it is defined as

$$I_2 = (\sum_j p_{ij}/n) \,/\, (\sum_{i,j} p_{ij}/n^2), \qquad \text{(v)}$$

The numerator gives the mean for the ith row of the Leontief Inverse and the denominator is the grand mean of all rows. I_2 shows the extent to which the output of sector i is increased by the expansion in the system of industries. $I_2 > 1$ means the forward linkage of the ith sector is greater than the average forward linkage.

A sector can exhibit a high backward linkage if it draws its inputs from a few sectors, whereas another sector, which draws inputs from a large number of sectors, can also have a high backward linkage. In the latter case, the high backward linkage effects are well spread over a large number of sectors than the first one. Therefore, the variability of the linkage inducements is required to be measured to supplement the backward and forward linkages. The coefficient of variation for each column and coefficient of variation for each row are usually used to measure the variability of backward and forward linkages respectively.

Coefficient of variation for each column is

$$CV_1 = [(1/n-1) \sum_i \{p_{ij} - (1/n) \sum_i p_{ij}\}^2]^{1/2} [(1/n) \sum_i p_{ij}]^{-1} \quad \text{(vi)}$$

For each row coefficient of variation is measured as

$$CV_2 = [(1/n-1) \sum_j \{p_{ij} - (1/n) \sum_j p_{ij}\}^2]^{1/2} [(1/n) \sum_j p_{ij}]^{-1} \quad \text{(vii)}$$

2.2 Augmented Input-Output Model

The first fundamental equation of the Leontief model which shows the balance between the gross output of a sector and its disposal as intermediate input of the other sectors and as final use of the open sector can be rewritten as, i.e. equation (i) can also be presented as

$$x = X e + D_c + D_o \quad \text{(viii)}$$

where D_c is the final private consumption demand vector of order (n × 1) and D_0 is the other final demand vector of order (n × 1). e is the unit column vector. In the Augmented model the final private consumption demand vector are split into two components – final private consumption demand for non-durable goods and final private consumption demand for durable goods. The first class includes the final outputs of the sectors 1-26, 28, 30-37, 59 and 61-72, which produce either raw materials or non-durable consumer goods. The second class includes the final outputs of the sectors 27, 29, 38-58 and 60, which produce either capital goods or durable consumer goods. The classification in detail is given in the appendix.

In the Augmented model the private consumption demand for the non-durable sectors are endogenised to form an additional vector in the transaction matrix and that of the durable sectors are treated as exogenous. This generates an augmented matrix of order (73 × 73). The justification of incorporating the final consumption demand for the non-durable sectors only into the Input-Output matrix is that the day-to-day demand for non-durable goods and services by the households depends simply on the income whereas, the demand for the durables depends on many long-term factors.

In matrix notation, we can rewrite the open model as

$$x_a = X_a e + D_a \qquad \text{(ix)}$$

where x_a is the vector of final output, X_a represents the transaction matrix in the Augmented structure whose last column consists of purchases of non-durable commodities by the final private consumers and the last row consists of the value added of the sectors producing the non-durable goods. D_a is the final demand in the augmented structure, which is obtained by subtracting the private consumption demand of the non-durable goods from the total final demand. The matrix of technical coefficient is defined as

$$A_a = X_a \hat{x}^{-1}{}_a, \qquad \text{(x)}$$

where A_a is an augmented matrix whose final column contains non-durable goods bought by the domestic final users.

Therefore,

$$x_a = A_a\, x_a + D_a,$$

or,

$$x_a = (I - A_a)^{-1} D_a \qquad \text{(xi)}$$

Equation (xi) represents the fundamental equation in the Augmented model where $(I - A_a)^{-1}$ is the Inverse Matrix obtained in the Augmented model.

(a′) Backward Linkage in the Augmented Model: The revised measure for backward linkage for sector j in the Augmented model is defined as,

$$I_3 = (\sum_i q_{ij}/n_1)/(\sum_{i,j} q_{ij}/n_1^2), \qquad \text{(xii)}$$

where q_{ij} is an element of the Inverse Matrix of the Augmented structure and $n_1 = n + 1$, the number of sectors in the Augmented model.

(b′) Forward Linkage in the Augmented Model: The revised forward linkage for sector i in the Augmented model is as follows:

$$I_4 = (\sum_j q_{ij}/n_1)/(\sum_{i,j} q_{ij}/n_1^{2}) \qquad \text{(xiii)}$$

In order to measure the variability of linkages obtained in the Augmented model we have calculated the coefficient of variations for backward linkages and forward linkages, which are defined as,

$$CV_3 = [\,(1/n{-}1)\sum_i \{p_{ij} - (1/n)\sum_i p_{ij}\}^2]^{1/2}\,[(1/n)\sum_i p_{ij}]^{-1} \qquad \text{(vi)}$$

$$CV_4 = [\,(1/n{-}1)\sum_j \{p_{ij} - (1/n)\sum_j p_{ij}\}^2]^{1/2}\,[(1/n)\sum_j p_{ij}]^{-1} \qquad \text{(vii)}$$

3. EMPIRICAL RESULTS AND DISCUSSION

In this section, we have identified the key sectors of the Indian economy in the Conventional and Augmented models where investment should be concentrated. First, we have chosen the key sectors in terms of backward and forward linkages in the Conventional model, followed by identifying those in the Augmented model.

The rationale behind identifying the sectors with highest linkages as key sectors is that an increase in investment on these sectors would spread more over the rest of the sectors than in the case of sectors having low linkage values and thereby the key sectors have a large multiplier effect on the gross output. We have discussed earlier that the high linkage inducements do not necessarily mean the linkage effects are uniformly distributed over all sectors. It may happen that a few numbers of sectors is highly benefited from the investment made on the sectors with high linkages while the impact on the production of the remaining sectors is negligible. Therefore, the criteria of choosing the key sectors should not solely be the high linkage values, but the variability of linkage strength provided by a sector should be taken into account, which is measured by the coefficient of variation. Smaller the value of coefficient of variation of linkages with other sectors, lesser the variability of the linkage effects spread over the rest of the sectors. Therefore, in terms of backward linkages (or forward linkages) the sector with highest linkage is ranked first while the sector with lowest value of coefficient of variation tops the list when the sectors are arranged according to the corresponding coefficient of variation. In an attempt to give equal weight to both the criteria while choosing the key sectors, the ranks according to backward linkages (or forward linkages) and the corresponding coefficient of variation are added for each sector. Then the sectors are arranged in ascending order according to the number scored by them by adding the ranks, i.e. the sectors scoring lowest number tops the list. Diamond (1975) used a similar method where he took the difference between the two ranks. The top ten sectors according to the combined ranks are identified and regarded as the Key sectors according to backward linkages (or forward linkages) in the subsequent analysis as these sectors reveal greater and more stable linkages with the rest of the economy in terms of backward linkages (or forward linkages).

3.1 Backward Linkage Results

The key sectors according to backward linkages of the Conventional model for 1983-84, 1993-94 and 1998-99 are chosen and presented in Table 1. The key sectors according to backward linkages in 1983-84 are as follows: Coal tar products, Fertilizers, Soaps, cosmetics and glycerin, Machine tools, Electrical industrial machinery, Miscellaneous manufacturing, Industrial machinery, Rubber and plastic products, Motor vehicles, Tractors and Agricultural implements and Hotels and restaurants. The last two sectors in the list of top ten sectors have the same ranking that is why the list contains twelve sectors. Among these sectors Coal tar products, Soaps, cosmetics and glycerin, Electrical industrial machinery and Tractors and Agri. Implements have retained their importance in 1993-94 and 1998-99 as well.

Between 1983-84 and 1993-94, Machine tools, Miscellaneous manufacturing, Industrial machinery, Rubber and plastic products and Hotel and restaurants have omitted from the group of key sectors while Electrical wires, cables and appliances, Batteries,

TABLE 1

Key Sectors According to Backward Linkages in the Conventional Model

1983-84		*1993-94*		*1998-99*	
Sec. No.	*Key Sectors*	*Sec. No.*	*Key Sectors*	*Sec. No.*	*Key Sectors*
28	Coal tar products	28	Coal tar products	53	Electronic equipments (incl. TV)
30	Fertilizers	49	Electrical wires, cables and appliances	33	Drugs and medicines
34	Soaps, cosmetics & glycerin	34	Soaps, cosmetics & glycerin	34	Soaps, cosmetics & glycerin
45	Machine tools	50	Batteries	48	Electrical industrial machinery
48	Electrical industrial machinery	53	Electronic equipments (incl. TV)	43	Tractors and agri. implements
59	Miscellaneous manufacturing	42	Hand tools and other metal products	28	Coal tar products
44	Industrial machinery	31	Pesticides	49	Electrical wires, cables and appliances
26	Rubber and plastic products	30	Fertilizers	32	Paints, varnishes and lacquers
56	Motor vehicles	43	Tractors and agri. implements	56	Motor vehicles
43	Tractors and agri. implements	48	Electrical industrial machinery	55	Rail equipments
67	Hotels and restaurants				

Electronic equipments, Hand tools and other metal products and Pesticides have included in this group during this period. However, Batteries, Electronic equipments, Hand tools and other metal products and Pesticides have reduced in importance in 1998-99 while Drugs and medicines, Paints, varnishes and lacquers and Rail equipment have featured in top ten groups in this year. Motor vehicles have regained its importance as key sector in 1998-99.

The above-mentioned key sectors of the Conventional model and their changing pattern apparently reflects a more or less modern character of India's production structure, as the groups of top ten sectors mostly consist of modern technology and capital-based industries.

The key sectors according to backward linkages of the augmented model are shown in Table 2. In 1983-84, the identified key sectors according to backward linkages of this model are as follows: Coal tar products, Fertilizers, Soaps, cosmetics and Glycerin, Machine tools, miscellaneous manufacturing, Cement, Water supply, Tractors and agricultural implement, Jute, hemp and mesta textiles and Pesticides. Six out of these ten sectors feature in the corresponding list in the Conventional model. The exceptions are Cement, Water supply, Jute, hemp and mesta textiles and Pesticides.

In 1993-94, the group of key sectors in the Augmented model is dominated by the presence of agro-based sectors like Tea and coffee processing, Other food products and beverages, Animal services (agricultural), Cotton textiles, Jute, hemp and mesta textiles, Other textiles, Sugar and Khandsari boora and Leather products. The other sectors belonging to the category of key sectors in 1993-94 are: Fertilizers, Coal tar products and other chemicals.

However, most of the traditional agro-based sectors except Animal services (agricultural) and Jute, hemp and mesta textiles, identified as key sectors in 1993-94 are dropped from the group of key sectors in 1998-99. The traditional sectors which feature in the top ten groups in this year are Wheat and Tobacco products. The list also includes Drugs and medicines, Medical and Health, Fertilizers, Electronic equipments (incl. TV), Electricity and Hotels and restaurants.

While comparing the key sectors of the Conventional model

TABLE 2

Key Sectors According to Backward Linkages in the Augmented Model

1983-84		1993-94		1998-99	
Sec. No.	*Key Sectors*	*Sec. No.*	*Key Sectors*	*Sec. No.*	*Key Sectors*
28	Coal tar products	28	Coal tar products	33	Drugs and medicines
30	Fertilizers	15	Tea and coffee processing	20	Jute, hemp, mesta textiles
34	Soaps, cosmetics & glycerin	30	Fertilizers	70	Medical and health
45	Machine tools	17	Other food products and beverages	18	Tobacco products
59	Miscellaneous manufacturing	6	Animal services (agricultural)	30	Fertilizers
38	Cement	19	Cotton textiles	2	Wheat
63	Water supply	20	Jute, hemp, mesta textiles	6	Animal services (agricultural)
43	Tractors and agri. implements	21	Other textiles	53	Electronic equipments (incl. TV)
20	Jute, hemp, mesta textiles	16	Sugar, khandsari boora	61	Electricity
31	Pesticides	25	Leather products	67	Hotels and restaurants
		36	Other chemicals		

with that of the Augmented model, it is observed that the group of the key sectors of the latter model contains mostly traditional agro-based industries along with a few modern industries. Also, an observation on the changing pattern of the key sectors of the Augmented model over the years reveals that the groups of key sectors for 1993-94 and 1998-99 contain more traditional industries as compared to 1983-84 whereas, in the conventional model the structural shift is found to have taken place in the direction of some modern industries.

3.2 Forward Linkage Results

The top ten sectors according to forward linkages of the Conventional and Augmented models in 1983-84, 1993-94 and 1998-99 are enlisted in Tables 3 and 4 respectively.

In 1983-84, the group of key sectors in terms of forward linkages in the Conventional model consists of Trade, Transport services, Electricity, Iron and Steel, Other services, Banking and Insurance, Petroleum products, Other crops, Commercial crops and Coal and Lignite.

Out of these ten sectors, seven sectors have retained their importance in 1993-94 and 1998-99 also, showing almost an unaltered structure over the decade of the 1980's and the 1990's. Heavy chemicals and Crude petroleum and natural gas have replaced Petroleum products and Commercial crops from the group of top ten sectors in 1993-94 as compared to 1983-84 and Non-ferrous basic metal is included in the corresponding group in 1998-99 in place of other crops.

The results regarding the key sectors according to forward linkages in the Augmented model corroborates almost an unvarying production structure during 1983-84 to 1998-99 because seven out of the top ten sectors have retained their importance as key sectors over this period. They are Household sectors, Trade, Transport services, Other crops, Other services, Milk and milk product and Public administration. While Commercial crops and Wheat have dropped from the top ten groups in 1993-94, Paddy, another agricultural crop has omitted from the corresponding list in 1998-99. Other food products and beverages, which has declined in importance in 1993-94, has regained it in 1998-99. The sectors, which have promoted in the group of key sectors in 1993-94 and retained their importance in 1998-99 as well, are Electricity, Banking and Insurance.

TABLE 3

Key Sectors According to Forward Linkages in the Conventional Model

1983-84		*1993-94*		*1998-99*	
Sec. No.	*Key sectors*	*Sec. No.*	*Key sectors*	*Sec. No.*	*Key sectors*
66	Trade	66	Trade	66	Trade
64	Transport services	64	Transport services	61	Electricity
61	Electricity	61	Electricity	64	Transport services
40	Iron and steel	40	Iron and steel	40	Iron and steel
71	Other services	68	Banking and insurance	68	Banking and insurance
68	Banking and insurance	11	Crude petroleum, natural gas	29	Heavy chemicals
27	Petroleum products	71	Other services	71	Other services
3	Other crops	3	Other crops	41	Non-ferrous basic metals
4	Commercial crops	29	Heavy chemicals	11	Crude petroleum, natural gas
10	Coal and lignite	10	Coal and lignite	10	Coal and lignite

TABLE 4

Key Sectors According to Forward Linkages in the Augmented Model

1983-84		*1993-94*		*1998-99*	
Sec. No.	*Key Sectors*	*Sec. No.*	*Key Sectors*	*Sec. No.*	*Key Sectors*
73	Household sector	73	Household sector	66	Trade
66	Trade	66	Trade	73	Household sector
3	Other crops	64	Transport services	64	Transport services
64	Transport services	3	Other crops	71	Other services
71	Other services	71	Other services	3	Other crops
1	Paddy	61	Electricity	17	Other food products and beverages
17	Other food products and beverages	68	Banking and insurance	68	Banking and insurance
5	Milk and milk products	1	Paddy	61	Electricity
4	Commercial crops	5	Milk and milk products	72	Public administration
2	Wheat	72	Public administration	5	Milk and milk products
72	Public administration				

Unlike the Backward linkage results, the forward linkage results of both the Conventional and the Augmented models indicates a common point that the structure of the Indian economy has remained almost unchanged over the period 1983-84 to 1998-99. At the same time, it is also observed that whatever minor structural changes have occurred, the shift was in the direction of modern industries like heavy chemicals, Non–ferrous basic metals, etc. in the Conventional model, whereas in the Augmented model the shift was in favour of Electricity, Banking and Insurance and Food products.

4. CONCLUSIONS

In this paper, an attempt has been made to study the structural changes of the Indian economy over the decade of the 1980's and the 1990's. Along with the Conventional Input-Output open model, the structural relationships have also been studied with an Augmented Input-Output framework, which are expected to be more suitable for exploring the structure of developing country like India. In the Augmented model the final private consumption demand on the non-durable consumer goods are endogenised while the other components of final demand are treated as exogenous. The study identifies the key sectors of the Indian economy where the investment should be concentrated to set India on a high growth path, by using Rasmussen's backward and forward linkage measures.

The study reveals the following results:

First, high-technology intensive machine industries have strong linkage inducements over the other sectors as these industries dominate the groups of key sectors according to backward linkages in the Conventional model which reflects a well-diversified and modern structure of the Indian economy. In sharp contrast to this, the key sectors as identified in the augmented model are of more traditional in character. However, it should also be mentioned that some non-traditional sectors like Fertilizers, Electronic equipments have gained in importance as the key sectors over the years in the augmented framework.

Secondly, in case of forward linkages, service sectors like Trade, Transport services, Other services, Banking and Insurance,

Electricity, etc. dominate the group of the key sectors in both the models. In this regard inter-temporal studies in both the Conventional and the Augmented models show that the structure of the Indian economy is almost unvarying over the period 1983-84 to 1998-99.

The decade of the 1980's and 1990's witnessed a significant change in the macro-economic policies of the Indian Government, the major thrust of which was to shift the economy to a more liberalized system. India had started to adopt reform measures from mid 1980's, which got its momentum in 1991 after introduction of the New Economic Policy. The changes were expected to bring about modernization and diversification in the structure of the Indian economy. However, the study reveals that the Reforms measures have not ushered any significant change in the structure of the Indian economy. This may be an indication of the existence of some bottlenecks in the programme of Reforms, which have hindered any major shift in the economic structure.

The Input-Output methodology-based analysis about the structure of the Indian economy displays that India's production structure is neither traditional nor a highly modernized one. Some machine industries, chemical industries, metal-based industries and service sectors are found to have a large multiplier effect on growth along with the traditional agro-based sectors. The study also concludes that the Indian economy has not experienced any major structural change during the decade of the 1980's and 1990's even after adoption of reform measures during this period.

REFERENCES

Bharadwaj, K. (1966), "A Note on the Structural Interdependence and the Concept of a Key Sector", *Kyklos*, Vol. 19, No. 2.

CSO, *Input-Output Transaction Tables of 1983-84, 1993-94 and 1998-99*, Central Statistical Organization,

Dhawan, S. and K.K. Saxena (1992), "Structural Linkages and Key Sectors of the Indian Economy", *Indian Economic Review*, Vol. 27, No. 2, pp. 195-210.

Diamond, J. (1975), "Linkages in Industrialization: A study of Selected Developing Countries", *United Nations Journal of Development Planning*.

Ghosh, Ambika (1964), *Experiments with Input-Output Model*, Cambridge University Press, U.K.

Hashim, S.R. (1970), "Inter-regional Linkages and the Changes in the

Pattern of Commodity Flows in India, 1950-51 to 1959-60", *Indian Economic Journal*, Vol. 4, No. 2, Oct.-Dec.

Hazari, B. (1970), "Empirical Identification of key sectors of the Indian Economy", *The Review of Economics and Statistics*, Vol. 52, No. 3, pp. 173-95.

Leontief, W. (1951), *The Structure of the American Economy, 1919-39*, 2nd edition, Oxford University Press, New York.

Mehta, B.C. (1977), *Structure of Rajasthan's Economy: An Input-Output Analysis*, Research Books, Jaipur.

Ministry of Statistics and Programme Implementation, Government of India.

Rasmussen, P.N. (1956), *Studies in Intersectoral Relations*, Amsterdam, North Holland.

Sastry, D.V. S., Balwant Singh *et al.* (2003), "Sectoral Linkages and Growth Prospects, Reflections on the Indian Economy", *Economic and Political Weekly*, June 14, 2003, pp. 2390-97.

Saxena, K.K and I. Bhatnagar (1987), "Comparison of Regional Input-Output Tables—Rajasthan, Punjab and Haryana", *Anvesak*, Vol. 17, No. 2, December.

Venkatramaiah, P. and L. Argade (1979), "Changes in Input-Output Coefficients and their Impact on Production Levels", *Arth Vijnana*, Vol 21, March.

APPENDIX
Classification of Sectors in the Augmented Structure

Sec. No.	*Non Durable Sectors*	*Sec. No.*	*Durable Sectors*
1	Paddy	27	Petroleum products
2	Wheat	29	Heavy chemicals
3	Other crops	38	Cement
4	Commercial crops	39	Other non-metallic mineral prods.
5	Milk and milk products	40	Iron and steel
6	Animal services (agricultural)	41	Non-ferrous basic metals
7	Other livestock products	42	Hand tools and other metal products
8	Forestry and logging	43	Tractors and agri. implements
9	Fishing	44	Industrial machinery
10	Coal and lignite	45	Machine tools
11	Crude petroleum, natural gas	46	Office computing machines
12	Iron ore	47	Other non-electrical Machinery
13	Other metallic minerals	48	Electrical industrial Machinery
14	Other non metallic minerals	49	Electrical wires, cables and appliances
15	Tea and coffee processing	50	Batteries
16	Sugar and khandsari boora	51	Communication equipments
17	Other food products and beverages	52	Other electrical machinery
18	Tobacco products	53	Electronic equipments (incl. TV)
19	Cotton textiles	54	Ships and boats
20	Jute, hemp, mesta textiles	55	Rail equipments
21	Other textiles	56	Motor vehicles
22	Wood and wood products	57	Other transport equipments
23	Paper, paper prods. & newsprint	58	Watches and clocks
24	Printing and publishing	60	Construction
25	Leather products		
26	Rubber and plastic products		
28	Coal tar products		
30	Fertilizers		
31	Pesticides		
32	Paints, varnishes and lacquers		
33	Drugs and medicines		
34	Soaps, cosmetics & glycerin		
35	Synthetic fibers, resin		
36	Other chemicals		
37	Structural clay products		
59	Miscellaneous manufacturing		
61	Electricity		
62	Gas		
63	Water supply		
64	Transport services		
65	Communication		
66	Trade		
67	Hotels and restaurants		
68	Banking and insurance		
69	Education and research		
70	Medical and health		
71	Other services		
72	Public administration		

Structural Analysis of the Indian Economy in Input-Output Framework

VIJAY S. SATHE

INTRODUCTION

Wassily Leontief Russia born and America settled, was honoured by a Nobel Prize in Economics in 1973 for explaining the economy using his Input-Output model. There are two applications of the Leontief model, a closed model and an open model. A closed model deals only with the income of each industry whereas the open model finds the amount of production needed to satisfy an increase in demand. The most useful application of Input-Output analysis for the economist is the ability to be able to see how the change in the demand or the industry affects the entire economy.

Input-Output analysis can be applied to any size economy from business, district to the entire world. It is most often used for city planning and analysis of our national economy. After winning a Nobel Prize Leontief delivered a lecture on "Future of the World Economy". Some writers have written on Sectoral Interdependence and Growth of Orissan Economy. Some have explained the structure of Indian economy with the help of I-O techniques. Some have studied on Inter-Sectoral terms of trade in I-O framework. Some have selected a company's effect on other sectors and so on.

TERMINOLOGY

What is Leontief Inverse? The Leontief static open production model provides us with a powerful economic analysis tool in the form of I-O analysis. One needs to understand matrix and linear algebra for this technique. The terminologies in the formula are as follows:

1. Technology Coefficient Matrix (A)

This describes the relations a sector has with all other sectors. This matrix A is a matrix such that each column vector represents a different industry and each corresponding row vector represents what that industry inputs has a commodity into the column industry.

2. The Final Demand Vector (F)

The final demand vector is represented by F and is the amount of product the consumers will need.

3. The Total Production Vector (X)

The production vector X represents the total production that will be needed to satisfy the demand vector F.

Input-Output Technique developed by Leontief is an important analytical tool to understand the nature and the degree of integration of an economy. The concepts of backward and forward linkages related to this method are very useful for assessing the impact associated with the growth of a particular sector. This helps to formulate different economic policies. This matrix is a group of linear simultaneous equations.

MODEL

Leontief Static Open Input-Output Model is as follows:

$$x = [X]e + f,$$

where $[X]$ is $(n \times n)$ transaction matrix; e is the $(n \times 1)$ unit vector; f is the final demand vector $(n \times 1)$; and x is the total product.

The solution is

$$x = (I - A)^{-1} f$$

where A is the $(n \times n)$ technical coefficient matrix or fixed input coefficient matrix where each element is $a_{ij} = X_{ij}/x_j$. The elements of A indicate only the direct requirements per unit of output. While the elements of $(I - A)^{-1}$ matrix give both direct and indirect requirement per unit of output.

Weighted Inverse Leontief Model is as follows. The above model is presented as $(I - A^w)^{-1}$ in which each element is

$$a^w_{ij} = X^W_{ij}/x^w_j$$

In the present study weighted Leontief Inverse Matrix is taken into consideration.

DATA AND METHODOLOGY

Data

CSO, Ministry of Statistics and Programme Implementation, Government of India had published the first Input-Output transaction table (IOTT) in 1968-69. Thereafter the reports on IOTT for the reference years 1978-79, 1983-84, 1989-90 and 1993-94 were published. The last publication contains the IOTT for the year 1998-99. Our data source is the last publication, i.e. 1998-99 year of Indian Economy. We have used mainly the inverse Leontief matrix (Appendix 7) data from the report. The column vectors of final demand and total production are taken from transaction matrix 1 for 115 sectors.

Sectoral Dependence Measures (Linkages)

The forward linkages and backward linkages in Leontief framework measure the degree of integration of a particular sector in the rest of the economy. The widely used measures of Inter-Sectoral dependence are the backward, forward and total linkages indices.

(a) Backward Linkages

Backward linkage of a sector shows the relationship between the activities in the sector and its purchases. Backward linkage of a particular sector is defined as change in gross output of all sectors in an economy if the final demand for that particular sector increases by a unit. Backward linkage of a sector measures the inducement to production in other sectors, which is absorbed as an input to the former. In matrix notation the backward linkages are defined as

$$Q = e' (I - A^{w})^{-1}$$

where e is the unit vector and Q is the vector for backward linkages. Leontief Inverse is pre-multiplied by the transpose of unit vector, i.e. the backward linkages are nothing but the column-sums of the Leontief inverse. The Kth column sum would indicate a change in output of the whole economy if the final demand of the kth sector increases by one unit. The backward linkages are also treated as output multipliers in the input-output framework.

(b) Forward Linkages

Forward linkage shows the relationship between the total output of a sector and the sale of its output as intermediate input to other sectors. The measure of forward linkages in demand led model is defined as the row-sums of the Leontief inverse, i.e. forward linkage of a particular sector shows the change in the total output of the sector if the final demand of each sector increases by one unit. In matrix notation the forward linkages in the demand led model are

$$R = (I - A^{w})^{-1} e$$

where the vector for the forward linkages is denoted by R.

(c) Backward and Forward Linkage Indices

Backward and forward linkage indices reveal the relative linkage strength of a particular sector in terms of backward and forward linkages respectively. Backward linkage index is defined by the ratio of average of jth column of Leontief inverse to the total average, that is,

$$I_1 = c/L$$

where $c = \Sigma\, a^w_{ij}/n$, the column-wise average and

$$L = \Sigma\, a^w_{ij}/n^2$$

The total average and a^w_{ij} denotes the elements of weighted Leontief inverse. Similarly, the index constructed for measuring the strength of forward linkage in the demand side model is defined as the ratio of average of ith row sum of Leontief Inverse to the total average.

$$I_2 = r/L$$

where $r = \Sigma\, a^w_{ij}/n$ the row-wise average. Rasmussen however has labeled these two types of indices as the 'power of dispersion' and 'sensitivity of dispersion' respectively. If the column-wise average is greater than the total average, then the sectors are said to have a strong integration with the rest of the economy in terms of backward linkages. If the row-wise average is greater than the total average, the sectors are said to have a strong integration with the rest of the economy in terms of forward linkage while the other sectors have either moderate or weak linkage strength.

Strong: LI >= 1
Moderate: 1 > LI >= 0.8
Weak: LI < .8,

where LI = Linkage Indices.

(d) Coefficient of Variation (CV)

As averages are said to be sensitive to extreme values, a measure for variability of the linkages is required to measure the stability of the linkages strength provided by the sectors. For this purpose coefficient of variation for the Leontief backward and forward linkage indices are measured. They are denoted by CV_1 and CV_2 respectively.

CV = Standard Deviation/Average

The coefficient of variation index measures the relative evenness with which the sales or purchases to or from other sectors. Obviously the key sectors with low coefficient of variation index score a point in priority over the sectors with high coefficient of variation index. Smaller the value of coefficient of variation, greater is the stability of the linkage provided by the sector.

(e) Total Linkages

The total linkage is the sum of backward linkage and forward linkage. The total linkage index (TLI) is derived from backward and forward linkage indices.

Total linkage index = Forward linkage index + Backward linkage index

If (TL > 2), the sector is identified as a 'key sector'. The forward and backward linkage indices and their co-variations, total linkages are all ranked in descending order.

By applying CSO data, the various measures are calculated. They are all in Appendix Tables 1, 2 and 3. The findings from the calculations are as under.

EMPIRICAL FINDINGS

Backward, Forward and Total Linkages

Both the backward and forward linkages accounts for both direct and indirect linkages. In case of Leontief backward linkage indices, out of 115 sectors the number of sectors with strong backward index is 43, i.e. around 37.39% of the total sectors have capacity of affecting the gross output of the economy significantly. Any changes in the final demand in these sectors will effectively influence the economic activities of other sectors. 22 sectors are found to be moderately linked and 49 sectors are found weakly linked with the rest of the economy in terms of backward linkages. The sectors having backward sector index greater than unity are key sectors of the economy. The index value of backward linkage has varied between –0.21 (Crude petroleum and natural gas) to 4.89 (Construction). In terms of index of forward linkage it is observed:

1. That out of 115 sectors, 9 sectors have index value 2 or more. They are Trade, Other transport service, Other crops, Construction, Other services, Banking, Electrical, Misc. food products and Public Administration.
2. Out of 115 sectors 3 sectors have index between 1 and 2. They are Paddy, Wheat, Milk and Milk products. The index value of forward linkage varied between –2.35 (Non-ferrous basic metals) and 35.80 (Trade).
3. The rest sectors about 95 sectors are in weak integration.

In case of total linkage index, it is observed that 21 sectors out of total 115 sectors have an index above 2. These 21 sectors are identified as key sectors. They are in order of merit as Trade, Other transport services, Construction, Other crops, Other services, Banking, Misc. food products, Public administration, Medical and health, Milk and milk products, Electricity, Education and research, Ownership of dwellings, Hotels and restaurants, Cotton textiles, Misc. manufacturing, Other livestock products, Edible oils other than vanaspati, Animal services agriculture and Wheat. Other sectors have weak integration. The total linkage value has varied from –2.21 (Non-ferrous basic metals) to 39.25 (Trade). We will focus on these key sectors. Out of these 21 key sectors 7 sectors are from agricultural sector, 5 from industrial sector and 9 from service sectors. Sector number 1, 2, 17, 18, 19, 20, 36 are from agricultural sector, sector number 99, 38, 100, 42, 98 are from industry sector and sector number 104, 114, 109, 115, 113, 112, 111, 108 are from service sectors. Because of this it is seen that the economic growth is service-led growth.

Coefficient of variation index measures the relative evenness with which the sales or purchases to or from other sectors. Obviously the key sectors with low coefficient of variation index score a point in priority over the sectors with high coefficient of variation index. All these CVs are in appendix table. We have prepared a table of ranks of backward index, forward index and their respective CVs. The best combination of linkage index and corresponding CV will be 1 and 115 (ranks) because backward index's rank 1 will have the highest value and rank no. 115 in CV will have the lowest value. We have prepared a table of these combinations in case of 21 key sectors.

TABLE 1

Ranking Table

Sector No.	*Sector*	*Backward index*	*IBCV*	*Forward index*	*IFCV*
107	Trade	1	4	1	96
104	Other transport services	4	10	2	93
99	Construction	1	6	4	87
17	Other crops	7	5	3	91
114	Other services	14	18	5	92
109	Banking	41	13	6	94
38	Misc food product	3	38	8	55
115	Public administration	9	3	9	3
113	Medical and health	5	32	16	28
1	Paddy	13	9	10	56
18	Milk and milk products	11	11	11	52
100	Electricity	44	81	7	95
112	Education and research	12	7	13	9
111	Ownership of dwelling	10	8	14	2
108	Hotels and restaurants	8	97	18	64
42	Cotton textiles	17	63	15	83
98	Misc. manufacturing	23	20	12	86
20	Other livestocks products	21	35	17	82
36	Edible oil other than vanaspati	15	65	20	60
19	Animal Services Agriculture	6	16	96	—
2	Wheat	25	17	19	57

Source: Compiled from appendix table.

The above table is compiled to know which of the above sectors have been given the priority. Priority is always given to that sector which has the highest backward index, i.e. the lowest rank accompanied by backward CV of the lowest value, i.e. higher rank. If the backward linkage CV is low then there is sustainability in the sector. From the above table it is observed that:

1. Most of the key sectors are forward linkage-oriented and are sustainable due to low CVs. The exceptions are sectors 115, 112 and 111.
2. The following sectors are in this category. They are Trade, Other transport services, Construction, Other crops, other services, Banking, Mixed food product, Medical and health, Paddy, Milk and Milk products, Electricity and Misc. Manufacturing.
3. Only 30% of the key sectors are backward linkage-oriented with sustainability. The rest sectors are backward linkage-oriented but not sustainable. The sectors are Other transport services, Mixed food products, Medical and health, Hotel and restaurants, Cotton textiles, Edible oils other than vanaspati.
4. The top six sectors with forward and backward linkage-oriented with low dispersion are Trade, Other transport services, Construction, Misc. food products, Medical and health, Misc. Manufacturing.

Dependence on the Components of Final Demand

The driving force behind the entire analysis of linkages in I-O open framework is the final demand. The identification of the components of the final demand, affecting significantly the gross output of each sector is important from the point of view of policy-making. As the key sectors are supposed to drive the economy towards increasing Sectoral interdependence and generate greater growth and development, the components of final demand with greater stimulating effects for these sectors are required to be identified as far as policy-making is concerned. The final demand is defined as follows:

Final Demand (f) = Private consumption demand (f_1) + Govt. consumption demand (f_2) + Gross domestic capital formation (f_3) + Change in Stock (f_4) + Export demand (f_5) – Import demand (f_6)

The six components influence the gross output of a sector in varying degrees. The vector that shows the gross output produced by different sectors to meet total final demand is $(I - A^w)^{-1}$ f.

CONCLUSION

The present study of linkages has identified key sectors and their nature. Top six sectors and one sided linkage sectors show that Indian economy is not completely diversified. The service-led sectors have dominated before industrial sectors have developed. In the developed countries the picture is little different. The study has simply touched the final demand area which has to be studied intensively. The study however has helped in identifying the role of intermediate or input sector because this sector has significant share in total production.

REFERENCES

Arrous Gean (2000), *Energy Input Output Economics.*

Bhagabata Partro (2005), "Sectoral Interdependence and Growth of Orissan Economy".

Bart Los (2000), "Endogenous Growth and Structural Change in a Dynamic Input-Output Model".

Chitro Majumdar (2002), "Combinational Optimization, Cumulative Inflation and Dynamic Input-Output Modeling".

CSO, Govt. of India (2004), *Input-Output Transaction Table, 1998-99.*

Irs Jenson (2001), "The Leontief Open Production Model or Input-Output Analysis".

Klien, L.R. (2002), "Leontief and the Future of World Economy".

Prasad, K.N. (2000), "Inter-Sectoral Terms of Trade in Input-Output Framework".

Paramita Dasgupta (2005), "The Structure of Indian Economy".

Pal, D.P. (2003), "Economic Integration. A Systemic Measure in I-O Framework."

Prakash, S. (2003), "Input-Output Modeling of Employment and Productivity as Base of Growth".

Ram Subramaniyam (2005), "Macro-Contribution of a Micro-Level Company".

Sanjay K. Hansda (2003), "Sustainability of Services-led Growth: An Input-Output Analysis of the Indian Economy," RBI Publication.

APPENDIX TABLES

Table 1: Backward, Forward and Total Linkages—Activity-wise Indices

Sec./ Code	*Commodity*	*Backward Index*	*Rank*	*Forward Index*	*Rank*	*Total Index*	*Overall Rank*
1	*2*	*3*	*4*	*5*	*6*	*7*	*8*
1	Paddy	1.83	13	1.84	10	3.67	10
2	Wheat	1.25	25	1.05	19	2.30	21
3	Jowar	0.68	76	0.11	56	0.79	74
4	Bajra	0.63	83	0.06	67	0.69	82
5	Maize	0.64	81	0.10	59	0.74	78
6	Gram	0.40	96	0.12	54	0.52	90
7	Pulses	0.82	63	0.25	36	1.07	51
8	Sugarcane	0.51	91	0.63	24	1.14	47
9	Groundnut	0.50	92	0.09	63	0.59	87
10	Jute	0.38	98	0.00	98	0.38	99
11	Cotton	0.37	99	0.02	84	0.39	98
12	Tea	0.17	111	-0.01	102	0.15	111
13	Coffee	0.39	97	0.03	79	0.42	95
14	Rubber	0.12	113	0.00	100	0.11	112
15	Coconut	0.36	101	0.10	58	0.46	92
16	Tobacco	0.16	112	0.01	90	0.17	110
17	Other crops	2.28	7	10.85	3	13.12	4
18	Milk and milk products	1.87	11	1.78	11	3.64	11
19	Animal Serv.)	2.39	6	0.00	96	2.39	20
20	Other livestock products	1.34	21	1.36	17	2.71	18

21	Forestry and logging	0.50	93	0.47	28	0.97	60
22	Fishing	0.58	88	0.42	29	1.00	56
23	Coal and lignite	0.34	102	-0.03	105	0.32	107
24	Crude petroleum	-0.21	115	-1.79	114	-2.00	114
25	Iron ore	0.36	100	0.01	86	0.37	100
26	Manganese ore	0.21	108	0.00	93	0.21	109
27	Bauxite	0.33	105	0.00	97	0.33	105
28	Copper ore	0.42	95	-0.01	103	0.40	96
29	Other metallic minerals	0.34	103	-0.01	101	0.33	106
30	Lime stone	0.33	104	0.00	94	0.33	104
31	Mica	0.29	107	0.00	95	0.29	108
32	Other non-metallic min.	-0.18	114	-0.81	113	-0.99	113
33	Sugar	1.04	42	0.24	38	1.27	40
34	Khandsari, boora	1.15	31	0.03	80	1.17	45
35	Hydrogenated oil	1.73	16	0.09	62	1.82	24
36	Edible oils	1.79	15	0.73	20	2.52	19
37	Tea and coffee	1.09	36	0.18	46	1.27	39
38	Miscellaneous food products	3.34	3	2.20	8	5.54	7
39	Beverages	1.23	27	0.24	39	1.47	31
40	Tobacco products	1.13	32	0.37	31	1.50	30
41	Khadi, cotton textiles	1.05	39	0.08	65	1.13	48
42	Cotton textiles	1.63	17	1.41	15	3.04	16
43	Woolen textiles	1.20	28	0.04	72	1.24	42
44	Silk textiles	0.96	46	0.02	81	0.99	57
45	Art silk, synthetic fiber textiles	1.38	20	0.49	27	1.87	23
46	Jute, hemp, mesta textiles	0.91	52	0.01	89	0.92	64
47	Carpet weaving	0.94	50	0.03	75	0.98	59

(Contd.)

TABLE 1 (*Contd.*)

1	2	3	4	5	6	7	8
48	Readymade garments	1.57	18	0.42	30	1.98	22
49	Miscellaneous text. products	1.20	29	0.23	40	1.43	33
50	Furniture and fixtures—wooden	0.71	74	0.15	49	0.85	70
51	Wood and wood products	0.58	86	0.05	70	0.63	86
52	Paper, paper prods	0.90	53	-0.03	104	0.87	67
53	Printing and publishing	0.85	60	0.18	47	1.03	54
54	Leather footwear	1.18	30	0.09	61	1.28	38
55	Leather and leather products	1.40	19	0.13	51	1.52	29
56	Rubber products	1.13	33	0.22	41	1.35	36
57	Plastic products	0.86	57	0.25	35	1.11	49
58	Petroleum products	0.20	110	0.15	48	0.35	103
59	Coal tar products	0.88	54	-0.14	107	0.74	77
60	Inorganic heavy chemicals	0.66	78	-0.23	109	0.43	94
61	Organic heavy chemicals	0.63	82	-0.23	110	0.40	97
62	Fertilizers	0.60	84	-0.25	111	0.35	102
63	Pesticides	0.77	69	0.04	74	0.80	72
64	Paints, varnishes etc.	0.77	68	0.04	73	0.81	71
65	Drugs and medicines	1.06	38	0.25	37	1.31	37
66	Soaps, cosmetics & glycerin	1.06	37	0.29	32	1.35	35
67	Synthetic fibers, resin	0.65	79	-0.21	108	0.44	93
68	Other chemicals	1.24	26	0.22	43	1.46	32
69	Structural clay products	0.58	87	0.00	91	0.58	88
70	Cement	0.74	71	0.00	99	0.74	76
71	Other non-metallic min. prod.	0.76	70	0.26	34	1.02	55

72	Iron, steel and ferro alloys	0.80	66	-0.29	112	0.51	91
73	Iron and steel casting, forg.	0.85	61	0.02	82	0.87	69
74	Iron and steel foundries	0.85	59	-0.06	106	0.79	73
75	Non-ferrous basic metals	0.20	109	-2.35	115	-2.15	115
76	Hand tools, hardware	0.78	67	0.10	57	0.88	66
77	Miscellaneous metal products	1.04	40	0.73	21	1.77	27
78	Tractors and agri. implements	0.96	47	0.14	50	1.10	50
79	Industrial machinery (F&T)	0.88	55	0.08	66	0.95	62
80	Industrial machinery (others)	0.94	49	0.04	71	0.98	58
81	Machine tools	0.81	65	0.06	68	0.87	68
82	Office computing machines	0.68	75	0.01	87	0.70	81
83	Other non-electrical mach.	1.11	34	0.70	22	1.81	25
84	Electrical industrial machinery	0.97	45	0.28	33	1.25	41
85	Electrical wires & cables	0.59	85	0.08	64	0.67	85
86	Batteries	0.64	80	0.03	78	0.68	84
87	Electrical appliances	0.82	64	0.11	55	0.93	63
88	Communication equipments	0.87	56	0.19	45	1.06	52
89	Other electrical machinery	0.72	73	0.02	85	0.73	79
90	Electronic equip. (incl. TV)	1.00	43	0.22	42	1.22	43
91	Ships and boats	1.11	35	0.03	76	1.14	46
92	Rail equipments	0.83	62	0.13	52	0.96	61
93	Motor vehicles	1.27	24	0.52	26	1.79	26
94	Motor cycles and scooters	0.94	51	0.10	60	1.04	53
95	Bicycles, cycle-rickshaw	0.85	58	0.06	69	0.91	65
96	Other transport equipments	0.67	77	0.01	88	0.68	83
97	Watches and clocks	0.73	72	0.02	83	0.75	75
98	Miscellaneous manufacturing	1.27	23	1.67	12	2.94	17

(Contd.)

TABLE 1 (*Contd.*)

1	2	3	4	5	6	7	8
99	Construction	4.89	1	10.65	4	15.54	3
100	Electricity	0.99	44	2.61	7	3.61	12
101	Gas	0.32	106	0.03	77	0.36	101
102	Water supply	1.28	22	0.13	53	1.40	34
103	Railway transport services	0.95	48	0.62	25	1.57	28
104	Other transport services	2.98	4	16.04	2	19.02	2
105	Storage and warehousing	0.55	90	0.00	92	0.55	89
106	Communication	0.56	89	0.64	23	1.20	44
107	Trade	3.44	2	35.81	1	39.25	1
108	Hotels and restaurants	2.21	8	1.07	18	3.28	15
109	Banking	1.04	41	5.34	6	6.38	6
110	Insurance	0.50	94	0.22	44	0.71	80
111	Ownership of dwellings	1.88	10	1.55	14	3.43	14
112	Education and research	1.87	12	1.64	13	3.50	13
113	Medical and health	2.49	5	1.40	16	3.90	9
114	Other services	1.83	14	7.79	5	9.62	5
115	Public administration	2.13	9	2.13	9	4.25	8

Table 2: Indices of Backward and Forward Coefficient of Variation

Sec. Code	*Commodity*	*IBCV*	*Rank*	*IFCV*	*Rank*
1	*2*	*3*	*4*	*5*	*6*
1	Paddy	8.74	9	8.67	56
2	Wheat	7.51	17	8.67	57
3	Jowar	4.64	105	10.59	12
4	Bajra	4.76	96	10.60	11
5	Maize	4.68	103	10.45	20
6	Gram	4.62	106	9.64	42
7	Pulses	4.71	99	9.86	35
8	Sugarcane	6.57	26	6.14	76
9	Groundnut	4.85	91	7.70	68
10	Jute	5.11	77	-8.20	110
11	Cotton	5.17	75	6.37	75
12	Tea	5.61	52	-8.38	111
13	Coffee	4.18	112	9.97	33
14	Rubber	6.76	24	-9.19	114
15	Coconut	5.41	64	10.13	29
16	Tobacco	5.03	82	9.73	39
17	Other crops	9.76	5	2.79	91
18	Milk and milk products	8.54	11	8.90	52
19	Animal services (agricultural)	7.52	16	—	#N/A
20	Other livestock products	6.13	35	5.22	82
21	Forestry and logging	6.15	34	6.03	78
22	Fishing	7.62	14	10.27	26
23	Coal and lignite	4.89	88	-2.64	98
24	Crude petroleum, natural gas	-22.35	115	-2.99	100
25	Iron ore	4.69	101	8.93	51
26	Manganese ore	4.68	102	10.41	23
27	Bauxite	4.70	100	-10.41	115
28	Copper ore	4.76	95	-8.69	112
29	Other metallic minerals	4.62	107	-8.16	109
30	Lime stone	4.91	87	9.56	43
31	Mica	5.97	42	10.72	4
32	Other non-metallic minerals	-22.19	114	-4.87	106
33	Sugar	5.50	59	9.99	32
34	Khandsari, boora	5.41	66	10.34	24
35	Hydrogenated oil (vanaspati)	5.77	49	10.64	10
36	Edible oils other than vanaspati	5.41	65	8.07	60
37	Tea and coffee processing	5.34	68	10.41	22
38	Miscellaneous food products	6.06	38	8.72	55

(Contd.)

TABLE 2 (*Contd.*)

1	*2*	*3*	*4*	*5*	*6*
39	Beverages	4.39	109	10.31	25
40	Tobacco products	4.85	92	10.66	8
41	Khadi, cotton textiles (handlooms)	5.12	76	9.72	40
42	Cotton textiles	5.42	63	5.17	83
43	Woolen textiles	5.06	79	9.39	46
44	Silk textiles	4.67	104	10.48	19
45	Art silk, synthetic fiber textiles	4.92	86	7.90	65
46	Jute, hemp, mesta textiles	5.57	55	7.77	66
47	Carpet weaving	5.01	83	10.71	5
48	Readymade garments	4.88	90	10.50	16
49	Miscellaneous textile products	4.94	85	7.22	70
50	Furniture and fixtures—wooden	4.79	94	9.79	38
51	Wood and wood products	4.73	98	5.35	81
52	Paper, paper prods. & newsprint	5.54	57	-4.73	104
53	Printing and publishing	4.88	89	8.95	50
54	Leather footwear	5.65	51	10.68	7
55	Leather and leather products	6.06	39	8.86	53
56	Rubber products	5.31	69	6.83	71
57	Plastic products	5.04	80	6.10	77
58	Petroleum products	19.02	2	3.04	90
59	Coal tar products	6.61	25	-6.56	107
60	Inorganic heavy chemicals	6.31	31	-3.34	101
61	Organic heavy chemicals	6.51	27	-3.87	102
62	Fertilizers	7.61	15	-4.07	103
63	Pesticides	5.79	47	7.75	67
64	Paints, varnishes and lacquers	5.79	48	6.47	74
65	Drugs and medicines	5.28	72	8.10	59
66	Soaps, cosmetics & glycerin	4.84	93	9.86	36
67	Synthetic fibers, resin	6.48	28	-4.79	105
68	Other chemicals	5.28	71	3.45	88
69	Structural clay products	6.43	29	10.08	31
70	Cement	6.05	40	-9.01	113
71	Other non-metallic mineral prods.	5.26	74	7.95	63
72	Iron, steel and ferro alloys	6.85	22	-2.19	97
73	Iron and steel casting & forging	6.40	30	6.70	72
74	Iron and steel foundries	6.77	23	-6.89	108
75	Non-ferrous basic metals	34.61	1	-2.73	99
76	Hand tools, hardware	5.79	46	6.48	73
77	Miscellaneous metal products	5.67	50	4.77	85
78	Tractors and agri. implements	5.00	84	10.26	27
79	Industrial machinery (F&T)	5.56	56	9.40	45
80	Industrial machinery (others)	5.27	73	9.01	48

TABLE 2 (*Contd.*)

1	*2*	*3*	*4*	*5*	*6*
81	Machine tools	5.61	53	9.65	41
82	Office computing machines	6.08	36	10.53	14
83	Other non-electrical machinery	5.44	62	5.73	80
84	Electrical industrial machinery	5.51	58	8.23	58
85	Electrical wires & cables	8.02	12	7.62	69
86	Batteries	6.91	21	10.50	15
87	Electrical appliances	5.57	54	8.78	54
88	Communication equipments	5.49	60	9.20	47
89	Other electrical machinery	5.99	41	7.96	61
90	Electronic equipments (incl. TV)	5.35	67	10.10	30
91	Ships and boats	5.47	61	10.43	21
92	Rail equipments	5.87	45	7.95	62
93	Motor vehicles	5.09	78	9.00	49
94	Motor cycles and scooters	5.29	70	10.49	17
95	Bicycles, cycle-rickshaw	6.07	37	10.54	13
96	Other transport equipments	5.91	43	10.48	18
97	Watches and clocks	5.90	44	10.70	6
98	Miscellaneous manufacturing	7.07	20	4.58	86
99	Construction	9.37	6	4.33	87
100	Electricity	5.03	81	1.38	95
101	Gas	4.50	108	9.80	37
102	Water supply	7.30	19	9.51	44
103	Railway transport services	4.34	110	3.34	89
104	Other transport services	8.66	10	1.59	93
105	Storage and warehousing	4.26	111	9.90	34
106	Communication	6.21	33	5.02	84
107	Trade	9.99	4	1.01	96
108	Hotels and restaurants	4.75	97	7.91	64
109	Banking	7.86	13	1.50	94
110	Insurance	3.88	113	5.75	79
111	Ownership of dwellings	8.95	8	10.72	2
112	Education and research	9.34	7	10.65	9
113	Medical and health	6.23	32	10.24	28
114	Other services	7.32	18	1.82	92
115	Public administration	10.72	3	10.72	3

Table 3: Rank-wise Table of Backward, Forward and their Coefficient of Variations

Sec. Code	*Commodity*	*Backward Rank*	*IBCV Rank*	*Forward Rank*	*IFCV Rank*	*Total Rank*
1	*2*	*3*	*4*	*5*	*6*	*7*
107	Trade	2	4	1	96	1
104	Other transport services	4	10	2	93	2
99	Construction	1	6	4	87	3
17	Other crops	7	5	3	91	4
114	Other services	14	18	5	92	5
109	Banking	41	13	6	94	6
38	Miscellaneous food products	3	38	8	55	7
115	Public administration	9	3	9	3	8
113	Medical and health	5	32	16	28	9
1	Paddy	13	9	10	56	10
18	Milk and milk products	11	11	11	52	11
100	Electricity	44	81	7	95	12
112	Education and research	12	7	13	9	13
111	Ownership of dwellings	10	8	14	2	14
108	Hotels and restaurants	8	97	18	64	15
42	Cotton textiles	17	63	15	83	16
98	Miscellaneous manufacturing	23	20	12	86	17
20	Other livestock products	21	35	17	82	18
36	Edible oils other than vanaspati	15	65	20	60	19
19	Animal services (agricultural)	6	16	96	#N/A	20
2	Wheat	25	17	19	57	21
48	Readymade garments	18	90	30	16	22
45	Art silk, synthetic fiber textiles	20	86	27	65	23
35	Hydrogenated oil (vanaspati)	16	49	62	10	24
83	Other non-electrical machinery	34	62	22	80	25
93	Motor vehicles	24	78	26	49	26
77	Miscellaneous metal products	40	50	21	85	27
103	Railway transport services	48	110	25	89	28
55	Leather and leather products	19	39	51	53	29
40	Tobacco products	32	92	31	8	30
39	Beverages	27	109	39	25	31
68	Other chemicals	26	71	43	88	32
49	Miscellaneous textile products	29	85	40	70	33
102	Water supply	22	19	53	44	34
66	Soaps, cosmetics & glycerin	37	93	32	36	35

56	Rubber products	33	69	41	71	36
65	Drugs and medicines	38	72	37	59	37
54	Leather footwear	30	51	61	7	38
37	Tea and coffee processing	36	68	46	22	39
33	Sugar	42	59	38	32	40
84	Electrical industrial machinery	45	58	33	58	41
43	Woolen textiles	28	79	72	46	42
90	Electronic equipments (incl. TV)	43	67	42	30	43
106	Communication	89	33	23	84	44
34	Khandsari, boora	31	66	80	24	45
91	Ships and boats	35	61	76	21	46
8	Sugarcane	91	26	24	76	47
41	Khadi, cotton textiles (handlooms)	39	76	65	40	48
57	Plastic products	57	80	35	77	49
78	Tractors and agri. implements	47	84	50	27	50
7	Pulses	63	99	36	35	51
88	Communication equipments	56	60	45	47	52
94	Motor cycles and scooters	51	70	60	17	53
53	Printing and publishing	60	89	47	50	54
71	Other non-metallic mineral prods.	70	74	34	63	55
22	Fishing	88	14	29	26	56
44	Silk textiles	46	104	81	19	57
80	Industrial machinery (others)	49	73	71	48	58
47	Carpet weaving	50	83	75	5	59
21	Forestry and logging	93	34	28	78	60
92	Rail equipments	62	45	52	62	61
79	Industrial machinery (F&T)	55	56	66	45	62
87	Electrical appliances	64	54	55	54	63
46	Jute, hemp, mesta textiles	52	55	89	66	64
95	Bicycles, cycle-rickshaw	58	37	69	13	65
76	Hand tools, hardware	67	46	57	73	66
52	Paper, paper prods. & newsprint	53	57	104	104	67
81	Machine tools	65	53	68	41	68
73	Iron and steel casting & forging	61	30	82	72	69
50	Furniture and fixtures-wooden	74	94	49	38	70
64	Paints, varnishes and lacquers	68	48	73	74	71
63	Pesticides	69	47	74	67	72

(Contd.)

1	*2*	*3*	*4*	*5*	*6*	*7*
74	Iron and steel foundries	59	23	106	108	73
3	Jowar	76	105	56	12	74
97	Watches and clocks	72	44	83	6	75
70	Cement	71	40	99	113	76
59	Coal tar products	54	25	107	107	77
5	Maize	81	103	59	20	78
89	Other electrical Machinery	73	41	85	61	79
110	Insurance	94	113	44	79	80
82	Office computing machines	75	36	87	14	81
4	Bajra	83	96	67	11	82
96	Other transport equipments	77	43	88	18	83
86	Batteries	80	21	78	15	84
85	Electrical wires & cables	85	12	64	69	85
51	Wood and wood products	86	98	70	81	86
9	Groundnut	92	91	63	68	87
69	Structural clay products	87	29	91	31	88
105	Storage and warehousing	90	111	92	34	89
6	Gram	96	106	54	42	90
72	Iron, steel and ferro alloys	66	22	112	97	91
15	Coconut	101	64	58	29	92
67	Synthetic fibers, resin	79	28	108	105	93
60	Inorganic heavy chemicals	78	31	109	101	94
13	Coffee	97	112	79	33	95
28	Copper ore	95	95	103	112	96
61	Organic heavy chemicals	82	27	110	102	97
11	Cotton	99	75	84	75	98
10	Jute	98	77	98	110	99
25	Iron ore	100	101	86	51	100
101	Gas	106	108	77	37	101
62	Fertilizers	84	15	111	103	102
58	Petroleum products	110	2	48	90	103
30	Lime stone	104	87	94	43	104
27	Bauxite	105	100	97	115	105
29	Other metallic minerals	103	107	101	109	106
23	Coal and lignite	102	88	105	98	107
31	Mica	107	42	95	4	108
26	Manganese ore	108	102	93	23	109
16	Tobacco	112	82	90	39	110
12	Tea	111	52	102	111	111
14	Rubber	113	24	100	114	112
32	Other non-metallic minerals	114	114	113	106	113
24	Crude petroleum, natural gas	115	115	114	100	114
75	Non-ferrous basic metals	109	1	115	99	115

The Structure of the Orissan Economy: An Input-Output Analysis

ADITYA KUMAR PATRA

INTRODUCTION

Input-Output analysis is the brainchild of the Nobel Laureate Professor Wassily Leontief.[1] This is also known as inter-sectoral analysis or inter-industry analysis. The emphasis on inter-industry relations may be traced back to 1758, the year in which Francois Quesney published his *'Tableau Economique'*, a device, which is stressed the interdependence of economic activities. For more than a century nothing more is added to this literature. In 1874, Leon Walras published his *"Elements de'conomie Politique Pure"*. The model developed by Walras depicts a general equilibrium system. This attempts to demonstrate the mathematical nature of dependence between producing and consuming sectors of the economy with the help of a set of simultaneous linear equations. The works carried out in this area culminated finally in 1936, when Leontief published the first input-output table of the world for the American economy. Input-output analysis is the name given to the technique that attempts to take account of general equilibrium phenomena in the empirical analysis of production (Baumol, 1977). With the passage of time the input-output framework has been extended to deal with various fields of economic analysis such as energy consumption, environmental pollution, regional analysis, impact study etc.[2]

Thanks to the modern digital computer to make the input-output technique a handy device for use. Today the input-output model is widely applied throughout the world. The United Nations has promoted input-output as a practical planning tool for less developed countries. In India this technique is routinely applied in planning process ever since Fifth Five Year Plan. Input-output tables partial as well as complete were prepared for many states/regional economies in India to study the structure of the region and to use in planning exercise.[3]

An attempt has been made in this article to analyze the structure of Orissan economy with the help of inter-industry analysis and suggest a few steps to strengthen the poverty stricken underdeveloped economy of Orissa. The scheme of the paper is as follows: Section I briefly outlines the important features of the Orissan economy. Section II presents the analytical framework under which the study is undertaken. Section III highlights the empirical findings and Section IV concludes the paper.

SECTION I
MAIN FEATURES OF THE ECONOMY OF ORISSA

Orissa continues to be one of the most backward states in the country. The state appears to be suffering from the vicious circle of poverty. The lop-sided development in orissa and insurmountable misery of the people in the interior region has caused widespread condemnation. In spite of liberal financial assistance from the central government, the socio-economic variables in the state have not undergone any significant change. The tempo of industrialization has not set in and the employment prospect in the non-government sector has not increased much. All these means, the planning process in the state requires serious restructuring on the basis of interdependence of various sectors of the state economy. Till now, the preparation of state plans based on qualitative judgments of the planners. The quantitative analysis is very often relegated to background and not taken seriously. To achieve better result, the techno-economic analysis of the economy based on quantitative techniques is essential. Here we prefer input-output technique to identify the key sectors of Orissan economy. Planned investments based on the key sectors will solve the problem of designing a suitable investment policy for the state economy.

SECTION II
ANALYTICAL FRAMEWORK

The Leontief's analytical system stems from input-output table. The input-output table or the inter-industry transactions shows the flow of goods and services from a sector of the economy to all the other sectors over a specified period of time (say a year). It gives the systematic description of interdependence of different sectors of the economy by way of a two-way table.

The economy is segregated into a number of homogeneous sectors each of which is represented in the table by a row and a column. The rows of the table give the distribution of the output of the sector while the columns give the inputs consumed by the sector. Since each figure in any horizontal row is also a figure in vertical column, the output of each sector is shown to be an input in some other. The additional columns, known as final demand, record the sales by each sector to consumers. The additional rows, labeled Value Added, represents the other non-industrial inputs to production (for example labour).

The Leontief model is represented through the equation: $X = (I-A)^{-1}Y$ (Leontief, 1960), where, X and Y are column vector of outputs and final demand respectively. A is the square matrix of technical coefficient ($a_{ij} = X_{ij}/X_j$; X_{ij} is the output of sector i used in sector j as input and X_j is the total output of sector j).

The input-output table has been used for establishing the linkages between sectors of the economy. Linkage means the interconnection between a sector and other sectors. This linkage can be of two types: Backward & Forward. A sector is linked with the other sectors, which supply inputs to it, and also with those, which use its output as their own inputs. Thus the expansion of a sector induces a large demand for inputs for its input-supplying sectors and also provides large input supply to other sectors using its output. The former type of inducement is called backward linkage and the latter forward linkage. The potentiality of a sector in generating growth depends upon the strength of these stimuli (Harishman, 1958).

The aspect of interdependence between various sectors of the economy has led to explore the notion of key sector. The key sectors are those, which by their powerful linkages with other sectors are in a favourable position to induce the expansion of other sectors and sometimes even help the initiation of new industries. Once the key sectors are identified, it is suggested that these sectors be given priority in investment allocation and industrial promotion strategy. It is argued that if resources can be concentrated on these key sectors, output, income and employment in the economy will grow rapidly than if these resources were put elsewhere.

In this article following three methods have been employed to investigate the sectoral interdependence of the economy of Orissa:

(1) 'Chenery & Watanabe' method to study the structure of the economy (Chenery & Watanabe, 1958).

(2) 'Yan & Ames' technique to examine the economic interrelatedness among various sectors (Yan and Ames, 1965).

(3) 'Rasmussen Backward and Bulmer-Thomas Forward' linkages for specification of key sector (Rasmussen, 1957; Bulmer-Thomas, 1982).

Chenery and Watanabe Method

Under this method the sectors of the economy are classified into four categories on the basis of U-W statistics. U_j is defined as the ratio of intermediate input of sector j to the total output of sector j ($U_j = \Sigma X_{ij}/X_j$), whereas, W_i is defined as the total intermediate demand for output of sector i to the total demand for sector i ($W_i = \Sigma X_{ij}/X_i$). U_j represents backward linkage and W_i forward linkage. The tetra partite classification of sectors on the basis of U-W statistics is given below.

Chenery-Watanabe Two-way Classification of Productive Sectors

By output use → *By input type↓*	*Final* *Low W_i*	*Intermediate* *High W_i*
Manufacturing High U_j	III Final manufacturing (High backward & Low forward linkage)	II Intermediate manufacture (High backward & high forward linkage)
Primary production Low U_j	IV Final primary (Low backward & low forward linkage)	I intermediate primary (Low backward & high forward linkage)

Index of Interrelatedness

The Chenery and Watanabe indicators measure direct linkage only. A sector may sell to or buy directly from a few others, yet its customers and suppliers may be connected with many other sectors of the economy. Hence a particular sector may have a great influence over the economy through its indirect relations with other sectors. It is therefore highly essential to examine all direct and indirect relations of a sector *vis-a-vis* others to decide upon the importance of each sector. This is here termed as the 'interrelatedness' of a sector. The technique suggested by Yan & Ames to measure interrelatedness is used here.

Yan and Ames defined an order matrix M for any matrix A having non-negative elements. M has the same order as A. Yan and Ames have examined the sequence a_{ij}, a_{ij}^2, a_{ij}^3, . . . and finds the first non-zero term in the sequence. If this term is the kth ($k = 1, 2, 3, \ldots$) then set $m_{ij} = k$. If $a_{ij}^k = 0$, then set $m_{ij} \neq \infty$.

$$\text{Let } M \begin{pmatrix} i_1 & \cdots & i_r \\ j_1 & \cdots & j_r \end{pmatrix}$$

be an arbitrary sub-matrix of an order matrix M, then the interrelatedness function R corresponding to this sub-matrix is defined by

$$R \begin{pmatrix} i_1 & \cdots & i_r \\ j_1 & \cdots & j_r \end{pmatrix}$$

$$= \frac{1}{rs} \Sigma_{v=1 \text{ to } r} \Sigma_{w=1 \text{ to } s} \frac{1}{m_{ivjw}} = \frac{1}{rs} \Sigma_{k=1 \text{ to }} \phi \frac{n_k}{k} = \frac{n_1}{rs} + \Sigma_{k_\varsigma 1} \frac{n_k}{k_{rs}}$$

The first term in the right hand side referred as the index of diversification (direct relations) and the second term is referred as the index of indirect relatedness (indirect relations).

Specification of Key Sector

For specification of key sector Rasmussen method is used. This method captures both direct and indirect effect by using Leontief inverse matrix. This technique is based on the use of matrix multipliers instead of technical coefficients. The sum of the column of the matrix of multipliers should represent the power of the sectoral backward linkage. That is why he called this sum the index of the power of dispersion (P). The total of the row of the matrix of multipliers represents sectoral forward linkages and he named this sum the index of the sensitivity of dispersion (S). However, as revised by Bulmer-Thomas I have used the output matrix to determine the forward linkages. That is why the index of sensitivity of dispersion of the sector will be determined as the sum of the row of the output inverse matrix. After normalization both the indices are: $P_n = ne'Z/e'Ze$ and $S_n = nOe/e'Oe$, where, e is the column summation vector, denotes transposition, $Z = (I-A)^{-1}$, $O = (I-B)^{-1}$, A is input coefficient matrix and B is the output coefficient matrix.

SECTION III
RESULTS

The Government of Orissa has not attempted on preparation of an input-output table for the state economy. However, a small attempt is made at the academic level to bring out the technology matrix for the state with the help of secondary data. The study divides the Orissan economy into 23 sectors. The input-output coefficient matrix estimated from available data is computed at producers' prices for the year 1994-95 for the state of Orissa (Patra, 2002).

Table 1 depicts the classification of sectors of Orissan economy as per Chenery-Watanabe statistics. The C-W analysis concludes that all the major producing sectors of the Orissan economy like cereals, pulses, other agriculture, forestry and logging, fishing, construction, manufacture of beverage and other manufacture and repair services resulting in 49.27 percent of gross output are in the low backward and low forward linkage category. Similarly, the final manufacturing sector comprising of food processing industries, manufacture of textiles, wood and wood products, etc. responsible for 24.34 percent of gross output are in the high backward linkage and low forward linkage category. The intermediate manufacture sector, which has high backward and high forward linkage, comprises of animal husbandry, basic chemical and chemical products, plastic and related products is generating for a very small fraction, i.e., 12.28 percent of the gross output of the state economy. The rest 14.11 per cent of gross output are produced by four sectors having low backward and high forward linkages.

Table 2 represents the index of interrelatedness of various sectors in Orissa. The value of row index of the sector 15 and 23 is nearer to 1. it means Basic Chemical & Chemical Product (15) and Electricity (23) are almost used by all the sectors. Therefore, these two sectors are most important to other sectors as the supplier of intermediate inputs to them. Other important output supplying sectors are: Mining (7), Manufacture of Textiles (11), Paper and Paper Products (13), Plastic and related Products (16) and Manufacture of Metal Products (19).

The value of column indices reveals that all the sectors are important as users of intermediate products. This is because of the low variation, (0.355) between the highest and lowest indices. Some important users of the intermediate outputs are Construction (8), Food Processing Industries (9), Paper and Paper Products (13) and Non-Metallic Mineral Products (17).

Table 3 represents the linkage indices derived under Rasmussen and Bulmer-Thomas approaches. Column P_n gives the backward linkage and S_n gives forward linkage. It is clear from Table 4 that four sectors show high forward and high backward linkage. These are Basic Chemical and Chemical Products (15), Plastic and Related Products (16), Manufacture of Metal Products (19) and Electrical M-E Industry (21). These sectors are identified as key sectors by both Bulmer-Thomas and Rasmussen linkage indices.

SECTION IV
CONCLUSIONS

All the major producing sectors in Orissa are either in category III or IV accounting for 24.34, 49.27 per cent of gross output respectively signifying the fact that production in Orissa is not much round-about the relatively lower importance of category II (12.28 per cent of gross output) points towards the low level of development of the economy. This is also confirmed by the fact that primary final goods (category IV) account for almost half of the gross output (49.27 per cent). In all, primary products contribute 63.38 per cent of total output and 73.61 per cent of total output is for final uses. Hence Orissa is a primary producing economy with low capital formation.

However, various sectors are intensively interrelated. This can be verified from the index of interrelatedness. As the average value of column indices is equal to 0.664 and of row indices is equal to 0.687.

The conclusion emerging from linkage analysis states importance of the manufacturing sector in the state economy. The primary sector, particularly the agriculture sector reveals low output linkage, which may be due to continuation of traditional technique of production and less use of modern inputs in this sector. The agriculture sector also could not generate adequate forward linkage due to absence of processing the agricultural products produced in the state. The study indicates existence of potentiality in Animal Husbandry and Mining in the primary sector and Chemical, Electrical and Food Processing in the secondary sector.

The foregoing discussion clearly points out that while formulating policies in Orissa the objective should be to promote sectors belonging to high forward and high backward linkage category. More specifically, the sectors like Basic Chemical and Chemical Product, Electrical M-E Industry, Plastic and Related Products and Manufacture of Metal Products among manufacturing sector, Animal Husbandry among primary sector should be targeted for intensive development.

NOTES

1. Wassily Leontief was born into an academic family on August 5, 1905 in St. Petersburg. Leontief started his professional life at the Institute of World Economics, University of Kiel, engaged in research on the derivation of statistical demand and supply curves. The Nobel Prize in Economic Science was awarded to him in 1973
2. For an exhaustive discussion one may go through: (1) Richardson, H.W. (1985), Input-Output and Economic Base Multipliers: Looking Backward and Forward, *Journal of Regional Science*, Volume 25, No. 4, pp. 607-61.
3. The complete models have been constructed for Gujarat (Alagh & Kashyap, 1971), Haryana (Bhalla, 1974), Punjab (Bhalla, 1975), Maharashtra (Koti and Santanam, 1970), Rajasthan (Mehta, 1977), Bihar (Ghosh, 1974), Uttar Pradesh (State Planning Board, 1975), Assam (Barua, 1977), Karnataka (Panchamukhi, 1980), Madhya Pradesh (Shri Prakash & Patankar, 1978), West Bengal (Dhar, 1965 & State Planning Board, 1985).

   Partial Tables (Only industrial sectors) exist for Karnataka (Panchamukhi, 1975), Maharashtra (Venkatramaiah and Baldota, 1965), Rajasthan (Meheta and Bohara, 1971; Saxena, 1986) and West Bengal (Singh, 1972).

   Micro-level studies were undertaken for Ahmedabad city of Gujurat (Kashyap, 1975), East Godavari District of Andhra Pradesh (Subrahmanyan, 1985) and Parambikulam Aliyar Project region in Tamil Nadu (Mohandoss and Subramanian, 1979).

REFERENCES

Baumol, W.J. (1977), *Economic Theory and Operational Analysis*, Englewood Cliffs, NJ: Prentice Hall.

Bulmer-Thomas, V. (1982), *Input-Output Analysis in Developing Countries: Sources, Methods and Applications*, John Wiley & Sons Ltd., New York.

Chenery, H.B., and Watanable, T. (1958), "International Comparison of the Structure of Production", *Econometrica*, Vol. 26, No. 4, October, pp. 487-521.

Hirschman, A.O. (1958), *The Strategy of Economic Development*, New Haven, Yale University Press.

Leontief, W. (1966), *Input-Output Economics*, Oxford University Press, New York.

Miller, R.E. and Blair, P. (1985), *Input-Output Analysis: Foundations and Extensions*, Englewood Cliffs, NJ: Prentice Hall.

Patra, Aditya Kumar (2002), "*Regional Dimension of Input-Output Analysis in India: A Model for Orissa*", Unpublished Ph.D. Dissertation submitted to Berhampur Univrersity.

Rasmussen, P.N. (1957), *Studies in Intersectoral Relations*, North-Holland Publishing Company, Amsterdam

Yan, C. and Ames, E. (1965), "Economic Interrelatedness", *The Review of Economic Studies*, Vol. 32, No. 4, pp. 290-310.

APPENDIX

TABLE 1

Classification of Sectors of the Orissan Economy According to C-W Statistics

	Sector No.	*Sector Name*	U_j	W_i
1.	**Intermediate Manufacture (II): High backward and High forward (12.28 Percent of gross output)**			
	4	Animal husbandry	.526	.442
	15	Basic chemical and chemical product	.607	.835
	16	Plastic and related products	.435	.589
	19	Manufacture of metal product	.380	.658
	21	Electrical M-E industry	.466	.626
2.	**Final Manufacture (III): High backward and Low forward (24.34 percent gross output)**			
	9	Food processing industries	.702	.201
	11	Manufacture of textiles	.541	.125
	12	Wood and wood product	.354	.262
	13	Paper and paper product	.427	.123
	14	Leather and leather product	.448	.099
	18	Basic metal and alloys industries	.460	.307
3.	**Intermediate primary production (I): Low backward and High forward (14.11 percent of gross output)**			
	7	Mining	.215	.866
	17	Non-metallic mineral product	.313	.444
	20	Non-electrical M-E industries	.291	.711
	23	Electricity	.338	.887
4.	**Final Primary production (IV): Low backward and low forward (49.27 percent of gross output)**			
	1	Cereals	.168	.228
	2	Pulses	.151	.084
	3	Other Agriculture	.183	.327
	5	Forestry & logging	.036	.249
	6	Fishing	.084	.139
	8	Construction	.320	.013
	10	Manufacture of beverage	.328	.122
	22	Other manufacture and repair	.348	.130

TABLE 2

Interrelatedness (R) in the Orissan Economy: 1993-94

Sector No.	*Sector Name*	*Column Index*	*Row Index*
1	Cereals	0.493	0.609
2	Pulses	0.493	0.565
3	Other Agriculture	0.493	0.652
4	Animal Husbandry	0.514	0.630
5	Forestry & Logging	0.739	0.739
6	Fishing	0.710	0.565
7	Mining	0.688	0.826
8	Construction	0.848	0.652
9	Food Processing Industries	0.804	0.630
10	Manufacture of Beverage etc.	0.739	0.565
11	Manufacture of Textile	0.630	0.826
12	Wood & Wood Product Industries	0.630	0.783
13	Paper & Paper Products	0.804	0.826
14	Leather & Leather Products	0.710	0.043
15	Basic Chemical & Chemical Products	0.717	0.978
16	Plastic & Related Products	0.623	0.826
17	Non-Metallic Mineral Products	0.804	0.674
18	Basic Metal & Alloys Industries	0.652	0.739
19	Manufacture of Metal Product	0.717	0.826
20	Non-Electrical M-E Industry	0.659	0.609
21	Electrical M-E Industry	0.703	0.696
22	Other Manufacture & Repair Services	0.609	0.630
23	Electricity	0.493	0.913
	Average	**0.664**	**0.687**

TABLE 3

Rasmussen Backward and Bulmer-Thomas Forward Linkages of Orissan Economy

Sector No.	*Name*	S_n	P_n
1	Cereals	0.835(12)	0.829(19)
2	Pulses	0.687(22)	0.787(21)
3	Other Agriculture	0.882(11)	0.820(20)
4	Animal Husbandry	0.992(8)	1.080(8)
5	Forestry & Logging	0.820(13)	0.679(23)
6	Fishing	0.738(18)	0.728(22)
7	Mining	1.565(3)	0.862(18)
8	Construction	0.637(23)	0.970(13)
9	Food Processing Industries	0.819(14)	1.295(2)
10	Manufacture of Beverage etc.	0.714(20)	0.980(12)
11	Manufacture of Textile	0.727(19)	1.126(6)
12	Wood & Wood Product Industries	0.818(15)	0.945(17)
13	Paper & Paper Products	0.745(17)	1.045(10)
14	Leather & Leather Products	0.695(21)	1.143(5)
15	Basic Chemical & Chemical Products	1.553(4)	1.337(1)
16	Plastic & Related Products	1.306(6)	1.151(4)
17	Non-Metallic Mineral Products	0.953(9)	0.956(16)
18	Basic Metal & Alloys Industries	0.888(10)	1.103(7)
19	Manufacture of Metal Product	1.353(5)	1.062(9)
20	Non-Electrical M-E Industry	1.724(1)	0.961(14)
21	Electrical M-E Industry	1.105(7)	1.159(3)
22	Other Manufacture & Repair Services	0.761(16)	1.024(11)
23	Electricity	1.684(2)	0.957(15)

Note: Numbers in parenthesis indicate rank.

TABLE 4

Linkage Analysis of Orissan Economy, 1994-95

Linkage Effect	*Sector No. & Rank*
High Forward Linkage ($S_n > 1$)	7(3), 15(4), 16(6), 19(5), 20(1), 21(7), 23(2).
High Backward Linkage ($P_n > 1$)	4(8), 9(2), 11(1), 13(10), 14(5), 15(1), 16(4), 18(7), 19(9), 21(3), 22(11).
High Forward & Backward Linkage (S_n & $P_n > 1$)	15, 16, 19, 21.

Note: Numbers in parenthesis indicate rank.

SECTION IV

ENVIRONMENT AND INTERNATIONAL TRADE

Economic Thoughts of W.W. Leontief with Special Reference to Environment

PUSHPA RANADE

INTRODUCTION

In 1973, Wassily Leontief received the Nobel Prize in Economics for his inter-industry analysis usually called input-output system. Conventional input-output system is related to all industrial products and services. It has its own framework of matrix structure. It deals with production and consumption. It describes the flow of goods and services between all individual sectors of the economy over a specific period of time say a year. It is a system that systematically quantifies the mutual interrelationships among the various sectors of the economy. It is applied to systems, which may be as large as a nation or even a world or even a small industry or enterprise.

In all instances the approach is the same. It basically describes the relationship between the input that the system absorbs and the output that the system produces. The sectors in the economy are interdependent and the relationship between these sectors is described by a set of linear equations. These equations express the balances between the total output and the aggregate output of each commodity within a specific period of time.

The technical structure of this system can be represented in matrix form. The matrix of technical input and output coefficients of all the sectors constitutes the input-output table. The inter-sectoral flows as represented in an input output table can be measured in physical terms but in practice they are constructed in value terms. The input-output table expressed in value terms can be interpreted as a system of national accounts. What input-output analysis does is to relate each industry's output and also to relate these outputs to final demands by consumers. With this, the effects of changes in individual industries on each of the other industries can be assessed. Some of the changes in the final demand also can be assessed in each industry. This technique is quite general.

BASIC MODEL

Presently National Input-Output tables are constructed in some 80 countries. The number of sectors has also been increased in recent years. Suppose there are 'n' sectors in the economy, then 'n+1'th sector is a final demand sector. For mathematical manipulation, suppose rows are indicated by 'i' and columns are indicated by 'j' respectively, then the physical output of sector "i" is usually represented by 'x_i' while the symbol 'x_{ij}' stands for the amount of the produce of sector 'i' that is absorbed as its input by sector 'j'. The quantity of the produce of sector 'i' delivered to the final demand sector '$x_{i,\, n+1}$' is identified as 'y_i'.

The Concept of Structural Matrix

A complete set of input coefficients of all sectors arranged in the form of rectangular matrix format is called a structural matrix. Structural matrices are normally described in value terms.

The Concept of Technical Coefficients

Let 'x_{ij}' be the quantity of the output of sector 'i' that is absorbed by sector 'j'. Now to get the amount of inputs to produce one unit of production, we have to divide 'x_{ij}', the quantity of produce by sector 'j' using the quantity of inputs from sector 'i', by the total output 'X_j'. Then we get 'a_{ij}' which is called a technical coefficient as,

$$a_{ij} = x_{ij}/\Sigma X_j$$

The matrix 'A' of technical coefficients a_{ij} is called the technical matrix.

The balance between the total output and the combined inputs of each sector can be described by the set of equations. If there is 'n' number of industries, then there will be 'n' set of equations. For example,

$$x_{11} + x_{12} + x_{13} \ldots + x_{1n} + x_{1,\, n+1} = X_1$$

where, $x_{1,n+1}$ is the quantity demanded by household that is, it is final demand denoted by 'y_1'. To get the quantity demanded by household we have to subtract all combined inputs from total output X_1. Then the equation will be,

$$(X_1 - x_{11}) - x_{12} - x_{13} \ldots x_{1n} = y_1$$

We can get the set of equations with 'n' general equilibriums. The final demand is denoted by the variables; $y_1, y_2, \ldots y_n$, it means, the quantities of all the different kinds of goods absorbed by household and all other sectors, if they are assumed to be given, then the system can be solved for the 'n' total outputs x_1, $x_2, \ldots x_n$. For the unknown 'x's in terms of the given 'y's, the general solution is: $x_i = \Sigma A_{ij}$, where I = 1 to n, j = 1 to n. That is,

$$X_1 = A_{11}y_1 + A_{12}y_2 + \ldots + A_{1n}, y_n \text{ and so on.} \ldots$$

The constant A_{ij} indicates that, how much the output x_i of the 'i'th sector would increase if the final demand for 'j'th sector would increased by one unit. Such an increase would affect the sector 'i' directly. To compute the magnitude of each coefficient 'a_{ij}' in the above solution depends upon all the input coefficients in 'A'. To get the value of $x_1, x_2 \ldots x_n$, we have to take inverse of the matrix of the set of equations:

$$(X_1 - x_{11}) - x_{12} - x_{13} \ldots x_{1n} = y_1$$

This solution is called the inversion of the coefficient matrix of the original equation, which permits us to determine the outputs of all sectors. If these outputs are multiplied by the magnitude of final demand of the respective sectors then we can get the total output with final demand.

The input output approach was being implemented empirically for different quantitative inter industry analysis. Thereafter Leontief had applied it, to quantify environmental problems. Whether input output (I-O) models will be successfully applied to environmental problems depends first on whether the detailed information they require will be available and second on whether the well known defects of input-output analysis are thought to render their results too untrustworthy.

Prof. Wassily Leontief is the pioneer in this field. He built I-O model on the basis of following assumptions:

1. There are constant returns to scale.
2. Production functions are linear and homogenous.
3. Only one process is available to each sector.

Input-Output analysis for an entire economy is based on an accounting of the flow of goods and services in dollar term at a given time. Part of this flow is an inter industry flow, transferred from an industry to be used in the production process. The remainder flows to an exogenously defined as final demand sector. This sector generally includes households, Governments and Foreign trade. The main function of the table is to estimate the levels of output of different sectors on the basis of given vector of final demand.

Let us study how the input-output framework is useful to explain the inter-industry relationship. For an "n" sector economy the inter-industry I-O table is arranged as follows:

TABLE 1

An Input-Output Transaction Matrix

Output → *Input ↓*	*1*	*2*	...	*n*	*F.D.*	*Total*
1	a_{11}	a_{12}	...	a_{1n}	D_1	X_1
2	a_{21}	a_{22}	...	a_{2n}	D_2	X_2
...	...	...	...	...	...	...
N	a_{n1}	a_{n2}	...	a_{nn}	D_n	X_n

The first column of this matrix says that to produce dollar worth of commodity 1, inputs of a_{11} units of commodity 1, a_{21} of commodity 2 etc. are needed. Frequently the matrix is set-up in such away that no industry uses its owned output.[3] In this case, the elements from the upper left hand to the lower right hand corner are zero. If industry 1 is to produce an output of just sufficient to meet the input of the "n" industries as well as final demand (F.D.) of the open sector, it's total output designated X_i must satisfy the following equation.

$$X_i = a_{11}X_1 + a_{12}X_2 + \ldots + a_{1n}X_n + D_1$$

It can be rewritten as,

$$(1 - a_{11})\ X_1 - a_{12}X_2 - \ldots -a_{1n}X_n = D_1$$

If we rewrite the equation for industry 2, 3, . . . n, then we will get the same results, as above, but diagonal components are deducted from one. This matrix is similar to matrix (I – A) because when matrix is deducted from "I" matrix (Identity matrix), then we get results similar to the above one. Thus we can write:

$$(I - A)\ X = D$$

where, I = n is an n identity matrix; A = n × n coefficient matrix; and X, D are both vectors. 'X' is the variable vector and 'D' is final demand vector. If (I – A) has the rank 'n' its inverse can be found and the system of 'n' simultaneous equations represented by the above matrix equations will have the solution.

$$X = (I - A)^{-1} D$$

Providing solutions for "n" simultaneous equations representing commodity and services flows from industries to industries and to final demand, the inverse matrix $(I-A)^{-1}$ has great importance. Once it is available 'D' can be multiplied by this inverse and a new solution vector produced for the industry, output 'X' always on the assumption that the coefficients of 'A' matrix will not change.

EXTENSION OF THE MODEL TO THE PROBLEMS OF ENVIRONMENT

In 1970, Leontief proposed an extension of the basic open input-output model. This would permit forecasting of residual emissions and at least gross effects of certain types of policy measures with respect to them. Pollution produced directly by households and other final users is not considered in it. Pollution and other external effects of production or consumption activities should for all practical purposes be considered as a part of the economic system. He has extended input-output table to include a pollution abatement sector. This is an important departure since pollution abatement is itself an industry, requiring inputs from other industries. He estimated pollution coefficients. He relates tons of pollutants to some unit of value of industrial output.

I-O table with pollution abatement sector:

A_{11}	A_{12}
A_{21}	A_{22}
$V_1, V_2 \ldots V_M$	$V_{M+1}, V_{M+2} \ldots V_N$

where:

A_{11} is a usual matrix of inter-industry coefficient;

A_{21} is the matrix of direct pollution output coefficient;

A_{12} is the input structure coefficient of specific anti-pollution activities;

A_{22} is the pollution output coefficient matrix for the anti-pollution activities;

$V_1, V_2 \ldots V_M$ represents the value-added in each industry per unit of output produced; and

$V_{M+1}, V_{M+2} \ldots V_N$ represents the value-added in each anti-pollution sector per unit of pollution eliminated by it.

Substances described as pollutants can be sometimes utilized as inputs in the production of useful goods. The corresponding input coefficient must be accordingly entered in the matrix A_{21} but with negative sign. In the description of pollution eliminating actually the coefficients entered into corresponding columns of A_{12} and A_{22} describe all inputs and outputs per unit eliminated pollutant. Entries in A_{22} matrix can represent the trade-off between the levels of output of different pollutants, permitting determination.

With the help of the availability of the data of matrices A_{11} and A_{21}, Leontief had presented an empirical example and implemented it to the environmental dimension. He had presented 5 types of air pollutants and made a preliminary report depending upon these five types of pollutants. The basic I-O data for the year 1963 he had referred was published by the US department of Commerce. On the basis of data he has presented 5 tables and had shown the prices are altered. The industrial pollution abatement costs were included in the prices. He had not taken into consideration that the processes used to control one kind of pollutant often generate other kinds of pollutants; but information was not available on the values of coefficients in matrices A_{12} and A_{22}.

To quote Leontief, "Once appropriate sets of pollution output and abatement coefficients have been compiled a more detailed and differentiated study of environmental repercussions can be undertaken; within the framework of multi-regional, regional and metropolitan. From purely formal point of view, the system can be easily extended to cover the relationship between the net output of pollutants on one hand and public health and corresponding demand for health care on the other."

The cost of elimination of pollutants originating in various sectors can be paid for either directly by the final users or by the producing sectors in which they are being generated. In latter case the cost will be included in the price of finished goods and if the prices are expected to be paid by final users they must cover the costs of eliminating all additional pollution generated in the process of their production. Otherwise consumer would get an additional delivery of pollutants. Hence the prices should be computed on the assumption that each industry bears the full cost of eliminating all pollutants generated by it.

Once the prices of all outputs have been determined they can be reflected in value terms. The outputs of all pollutants will be represented by negative figures (in value). The amount of pollutants eliminated will be represented by positive (value) figures. Then the net output of pollutants delivered to final users will add up a negative figure. It can be interpreted as representing the upper limit of the amount that would have to be spent (but in fact not spent) for the purpose if the final users decided to eliminate all pollution actually delivered to them. According to Leontief within the framework of the open I-O model, any reduction or increase in the output level of pollutants can be traced. It can change the technical structure of one more sector of the economy.

Effect of Pollution on Prices

Economists can anticipate the effect of output of pollutants on any given technology. With given value-added coefficients they can estimate the effect such a change on prices of various goods and services. Leontief had given a simple example to show, the effects of pollution elimination on prices. He has considered the simple two-sector economy. Taking numerical values the original state and structure is already explained. He assumed that the process has been introduced, permitting elimination of pollution and that amounts to 2 man-years of labour.

Combined with the previously introduced sets of technical coefficients this additional information yields the complex structure of matrix. Instead of describing complete elimination of all pollution, he introduced Y_3 as an un-eliminated pollutant. It is not demanded but tolerated. With this we can see the effects of reduction in the amount of pollution delivered to the final users would have on the total output levels of all other industries. It is accepted here that economic activities do generate some grams of pollutants.

Further he explained the price cost relationships within

agriculture and manufacturing sectors. He states that the price of eliminating 1 gram of pollution (p_3) should be just high enough to cover the value-added (V_3) that is the payments to labour and other primary factors employed directly by the antipollution industry. After calculations he gets the prices as p_1 = $2.00, p_2 = $ 5.00, p_3 = $ 3.00. Thus the price (cost per unit) of eliminating pollution turns out to be $3.00 per gram. The prices of agricultural and manufactured goods remain the same. That is to tolerate the cost of eliminating some part of the total pollution generated by system; the households have to suffer. These payments could be made directly or they might be collected in the form of taxes imposed on the households and used by the Government to cover the costs of privately or publicly operated anti-pollution industry.

The prices system would be different if voluntarily or by law each industry undertook to eliminate all or at least some fraction of the pollution at its own expense. The added cost would of course be included in price of its marketable products. After making relevant calculations we can see that the prices have changed.[3] P_1 = $ 3.234, P_2 = $ 5.923, P_3 = $ 3.185.

The prices are now higher than they were before. From the point of view of households the trial consumers the relation between real costs and real benefits remains the same, having paid for some anti-pollution activities indirectly, they will have to spend less on them directly.

CRITICAL EXAMINATIONS OF I-O MODELS

I-O models can be used to evaluate policies, if they are extended to contain some valuation procedure. We noted that one attempt in this direction that of Victor (1972), was rather weak, but there is possible scope for extending the basic idea of consensus expert valuation. Whether I-O models will be successfully applied to environmental problems depends,

1. The availability of detailed information.
2. The well-known defects of I-O analysis make their results too untrustworthy.
3. It has not accounted in a logically complete manner for the residual generated in the production and consumption in the initial attempts at application that is some residuals may not be accounted for.

4. It is usually not correct to think of residual control as taking place in a separate residual control activities. The residual output coefficients of I-O approach can change either from new application of existing technology or development of new technology.

The model focuses on residuals generation and discharge. It does not analyze to residuals once they enter into the environment nor does it incorporate any considerable damages. The model focuses on residual control costs but gives no attention to the value of loss in function of common property resources when their quality deteriorates due to the effects of residual discharges.

We have observed here that materials flow through the economy. To treat economic environment interaction in terms of extended I–O models the basic principles of I–O could be extended. It is true that not all extended I–O models, have observed the principles of material balance. Similarly, if we know the relationship between output and wastes the effects of changes in final demand on waste generation can also be estimated and further extensions might allow us to estimate the effects of various changes in resource demand.

Hence to conclude, the input-output model is designed to be implemented empirically and applications have been made to environmental problems. The success of this model depends upon the availability of detailed information.

References

Saluja, M.R. (1980), *Input-Output Tables for India: Concepts, Construction and Applications*, Wiley Eastern Ltd.

Kundu, A., Mathur, P.N., *et al.* (1976): *Input-Output Framework and Economic Analysis*, K.B. Publications, New Delhi.

Leontief W. (1985): Input-Output Economics.

—— (1951), *Input Output Analysis.*

—— (1967), *An Alternative to Aggregation in Input-Output Analysis and National Accounts.*

—— (1970), *Environmental Repercussions and the Economic Structure: An Input Output Approach.*

—— (1972), *Air Pollution and the Economics Structure: Empirical Results of Input-Output Computation.*

Environmental Analysis: An Input-Output Approach

B.P. CHANDRAMOHAN

INTRODUCTION

Every economic activity has pollution as its by-product or undesired output. The quantity of undesirable outcome of an economic activity of production or consumption can be measured in some ways. For example, the quantity of carbon-dioxide, carbon-monoxide released by different types of automobiles, the discharge of polluted water into streams by the paper mills, textile mill, etc. In all these there exist some definite direct technological relationship between the quantity of economic activity and the amount of pollutant. Wassily Leontief's input-output analysis helps to describe the level of output of each sector of an economy in terms of its relationship with the corresponding activities in all other sectors. The most complicated and multi-regional and dynamic versions of input-output analysis explain the spatial distribution of output and consumption of various goods and services. The outstanding benefit of the approach is the possibility of forecasting the growth or decline of the relationship over a period of time.

Often the link between the undesired by-products and the physical relationships that govern the day-to-day economic activities is unnoticed. The technical interdependence between the desirable and undesirable outputs can be described in terms of structural coefficients. The externalities can be incorporated into the conventional input-output analysis which yields results to some questions raised by undesirable environmental effects of the competing economies.

BASIC FRAMEWORK OF INPUT–OUTPUT ANALYSIS

The basic framework of the input-output analysis is explained by a simple economy consisting of two producing sectors (agriculture and manufacture) and households. Each one of the industries absorbs some of its annual output, supplies some portion to the other industry and the rest is given to the ultimate consumers or to the households. The inter-sectoral flows are conveniently entered in an input-output Table (Table 1).

TABLE 1

Input-Output Table

From	*Into*			*Total output*
	Sector I Agriculture	*Sector II Manufacture*	*Final Demand (Households)*	
Sector I Agriculture	25	20	55	100 units of wheat
Sector II Manufacture	14	6	30	50 meters of cloth

Table 1 gives the magnitude of total outputs of agriculture and manufacturing industries and two inputs absorbed into the production of wheat and cloth. The residue is allotted to the households. For instance, agriculture is assumed to require 0.25 (25/100) units of agricultural and 0.14 (14/100) of manufactured inputs to produce 100 units of wheat, while the manufacturing sector requires 0.40 (20/50) units of agricultural and 0.12 (6/50) units of manufactured product to make a meter of cloth. The two producing sectors can be presented in the following form as furnished in Table 2.

TABLE 2

Input Requirement per Unit of Output

From	*Into*	
	Sector I: Agriculture	*Sector II: Manufacture*
Sector I: Agriculture	0.25	0.40
Sector II: Manufacture	0.14	0.12

Table 2 presents the structural matrix of the economy. The numbers entered in the first column and second column show the technical input coefficients of agriculture and manufacturing sector respectively. The technical coefficients determine how large the total annual outputs of agriculture and manufactured goods must be if they are to satisfy the demand of the two sectors of the economy (the final demand of the two sectors of the economy) and the final demand of the households. The circular relationships are described precisely by the two equations.

$$X_1 - 0.25\ X_1 - 0.40\ X_2 = Y_1$$
$$X_2 - 0.25\ X_2 - 0.40\ X_1 = Y_2$$

While rearranging these two equations, we get:

$$0.75\ X_1 - 0.40\ X_2 = Y_1$$
$$-0.12X_2 - 0.40\ X_1 = Y_2$$

where X_1 is unknown total output of agriculture; X_2 is unknown total output of manufacturing sector; Y_1 is amount of agricultural products to be delivered to the final consumers; and Y_2 is the amount of manufactured products to be delivered to the final consumers.

These two linear equations with two unknowns can be solved, for X_1 and X_2 in terms of any given value of Y_1 and Y_2.

The general solutions can be written in the form of two equations.

$$X_1 - 1.457Y_1 + 0.662Y_2$$
$$X_2 - 0.232Y_1 + 1.242Y_2$$

As mentioned in Table 1, $Y_1 = 55$ and $Y_2 = 30$. By performing the necessary multiplications and additions one can find the corresponding magnitudes of X_1 and X_2.

The matrix developed is:

$$\begin{bmatrix} 1.457 & 0.662 \\ 0.232 & 1.242 \end{bmatrix}$$

It is called the inverse matrix of Leontief.

$$\begin{bmatrix} 0.75 & -0.40 \\ -0.14 & 0.88 \end{bmatrix}$$

Any change in the technology of either agriculture or manufacture entails a corresponding change in the structural matrix. Even if the final demand of agricultural (Y_1) and manufactured goods (Y_2) remained the same, their total outputs (X_1 and X_2) would have to change, if the balance between inputs and outputs were to be maintained. In other words, if Y_1 and Y_2 had changed, but the technology remained the same, the corresponding changes in X_1 and X_2 could be determined from the same general solution. In the real world, the effect to technical changes contains several hundred sectors, but the analytical approach remains the same. It can be explained by taking the example of pollution produced directly by the households.

Pollution is an undesirable effect of productive or consumption activities which is to be considered part of the economic system. The quantitative dependence of each kind of external output must be described by an appropriate technical coefficient. All these coefficients have to be incorporated in structural matrix of the economy in question. Let it be assumed that the preset technology of the manufacturing sector release into the air 0.20 gms of solid pollutant per meter of cloth while agricultural technology adds 0.50 gms per unit of wheat. X_3 is used to represent the yet unknown total quantity of this external output. When add to the original equations it becomes.

$$0.75X_1 - 0.40\,X_2 = Y_1$$
$$-\,0.14X_1 + 0.88X_2 = Y_2$$
$$0.50X_1 + 0.20X_2 - \bar{X}_3 = 0 \qquad (1)$$

In equation (1), the first term describes the amount of pollution produced by agriculture depending on X_1, while the second term represents the pollution of manufacturing sector as a function of X_2 and X_3 shows the total amount of pollution generated by the economic system as a whole. Given the final demands of Y_1 and Y_2 for agricultural and manufacture products, three equations can be solved by X_1, X_2 and X_3. The coefficients of the left hand side of the augmented input-output system form the matrix:

$$\begin{bmatrix} 0.75 & -0.40 & 0 \\ -0.14 & 0.88 & 0 \\ 0.50 & 0.20 & -1 \end{bmatrix}$$

A general solution of the system would consist of three equations. To determine the corresponding output of pollutions (X_3) entering the value of X_1 and X_2, mathematical static open input-output system with pollution-related activities.*

Notation

Commodities and services
1, 2, 3, . . . i . . . j . . . m + 1, m + 2 . . . g . . . k . . . n
useful goods undesired goods (pollutants)

Technical Coefficient

aiJ : input of good i per unit of output of j (produced by sector j);

aig : input of good (i) per unit of eliminated pollutant g. (eliminated by sector g);

agi : output of pollutant 'g' per unit of output of good (produced by sector);

agk : output of pollutant 'g' per unit of eliminated pollutant k (eliminated by sector k); and rgi, rgk : proportion of pollutant 'g' generated by industry 'i' or 'k' eliminated at the expense of that industry.

Variables

X_i : total output of good;
X_g : total amount of pollutant 'g' eliminated;
Y_i : final delivery of good 'i' (to households);
Y_g : final delivery of pollutant 'g' (to households);
P_i : price of good 'i';
P_g : the price of eliminating one unit of pollutant 'g';
V_i : 'value added' in an industry per unit of good 'i' produced by it; and
V_g : value-added in anti-pollution sector 'g' per unit of pollutant 'g' eliminated by it.

Vectors and Matrices

A_{11} = [aiJ] i, J = 1, 2, 3 . . . m;
A_{21} = [agi] i = 1, 2, 3 . . . m;
A_{12} = [aig] g = m+1, m+2, m+3 . . . n;
A_{22} = [agk] g, k = m+1, m+2, m+3 . . . n;
A_{21} = [qgi] i = 1, 2, 3 . . . m
g = m+1, m+2 . . . n;

where

qgi = rgiagi and qgk= rgkagk

An Input-Output Approach

$$X_1 = \begin{Bmatrix} x_1 \\ x_2 \\ \circ \\ \circ \\ \circ \\ x_m \end{Bmatrix} \qquad Y_1 = \begin{Bmatrix} y_1 \\ y_2 \\ \circ \\ \circ \\ \circ \\ y_m \end{Bmatrix} \qquad V_1 = \begin{Bmatrix} v_1 \\ v_2 \\ \circ \\ \circ \\ \circ \\ v_m \end{Bmatrix}$$

$$X_2 = \begin{Bmatrix} x_m+1 \\ x_m+2 \\ \circ \\ \circ \\ \circ \\ x_n \end{Bmatrix} \qquad Y_2 = \begin{Bmatrix} y_{1m}+1 \\ y_{1m}+2 \\ \circ \\ \circ \\ \circ \\ y_n \end{Bmatrix} \qquad V_2 = \begin{Bmatrix} v_m+1 \\ v_m+2 \\ \circ \\ \circ \\ \circ \\ v_n \end{Bmatrix}$$

Physical Input-Output Balance

$$\begin{pmatrix} I-A_{11} \\ \hline A_{21} \end{pmatrix} \begin{pmatrix} -A_{12} \\ \hline -I+A_{22} \end{pmatrix} \begin{pmatrix} X_1 \\ \hline X_2 \end{pmatrix} = \begin{pmatrix} Y_1 \\ \hline Y_2 \end{pmatrix}$$

$$\begin{pmatrix} X_1 \\ \hline X_2 \end{pmatrix} = \begin{pmatrix} I-A_{11} \\ \hline A_{21} \end{pmatrix} \begin{pmatrix} -A_{12} \\ \hline -I+A_{22} \end{pmatrix}^{-1} \begin{pmatrix} Y_1 \\ \hline Y_2 \end{pmatrix}$$

Input-Output Balance between Prices and Values-Added

$$\begin{pmatrix} I-A'_{11} \\ \hline -A'_{12} \end{pmatrix} \begin{pmatrix} -Q'_{21} \\ \hline -I+Q'_{22} \end{pmatrix} \begin{pmatrix} P_1 \\ \hline P_2 \end{pmatrix} = \begin{pmatrix} V_1 \\ \hline V_2 \end{pmatrix}$$

$$\begin{pmatrix} P_1 \\ \hline P_2 \end{pmatrix} = \begin{pmatrix} I-A'_{11} \\ \hline -A'_{21} \end{pmatrix} \begin{pmatrix} -Q_{21} \\ \hline I-Q'_{22} \end{pmatrix}^{-1} \begin{pmatrix} V_1 \\ \hline V_2 \end{pmatrix}$$

Supplementary Notation and Equations Accounting for Pollution Generated Directly by Final Consumption Notation

Technical Coefficient

99a_{gy} : output of pollutant generated by consumption of one unit of commodity i delivered to final demand.

Variables

y_g*: sum total of pollutant g 'delivered' from all industries to and generated within the final demand factor.

x_g*: total gross output of pollutant g generated by all industries and in the final demand sector.

$$A_y = \left\{ \begin{matrix} a_{m+1,y(1)} & a_{m+1,y(1)} & \cdots & a_{m+1,y(m)} \\ a_{m+2,y(2)} & a_{m+2,y(2)} & \cdots & a_{m+2,y(m)} \\ \cdot & \cdot & & \\ \cdot & \cdot & & \\ \cdot & \cdot & & \\ a_n\, y_1 & a_n\, y_2 & \cdots & a_n\, y_m \end{matrix} \right\}$$

$$Y_2^* = \begin{Bmatrix} y^*_{m+1} \\ y^*_{m+2} \\ \cdot \\ \cdot \\ y_n^* \end{Bmatrix} \qquad X_2^* = \begin{Bmatrix} x^*_{m+1} \\ x^*_{m+2} \\ \cdot \\ \cdot \\ x_n^* \end{Bmatrix}$$

In case some pollution is generated within the final demand sector itself the vector Y_2 has to be replaced by vector $Y_2 - Y_2^*$, where

$$Y_2^* = A_v Y_1 \tag{2}$$

The price-values added equations do not have to be modified final demand sector does not enter explicitly in any of the equation presented above; it can, however, be computed on the basis of the following equation,

$$X^* = [A_{21}: A_{22}]\ [X_1/X_2] + Y_2^* \tag{3}$$

INPUT-OUTPUT ANALYSIS: CO_2 EMISSION OF HOUSEHOLDS

Using input-output tables and energy flow matrices, the carbon-dioxide emission of individual households to different types of household items can be analyzed. Household characteristics have significant influence on the CO_2 emissions. The comparison demonstrates national differences in income and expenditure elasticities of both energy and CO_2. Recently several attempts to link household consumption choices and lifestyles with input-output modeling and energy and emission flow analysis in one integrated modeling framework has emerged (Weber and Perrels, 2000; Munksgard *et. al.*, 2000; Duchin, 1998; Lenzen, 1998). The present paper considers CO_2 emission from energy.

The model devised for the paper is an extension of the model used by Munksgard *et. al.* (2000). The present model concentrates on CO_2 emissions at the household level rather than focusing on CO_2 emission associated with the consumption all households. This model applies to various household types, making it possible to explore lifestyle effect on CO_2 emissions. It distinguishes between indirect and direct emission. The direct emissions are emissions associated with the consumption of energy commodities in the households i.e., electricity, LPG, Kerosene, Charcoal and other wood—fuels for heating, lighting, refrigeration, air-conditioning, etc. The indirect emissions are emissions associated with the production of all other commodities for households (furniture, clothes, foods and other services). It means the emissions that occur in the industries producing these commodities. The total CO_2 emissions from household type are defined as:

$$E_i = E_{ih} + E_{ip}$$

where, E_i is the total CO_2 emission from household 'i'; E_{ih} is the direct CO_2 emission from household 'i', and E_{ip} indirect CO_2 emission from household 'i'.

The analysis is carried out in two ways. Firstly, direct CO_2 emissions from household energy use are analyzed using simple energy-emission model. Secondly, indirect CO_2 emissions are analyzed using a generalized input-output model that also incorporates energy and emission matrices.

Direct CO_2 Emissions

Direct CO_2 emissions from household energy use are the product of total energy consumption and the composition of energy types in the household and energy supply sectors.

$$E_{ih} = Q_{ih} M_h F$$

where

- E_{ih} : a scalar of total direct CO_2 emissions from household i;
- Q_{ih} : a 1 × 5 vector including the consumption of five types of energy in household, i.e., electricity, LPG, Kerosene, Charcoal and Biofuels in units of GJ;
- M_h : a 5 × 40 matrix of fuel mix in the household sector, i.e., demand for 40 energy types per unit of total energy demand for five energy consumption categories; and
- F : a 40 × 1 vector of CO_2 emission factors in units of Kg CO_2/GJ for 40 energy types. The emission factor depends upon the carbon content of the fuel. The CO_2

emission factor depends upon the fuel mix in the energy supply sector and it has been changing over time.

The exogenous variable Q_{ih} is specific to household i, whereas M_h and F are general figures based on secondary data.

Indirect CO_2 Emissions

The indirect CO_2 emissions from household consumption by using the input-output model as are used in Munksgaard *et. al.* (2000):

$$Eip = F\ (Mp\ \#\ Rp)\ (1-A)^{-1}\ Cci$$

where

- \# : denotes the element-wise multiplication.
- Eip : denotes a scalar of total CO_2 emissions from production sectors as a consequence of production of goods and services used by household i,
- F : a 1 × 40 vector of CO_2 emission factors as above,
- Mp: a 40 × 130 matrix of fuel mix in the production sectors, i.e., the demand for 40 energy types per unit of total demand for energy for all production sectors,
- Rp: a 1 × 130 vector of energy intensities, i.e., total energy consumption per unit of production in all 130 sectors, in units of GJ,
- $(1-A)^{-1}$: the 130 × 130 sectors Leontief inverse matrix,
- C : a 130 × 72 matrix of the composition of consumption commodity aggregates apportioned by the production sectors, and
- Ci : 72 × 1 vector including consumption of 72 commodities in household i, in units of Rupees 1000.

The Integrated Model

The integrated model is explained in Chart I. It is extended in two ways. First matrices of energy consumption and emissions and added and second, final demand has been divided to a detailed level. Hence private consumption is given for 72 commodity groups and these groups are in all given for various household types. The number 'n' of household is open.

This method would help to quantify total CO_2 production

Chart I: Total CO_2 Emission of Households

	Intermediate commodities	Final demand						
		Private consumption						Other final demand
		Commodity # 1	Comm.#2				. . . Comm.	
		Household type#1,..., Household type #n	$H_1 \ldots H_n$				$H_1 \ldots H_n$	
Domestic production	Commodity Flows							
Foreign production								
Value added	Production factor flows							
Energy	Energy flows							
CO_2 emissions	Emission flows							

of households in a particular geographical boundary. It helps to understand the ratio of domestic production of CO_2 to foreign production, besides identifying CO_2 intensive fuel and non-fuel commodities used by households. Understanding the association of lifestyle variables on the usage of CO_2 emitting fuels and products will help the policy-makers to take suitable policy measures to arrest the production of CO_2. This model is equally applicable to other household emitting pollutants.

Notes

Under the World Bank—Ministry of Environment & Forests, Government of India Capacity Building Technical Assistance Project (2002); Faculty Upgradation Program in Environmental Economics, Course material, Madras School of Economics (Behind Government Data Centre), Gandhi Mandapam Road, Chennai-25, Vol. I, Concepts and Issues.

References

Duchin, F. (1998): *Structural Economics, Measuring Change in Technology, Lifestyles, and the Environment*, Washington D.C.: Island Press.

Lezen, M. (1998): "The Energy and Greenhouse Gas Cost of Living for Australia during 1993-94", *Energy*, 23:497-516.

Munksgaard, J., K.A. Pedersen and M. Wier (2000): "Impact of Household Consumption on CO_2 Emission", *Energy Economics*, 22:423-440.

Weber, C. and A. Perrels (2000): "Modelling Lifestyle Effects on Energy Demand and Related Emissions," *Energy Policy*, 28:549-566.

Service Sector Dynamics in India: Using Leontief Approach

INDERJEET SINGH, PARMOD KUMAR AND ANJU BANSAL

INTRODUCTION

The modern economists emphasize the catalytic role that technological changes play in the growth of an economy. The technological changes bring about an increase in per capita income, either by reducing the amount of inputs per unit of output or by yielding more output for a given amount of input (Leontief, W.W.). Technological change of an economy, therefore, refers to changes in the input-output relations of production activities. Consequently, as economy moves from lower to higher stages of development, there occurs a shift from simpler to more modern and complicated techniques of production on the one hand and from primary to secondary and/or to tertiary sectors on the other (Mathur, 1963). The excess growth of tertiary sector coupled with state-of-the-art technology has got its own implications for the future development patterns of the system (Mazumdar, 1984, 1995; Mitra, 1988; Nagraj, 1991; Sundram, 2002; Thakur, 1992).

In India, the share of tertiary sector in the gross domestic product has crossed the fifty percent mark. The nature and role of this excessive tertiarization has become a matter of concern. The work is an attempt to analyze the structure, linkage pattern and dynamics of the tertiary sector growth in India and its implications for the future.

COVERAGE

Keeping in view the broad objectives of the study, the secondary data on the Indian economy have been used. For the analysis of structure, the sector level data from 'National Accounts Statistics' (CSO) have been used. Input-output structure of the service sector and service intensity has been analyzed for the period 1998-99. To analyze the sectoral linkage pattern of the Indian economy six input-output tables have been used for the years 1973-74, 1978-79, 1983-84, 1989-90, 1993-94, and 1998-99. For analyzing the above data, tabular analysis has been supported with percentages, averages, growth rates and measures of forward and backward linkages.

MODEL

A Simple Leontief system in matrix notation can be briefly given as:

$$(I - A)\, X = C$$

where A is the matrix of coefficients; X is a vector of gross outputs and C is a vector of final demand. It is obvious from the above that once we have the matrix A and the vector of total output X, we can easily find the commodity available for final use. Similarly, when A and C are given we can solve for X. Similarly, by multiplying throughout $(I–A)\, X = C$ by $(I–A)^{-1}$, we can obtain:

$$X = (I - A)^{-1}\, C$$

where $(I - A)^{-1}$ is the Leontief inverse which gives the direct as well as the indirect requirements of the system. Service intensity can be evaluated following various alternative methodologies.

Two basic types of services intensity can be defined. The first type imputes productive services use, S_{ind}, to total output of economy, X. The second type imputes productive services use, S_{ind} to final demand F. That is

$$S_{ind} = SX$$

and

$$S_{ind} = S^{*} F$$

Here S is the vector of direct services requirements to produce one unit of goods by a sector. The vector S* represents the direct plus indirect services requirements to produce one unit of goods by a sector. It can be obtained as:

$$S^{*} = S\ (I-A)^{-1}$$

The vector S gives the direct services intensities of different industries for their production and the vector S* gives the direct plus indirect intensities of different industries for their production. The vectors S and S* have been calculated for the Indian economy from the input-output table 1998-99.

ANALYSIS

Trends in the distribution of Gross Domestic Product (GDP) by industrial origin show that the Indian economy has undergone a vast structural change over the last few decades (Table 1). In the year 1950-51, ours was predominantly an agricultural economy with 59.19 per cent share of the GDP originating from primary sector. The share of the secondary sector being 13.29 percent in the same year is indicative of the fact that manufacturing and allied activities were just in the developing stage. The share of tertiary sector, almost the double of secondary, stood at 27.50 per cent.

The share of primary sector that was 59.20 percent of GDP in the year 1950-51 came down to 56.11 percent in 19601-61; to 48.12 in 1970-71; to 41.82 in 1980-81; further to 34.92 in 1990-91; and finally to 24.03 in the year 2003-04. Thus over a span of past 55 years, the share of primary sector-related activities in general and the agriculture in particular in the GDP has come down to less than half of what it was initially. The decline of primary sector share with every increase in the GDP is indicator of a healthy economic development. It shows that a raw material producing/supplying economy is gradually shifting to a manufacturing and rigorous processing economy that has a higher value-added generation.

TABLE 1

Sectoral Shares in Gross Domestic Product in India (at 1993-94 Prices)

Year	*Primary*	*%*	*Secondary*	*%*	*Tertiary*	*%*	*GDP*
1950-51	83154	59.19	18670	13.29	38642	27.50	140466
1960-61	112848	56.11	34239	17.02	54016	26.85	201103
1970-71	142581	48.12	58997	19.91	94700	31.96	296278
1980-81	167770	41.82	86605	21.59	146753	36.58	401128
1990-91	242012	34.92	169703	24.49	281156	40.57	692871
2000-01	314585	26.24	298472	24.90	585535	48.85	1198592
2001-02	333274	26.28	309557	24.41	625114	49.30	1267945
2002-03	314578	23.86	329212	24.97	674572	51.16	1318362
2003-04	343806	24.03	351046	24.53	735696	51.42	1430548

Source: Economic Survey of India, 2004-05.

The share of secondary sector that was 13.29 percent of GDP in the year 1950-51 took a long span of 50 years to grow to 24.53 percent. The decades of 1970s and 1980s show that the pace of change in the share of secondary sector in the GDP was very negligible and was just near to stagnation. The share of secondary sector during the decades of 1970s and 1980s remained in the range of 20 to 22 percent of GDP. The structural change in India during the last half-century is characterized by a shrinking share of agriculture coupled with slow paced industrial development. Decade of 1990s and the last few years are indicative of the fact that the share of secondary sector as a percentage of GDP has stagnated around 24 percent.

The percentage share of tertiary sector in the GDP has almost doubled as compared to what it was in the year 1950-51. It has grown to 51.42 percent in 2003-04 as compared to mere 27.50

percent in 1950-51. In the initial years, i.e., during the decades of 1950s, 60s and 70s there was an overall rise of not more than 5 percent in this share. Most of the change in the tertiary sector has been during the last two decades. This implies that the tertiary sector has been the major beneficiary from the structural change.

Tertiary sector accounts for more than half of the India's GDP, it is comparable to any developed economy in terms of this share. It has grown by bypassing secondary sector. The Indian economy is passing through a transition to finally culminate into a service sector growth lead economy. The viability of such a service sector growth lead economy with weak primary and secondary sectors is a million dollar question that needs a thorough research at this juncture of time.

Relative Shares of Sub-Sectors of Tertiary Sector

Tertiary sector includes trade, hotels, transport and communication, financing, insurance, real estate and business services, public administration and defence and other services. Table 2 shows that the share of 'trade, hotels, transport and communication' improved from 11.94 percent in the year 1950-51 to 25.5 percent in 2003-04. During the period under analysis, its share has reached to level that is more than double what it was in the beginning. This increase in the share has been gradual and consistent. The share of trade, hotels, transport and communications was 18.40 per cent in 1980-81 and improved to 18.73 per cent in 1990-91 and finally to 22.79 percent in the year 2000-01. The rise in share during the nineties decade is attributable more to the trade, transport and communication than to hotels. In the recent years, it is the communication only that has witnessed a more growth as compared to other components of the sub-sector.

The share of financing, insurance, real estate and business services has also almost doubled during the last half century. The share of these services was 6.67 per cent of the total GDP in the year 1950-51 and increased to 12.84 per cent in 2003-04. As compared to real estate and insurance, it is the financing and business services that have registered a major share in this sub-sector. This is in response to the liberalization and privatization in the area of banking and finance. Many new business services have come into being, e.g., advertising, event management and so on. The share of public administration, defence and other services, including mainly the items of government expenditure, have reached at a level of 13.03 percent in the year 2003-04 as compared to 9.40 percent in 1950-51. The process of economic growth involves a rapid expansion of public administration, especially a rapid expansion of economic and welfare services such as education, health and family welfare.

TABLE 2

Gross Domestic Product in percentage Terms at Factor Cost by Industry of Origin (at 1993-94 prices)

Year	*Sector 1**	*Sector 2**	*Sector 3**	*Sector 4**	*Sector 5**	*GDPFC*
1950-51	59.19	13.29	11.94	6.67	9.40	100
1960-61	56.11	17.02	14.08	6.24	9.40	100
1970-71	48.12	19.91	15.55	5.93	10.68	100
1980-81	41.82	21.59	18.40	6.52	11.65	100
1990-91	34.92	24.49	18.73	9.66	12.17	100
2000-01	26.24	24.90	22.79	12.59	13.46	100
2001-02	26.28	24.41	23.48	12.44	13.37	100
2002-03	23.86	24.97	24.80	13.00	13.36	100
2003-04	24.03	24.53	25.55	12.84	13.03	100

* Sector Coding used.
1. Agriculture, forestry & fishing, mining and quarrying.
2. Manufacturing, construction, electricity, gas and water supply.
3. Trade, hotels, transport & communication.
4. Financing, insurance, real estate and business services.
5. Public administration and defence and other services.

GDPFC: Gross domestic product at factor cost.
Source: Economic Survey of India, 2004-05.

Growth profile of the components of the tertiary sector, given in Table 3, is indicative of the fact that 'trade, hotels, transport and communication' section that grew around five percent per annum in the decades of fifties, sixties and seventies rose to a level of 5.86 percent per annum in the decade of eighties and finally touched the growth level of 8.52 percent per annum in the recent years. Financing and real estate grew at a rate of 3 to 4 percent in the first three decades and suddenly touched the growth level of 10 percent per annum. Most of the growth of eighties decade was due to real estate segment. The financing and business services growth is phenomena of the nineties decade. During this decade, the growth of financing, insurance, real estate and business services has been 7.69 percent per annum. Public administration, defence and other services have grown from 3 to 5 percent per annum level in the first three decades; to 6.4 percent in eighties decade and to 7.00 percent in the last decade. Percentage share of components and the growth profile of the tertiary sector are indicative of the fact that half of the tertiary sector is formed by the financial sector and the government expenditure. The share of tradable services is just the half. If the economy has to achieve the highest level of service economy, i.e., the knowledge economy, it must increase the share of tradable services in the basket of tertiary sector.

TABLE 3

Sub-Sector Growth Rates (percent per annum) for the Tertiary Sectors at 1993-94 Prices

Sub-sectors of service sector	*1950-51 to 1960-61*	*1960-61 to 1970-71*	*1970-71 to 1980-81*	*1980-81 to 1990-91*	*1990-91 to 2003-04*
1. Trade, hotels, transport and communication	5.46	4.74	5.3	5.86	8.52
2. Financing, insurance, real estate and business services	3.03	3.21	4.3	10	7.69
3. Public administration and defence and other services	3.64	5.2	3.8	6.4	7

Source: Economic Survey of India, 2004-05.

Input Structure and Output Disposition of Tertiary Sector

Structure through input output matrices (Tables I and II in appendix) show, that the commodities have utilized 41.2 percent of commodity-output for intermediate consumption in 1998-99 as against 40.3 per cent in 1993-94, 42.5 percent in 1989-90, 40.3 per cent in 1983-84, 38 per cent in 1978-79 and 34.5 percent in 1973-74. The input use of commodities by commodity sector has improved from 34.5 percent in the year 1973-74 to 41.2 percent in

1998-99. On the other hand, the Service sector have utilized 13.2 per cent of service output for intermediate consumption in 1998-99 as against 11.7 per cent in 1993-94, 12.8 per cent in 1989-90, 13.1 per cent in 1983-84 15.5 per cent in 1978-79 and 9.4 per cent in 1973-74. Thus the use of services as input in the service sector has improved to 13.2 percent in the year 1998-99 as compared to the same as 9.4 percent in 1973-74. In the last quarter of a century, the intermediate input use of the commodity production has increased its dependence on the commodity sector and service sector has increased its dependence for its intermediate input use on the service sector. The intermediate-use of services in commodity sector has changed marginally in the entire period under consideration. The overgrowth of service sector output in the last decade is going more to the final use than to the intermediate input. This implies the emerging structure of the economy is going to be characterized by development of sectors that are loosely connected to the production and tightly connected to the consumption. The system is going to be a producer of final consumption goods rather than intermediate inputs.

The component of final use in the output shows a consistent decline with slight exceptions. Thus, the share of commodities in final use to total commodity output is 50.9 per cent in 1998-99 as against 52 percent in 1993-94; 51.4 per cent in 1989-90, 53.2 per cent in 1983-84; 56.1 per cent in 1978-79; and 60.2 per cent in 1973-74. The decrease in the share of commodities in final use indicates that production system of the economy is picking up. There is slight increase in the share of services in final use to total output of services, which is 63.2 per cent in 1998-99 as compared to 61.5 per cent in 1993-94. The final use of services during the same period has rather increased in the same period. Thus the emerging structure is gradually altering the final use basket by reducing the commodity consumption and increasing the share of services.

On the others hand, in the case of services producing industries the Gross Value Added (GVA) to output ratio is almost the same for 1998-99 and 1993-94 at 45.8 per cent and 43.9 per cent, respectively. The GVA to total output ratio of all commodities are almost the same for both the years. The component of commodities as input in the service producing industries has declined from 14.8 per cent in 1993-94 to 14:0 per cent in 1998-

99. But there is a slight increase in the component of services as input in the service producing industries from 12.4 per cent in 1993-94 to 14.2 percent in 1998-99. Commodity input requirement of the service sector is continuously on decline and service input requirement by the service sector is on the rise. Thus the service sector has very high value-added component as compared to the commodities. Further, the service sector has backward multiplier effect on the service sector and in the long-run it has a tendency to hamper the growth of commodity sector.

Looking into the composition of final use, it is observed that of the total final use 55 percent relates to commodities and 41 per cent to services in 1998-99. The corresponding figures for 1993-94, 1989-90, 1973-74, 1978-79 and 1973-74 were 58 per cent and 37 per cent; 64 per cent and 33 per cent; 64 per cent and 32 per cent; 66 per cent and 30 per cent and 70 per cent and 26 per cent respectively. The broad conclusion, which emerges is that the income from services have grown faster than commodity sector in the last decade. It appears that in general, the growth rate of service income is independent of the growth rate of commodity sector income. So gap between the growth rates of services and commodity sector has widened in the nineties as compared to the seventies and eighties. Emerging structure of the economy is characterized by continuous replacement of commodity production by service sector.

Sector-wise Linkage Patterns

A look on the sectoral linkages pattern highlights (Table III in appendix) the classification for the sector falling in each of the four categories: intermediate primary production; intermediate manufacturing; final manufacturing; and final primary production. This part of the analysis has been limited to the last three years, i.e., 1989-90, 1993-94 and 1998-99. Total backward and forward linkages have been worked out for three sector economy: primary sector; secondary sector and tertiary sector. In the first category, i.e., intermediate primary production, backward linkages are low and forward linkages are high. In Intermediate manufacturing both linkages are high, in final manufacturing backward linkages are high but forward linkages are low. In last category, i.e., final primary production both linkages are low.

The primary sector has low backward and low forward linkages with tertiary sector, i.e., primary sector takes less of inputs and also provides low outputs to tertiary sector. That is to say, Primary sector has weak linkage with tertiary sector. Further, the banking provides better services to primary sector and hotels and restaurants provide more of their services to tertiary sector. Other transport services and storage and warehousing takes services from tertiary sector and also provide services to it. Thus Primary sector has low backward and low forward linkages with tertiary sector, high linkages with itself and average linkages with the secondary sector. Secondary sector has low linkages with primary sector but high linkages with tertiary sector. Electricity alone has high linkages with all the three sectors.

Service Intensities

In this section, an attempt has been made to analyze the use of services by the other sectors, i.e., service intensity for production of different industries in the economy. Using the details given in the methodology, the vectors S and S* have been calculated for the Indian economy from the Input Output Transaction Table, 1998-99. Tables 4 and 5 show the variation across industries for two measures: direct services intensity (S) and direct plus indirect services intensity (S*). Table 4 highlights that S exhibit great variability in services consumption for production across different sectors. It is found that services use per unit of output produced varies from 3 percent for 'Other crops' (4) to 44 per cent for 'Coal tar production' (27). Table 8 shows that direct plus indirect services intensity (S*) varies from 5 percent for 'Other crops' (4) to 50 percent for 'Coal tar products' (27.) It is interesting to note that the direct (S) service intensity and direct plus indirect (S*) services intensity are highest according to the rank for 'Coal tar product' (27) and lowest according to the rank for the production of 'Other crops' (4). These variations are obviously due to variations in output and technologies. After 'Coal tar products', there is 'Leather and leather products' (24) that has 24 per cent service intensity. 'Tobacco products' (15), 'Cement' (33) and 'Cotton textiles' (16) comes at third, fourth and fifth rank respectively. Agriculture sector includes 'Cash crops' (2), 'Food crops' (1), 'Plantation crops' (3), 'Other crops' (4), 'Animal husbandry' (5), 'Forestry and logging' (6) and 'Fishing' (7), 'Coal and lignite' (8),

'Crude Petroleum and natural gas' (9), 'Iron ore' (10) and 'Other minerals' (11) have low service intensity and their ranks are in range of 40 to 47. Same condition can be seen in case of direct plus indirect services intensities.

TABLE 4

Sector-wise Direct Services Intensity in India, 1998-99

S. No.	*Sector*	*S*	*Rank*
1.	Food Crops	0.064	39
2.	Cash Crops	0.049	42
3.	Plantation Crops	0.043	43
4.	Other Crops	0.032	47
5.	Animal Husbandry	0.051	41
6.	Forestry and Logging	0.041	44
7.	Fishing	0.033	46
8.	Coal and Lignite	0.072	37
9.	Crude Petro, Natural Gas	0.034	45
10.	Iron Ore	0.081	36
11.	Other Minerals	0.052	40
12.	Sugar	0.167	22
13.	Food products (Excl. Sugar)	0.203	10
14.	Beverages	0.171	19
15.	Tobacco Products	0.235	3
16.	Cotton Textiles	0.231	5
17.	Wool, Silk & Synth. Textiles	0.207	9
18.	Jute, Hemp & Mesta Textiles	0.227	6
19.	Textile products	0.202	11
20.	Wood Prod. Excl. Furniture	0.126	33
21.	Furniture & Fixtures	0.130	31
22.	Paper and Paper Products	0.181	13
23.	Print, Publ. and Allied Act	0.147	27
24.	Leather and Leather products	0.243	2
25.	Plastic & Rubber Products	0.178	15
26.	Petro. Products	0.099	35
27.	Coaltar Products	0.435	1
28.	Inorganic Heavy Chemicals	0.154	26
29.	Organic Heavy Chemicals	0.126	32
30.	Fertilizers	0.158	24
31.	Paint Varnishes and Lacquers	0.141	28
32.	Pest. Drug & Other Chemicals	0.157	25
33.	Cement	0.232	4
34.	Non-Metallic Mineral Products	0.173	18
35.	Iron & Steel Ind. & Foundries	0.212	8

(Contd.)

S. No.	*Sector*	*S*	*Rank*
36.	Other Basic Metal Industry	0.138	29
37.	Metal Products Excl. Machinery	0.170	21
38.	Agriculture Machinery	0.174	17
39.	Machi. for Food & Text. Indus.	0.181	14
40.	Other Machinery	0.174	16
41.	Electronic & Elect. Machinery	0.163	23
42.	Railway Transport Equipment	0.132	30
43.	Other Transport Equipment	0.214	7
44.	Misc. manufacturing Industries	0.115	34
45.	Construction	0.171	20
46.	Electricity	0.185	12
47	Gas and Water Supply	0.066	38

Source: Computed.

TABLE 5

Sector-wise Direct Plus Indirect Service Intensities in India, 1998-99

S. No.	*Sector*	*S**	*Rank*
1.	Food Crops	0.11	39
2.	Cash Crops	0.078	41
3.	Plantation Crops	0.072	43
4.	Other Crops	0.051	47
5.	Animal Husbandry	0.073	42
6.	Forestry and Logging	0.05	46
7.	Fishing	0.058	44
8.	Coal and Lignite	0.122	38
9.	Crude Petro, Natural Gas	0.057	45
10.	Iron Ore	0.128	36
11.	Other Minerals	0.079	40
12.	Sugar	0.226	32
13.	Food products (Excl. Sugar)	0.290	20
14.	Beverages	0.259	29
15.	Tobacco Products	0.303	17
16.	Cotton Textiles	0.334	10
17.	Wool, Silk & Synth. Textiles	0.372	3
18.	Jute, Hemp & Mesta Textiles	0.299	19
19.	Textile products	0.350	6
20.	Wood Prod. Excl. Furniture	0.180	34
21.	Furniture & Fixtures	0.202	33
22.	Paper and Paper Products	0.325	12

S. No.	*Sector*	*S**	*Rank*
23.	Print, Publ. and Allied Act.	0.268	26
24.	Leather and Leather products	0.382	2
25.	Plastic & Rubber Products	0.314	15
26.	Ptero. Products	0.152	35
27.	Coaltar Products	0.501	1
28.	Inorganic Heavy Chemicals	0.265	28
29.	Organic Heavy Chemicals	0.252	30
30.	Fertilizers	0.281	22
31.	Paint Varnishes and Lacaquers	0.279	23
32.	Pest. Drug & Other Chemicals	0.278	24
33.	Cement	0.316	14
34.	Non-Metallic Mineral Products	0.250	31
35.	Iron & Steel Ind. & Foundaries	0.365	5
36.	Other Basic Metal Industry	0.277	25
37.	Metal Products Excl. Machinery	0.324	12
38.	Agriculture Machinery	0.344	8
39.	Machi. for Food & Text. Indus.	0.344	7
40.	Other Machinery	0.338	9
41.	Electronic & Elect. Machinery	0.324	11
42.	Railway Transport Equipment	0.304	16
43.	Other Transport Equipment	0.365	4
44.	Misc. manufacturing Industries	0.282	21
45.	Construction	0.266	27
46.	Electricity	0.300	18
47.	Gas and Water Supply	0.124	37

Source: Computed.

CONCLUSION

Thus, it may be concluded that both in primary and secondary sectors, a major part of total input comes from the tertiary sector. The growth rate in tertiary sector is higher in comparison to agriculture and industry. Therefore, considering high growth potential, it is concluded that tertiary sector is playing a very crucial role in the Indian economy. But the excessive growth of tertiary sector in India has a very complicated dynamics in terms of structure and linkages pattern thereof. The viability of such a service sector growth lead economy with weak primary and secondary sectors is a million dollar question that needs a thorough research at this juncture of time. An exercise fortified with a larger database is need of the time.

REFERENCES

Kuznets, S. (1979): *Modern Economic Growth-Rate, Structure and Spread,* Oxford and IBH Publishing Company, New Delhi.

Lewis, W.A. (1963): *The Theory of Economic Growth,* George Allen and Unwin.

Lewis, W.A. (1984): "The State of Development Theory", *American Economic Review,* 74.

Majumdar, Ashutosh (1984): "On the Relationship Between Economic Growth and Tertiary Sector's Contribution to GDP", *Journal of Income and Wealth,* Vol. 7, No. 2.

Majumdar, Krishna (1995): "Disproportional Growth of Service Sector in India: 1960-90", *Indian Economic Journal,* Vol. 43, No. 2.

Mathur, P.N. (1963): "An Efficient Path of Technological Transformation of an Economy", in Barna (ed.), *Structural Dependence and Economic Development,* Macmillan.

Mitra, Ashok (1988): "Dis-proportionality and the Service Sector: A Note", *Social Scientist,* Vol. 16, No. 4.

Nagaraj, R. (1991): "Excess Growth of Tertiary Sector?", *Economic and Political Weekly,* February 2.

Sundaram, Satya (2002): "Excess Growth of Tertiary Sector in India" in Jagdish Gandhi and P. Ganesan (ed.) *Service Sector in the Indian Economy,* Deep & Deep Publications Pvt. Ltd., New Delhi.

Thakur, Devendra (1992): "Tertiary Sector in India" in Devendra Thakur (ed.) *Tertiary Sector Development,* Deep & Deep Publications, New Delhi.

APPENDIX TABLES

TABLE I

Percentage Distribution of Output (Value in Rs. lakhs)

Item	*Year*	*Commodity*	%	*Services*	%	*Intermediate Use (3+4)*	%	*Final Use*	%	*Total Output (5+6)*	%
1	2	3		4		5		6		7	
Commodity	1973-74	23574.87	34.5	367570	5.3	2724999	39.8	4115190	60.2	6840184	100
	78-79	44554.12	38.0	696915	5.9	5152324	43.9	6589490	56.1	11741814	100
	83-84	97989.06	40.3	1809648	6.5	11608554	46.8	13208303	53.2	24816793	100
	89-90	236200.24	42.5	3429260	6.2	27049284	48.6	28583424	51.4	55632708	100
	93-94	39141400	40.3	7401400	7.6	46542700	48.0	50484100	52.0	97026800	100
	98-99	767758.03	41.2	14768124	7.9	91543927	49.1	94981175	50.9	186525116	100
Services	1973-74	476.54	21.2	210076	9.4	686611	30.6	1557617	69.4	2244228	100
	78-79	1136193	23.4	758083	15.5	1894276	38.9	2974871	61.1	4869147	100
	83-84	2524106	24.4	1454856	13.1	3978962	37.5	6634002	62.5	10612862	100
	89-90	6862580	27.8	3172877	12.8	10035457	40.6	14670854	59.4	24706311	100
	93-94	14214300	26.8	6198800	11.7	20413300	38.5	32574100	61.5	52984500	100
	98-99	26740166	23.6	14962635	13.2	41702801	36.8	715961681	63.2	113298967	100

(Contd.)

TABLE I (*Contd.*)

1	2	3		4		5		6		7	
Sub-total	1973-74	28334041	31.2	577646	6.4	3411609	37.6	5672803	62.4	9084412	100
	78-79	5591605	33.7	1454998	8.7	7046600	42.4	9564361	57.6	16610961	100
	83-84	12323012	35.5	3264504	8.5	15587516	44.0	19842305	56.0	35429655	100
	89-90	30482604	37.9	6602137	8.2	37084741	46.2	43254278	53.8	80339019	100
	93-94	53355800	35.6	13600100	9.1	66955900	44.6	83055500	55.4	150011400	100
	98-99	103515969	34.5	29730759	9.9	133246728	44.4	166577343	55.6	299824083	100
Net in direct Taxes	1973-74	239424	46.3	61247	11.9	300668	58.2	216173	41.8	516841	100
	78-79	521012	49.8	155997	14.5	677009	64.3	376335	35.7	1053344	100
	83-84	982426	48.5	278255	11.9	1260681	60.4	825846	39.6	2086527	100
	89-90	2729390	54.0	5352213	10.6	3264603	64.5	1794239	36.5	5058842	100
	93-94	1814000	23.3	1333700	17.1	3147800	40.4	4639700	59.6	7787500	100
	98-99	4177186	29.2	2587474	18.1	6764660	47.4	7521182	52.6	14285836	100
GVA	1973-74	3766793	70.1	1605342	29.9	—	—	—	—	5372135	100
	78-79	5629194	63.3	3258147	36.7	—	—	—	—	8887338	100
	83-84	11511293	63.0	41370210	37.0	—	—	—	—	18581503	100
	89-90	23984059	71.2	16005651	28.8	—	—	—	—	39989710	100
	93-94	44823722	56.1	35083977	43.9	—	—	—	—	79907700	100
	98-99	86604057	54.2	73208638	45.8	—	—	—	—	159812695	100

Source: IOTT, CSO, Various Issues.

TABLE II

Percentage Distribution of Inputs (Value in lakhs)

Item	Year	Commodity	%	Services	%	Sub-total	%	Final Use	%
1	2	3		4		5		6	
Commodity	1973-74	2357487	34.5	367570	16.4	2724999	30.0	4115190	69.9
	78-79	4455412	38.0	696915	14.1	5152324	31.0	6589490	66.3
	83-84	9798906	39.5	1809648	16.0	11608554	32.8	13208303	63.9
	89-90	23620024	41.3	3429260	14.8	27049284	33.7	28583424	63.5
	93-94	39141400	39.1	7401400	14.8	46542700	31.0	50484100	57.6
	98-99	76775803	39.5	14768124	14.0	91543927	30.5	94981175	54.6
Services	1973-74	476554	6.9	210076	9.4	686611	7.6	1557617	26.4
	78-79	1136193	9.7	758083	15.5	1894276	11.4	2974871	29.9
	83-84	2524106	10.2	1454856	13.7	3978962	11.2	6634002	32.1
	89-90	6862580	12.0	3172877	13.7	10035457	12.5	14670854	32.6
	93-94	14214300	14.2	6198800	12.4	20413300	13.6	32574100	37.1
	98-99	26740166	13.8	14962635	14.2	41702801	13.9	71596168	41.1
Sub-total	1973-74	28334041	41.4	577646	25.8	3411609	37.6	5672803	96.3
	78-79	5591605	47.7	1454998	29.6	7046600	42.4	9564361	96.2
	83-84	12323012	49.7	3264504	29.7	15587516	44.0	19842305	96.0
	89-90	30482604	53.3	6602137	28.5	37084741	46.2	43254278	96.0
	93-94	53355800	53.4	13600100	27.2	66955900	44.6	83055500	94.7
	98-99	103515969	53.3	29730759	28.2	133246728	44.4	166577343	95.7

(Contd.)

TABLE II (*Contd.*)

1	2	3	%	4	%	5	%	6	%
NIT	1973-74	239424	3.5	61247	2.7	300668	3.3	216173	3.7
	78-79	521012	4.5	155997	3.2	677009	4.1	376335	3.8
	83-84	982426	4.0	278255	2.4	1260681	3.6	825846	4.0
	89-90	2729390	4.8	535213	2.3	3264603	4.1	1794239	4.0
	93-94	1814000	1.8	1333700	2.7	3147800	2.1	4639700	5.3
	98-99	4177186	2.1	2587474	2.5	6764660	2.3	7521182	4.3
GVA	1973-74	3766793	55.1	1605342	71.5	5372135	59.1	—	—
	78-79	5629194	47.8	3258147	67.2	8887338	53.5	—	—
	83-84	11511293	46.3	41370210	67.9	18581503	52.4	—	—
	89-90	23984059	41.9	16005651	69.2	39989710	49.8	—	—
	93-94	44823722	44.8	35083977	70.1	79907700	53.3	—	—
	98-99	86604057	44.6	73208638	69.4	159812695	53.3	—	—
Total Output	1973-74	6840175	100	2244227	100	9084412	100	588976	100
	78-79	11741805	100	4869142	100	16610947	100	9940696	100
	83-84	24816731	100	10612969	100	35429700	100	20668151	100
	89-90	57196053	100	23143001	100	80339054	100	45048517	100
	93-94	99993473	100	50017898	100	150011371	100	87695200	100
	98-99	194297212	100	105526871	100	299824083	100	174098525	100

Source: IOTT, CSO, Various Issues.

TABLE III

Sector-wise Classification of Linkages

Category	*1989-90*		
	Primary	*Secondary*	*Tertiary*
1	2	3	4
I	2,35, 38, 40, 45, 48, 52, 54	9,18, 20, 27, 28,55,	14, 21, 26, 51, 53, 55
II	1, 4, 5,13, 26,30, 46	8, 22, 29, 31, 32, 33, 35, 36, 37, 39, 40, 46, 48	20, 22, 23, 25, 32, 42, 44, 46, 49, 50, 54, 58
III	3, 12, 14, 15, 16, 18, 20, 21, 22, 24, 27, 33, 34,53	2, 3, 11,14, 16, 17, 19, 23, 24, 25, 26, 30, 34, 38, 41, 42, 43, 44, 45, 47, 49, 58	12, 15 to 19, 27 to 31 33 to 37 39, 40, 41 43, 45, 47, 52, 59
IV	6, 7, 8, 9, 10, 11, 17, 19, 23, 25, 28, 29, 31, 35, 36, 37, 39, 41, 42, 43, 44, 47, 49, 50, 51, , 55 to 60	1, 4 to 7, 10, 12, 13, 15, 21, 50 to 54, 56, to 59, 60	1 to 11, 13, 24, 38, 48, 56, 57, 60

(Contd.)

TABLE III (*Contd.*)

Sector-wise Classification of Linkages

Category	*1993-94*		
	Primary	*Secondary*	*Tertiary*
1	*5*	*6*	*7*
I	2, 4, 11, 32, 38, 40, 54	2, 3, 8 to 11, 18, 20, 27, 33, 46, 55	21, 22, 23, 25, 26, 32, 42, 46, 47, 53
II	1, 5, 13, 18, 26, 30, 46	22, 28, 29, 31, 32, 34, 35, 36, 37, 39	44, 48 to 51, 54, 55, 59
III	12, 15, 16, 20, 21, 22, 27, 28, 33, 34, 35, 36, 53	14, 17, 19, 23, 24, 25, 30, 38, 40 to 45, 49, 58	8, 14, 15, 17, 24, 27, 28, 29, 34, 35, 37, 38, 39, 40, 41, 43, 52, 58
IV	3, 6, 7, 8, 9, 10, 14, 17, 19, 23, 24, 25, 29, 31, 37, 39, 41, 42, 43, 44, 45, 47, 48 to 52, 55 to 60	1, 4 to 7, 12, 13, 15, 16, 21, 26, 47, 48, 50 to 54, 56, 57, 59, 60	1 to 7, 9 to 11, 12, 13, 16, 18 to 20, 30, 31, 33, 36, 45, 56, 57, 60

(*Contd.*)

TABLE III (*Contd.*)

Sector-wise Classification of Linkages

Category	*1998-99*		
	Primary	*Secondary*	*Tertiary*
1	*8*	*9*	*10*
I	2, 4, 5, 11, 32, 38, 40, 48, 49, 52, 54	2, 3, 8 to 11, 18, 20, 27, 33	21, 26, 42, 44, 51, 53, 54, 59
II	1, 5, 18, 26, 30, 46	22, 28, 29, 31, 32, 35, 36, 39, 46, 48	22, 23, 25, 32, 40, 46, 49, 50, 55
III	12 to 16, 19 to 22, 27, 33, 34, 36, 53	14, 16, 17, 19, 21, 23, 24, 25, 30, 37, 38, 40 to 45, 47, 49	12 to 19, 24, 27, 28, 31, 33, 34, 35, 37, 38, 39, 41, 43, 45, 58
IV	3, 6, to 10, 17, 23, 24, 25, 28, 29, 31, 35, 37, 39 41 to 45, 47	1, 4 to 7, 12, 13, 15, 26, 34, 50 to 60	1 to 11 , 20, 29, 30, 36, 47, 48, 52, 56, 57, 60

The Relevance of Leontief Paradox in Modern International Trade

DEEPA RAWAT AND SHYAM SUNDER SINGH CHAUHAN

INTRODUCTION

W.W. Leontief is an eminent economist. One of his most important contributions to economics has been the 'Leontief Paradox'. Leontief paradox is a particular situation in international trade where capital-intensive countries import capital-intensive goods and export labour-intensive goods. The Leontief paradox was the total reversal of Heckscher Ohlin theory of international trade. The Heckscher Ohlin theory states that each country exports the commodity, which uses its abundant factors intensively. In other words, normally a capital abundant country would produce capital goods and export them too. Such countries try to bridge the demand gap by importing labour-intensive goods. The Heckscher Ohlin theory was generally accepted on the basis of casual empiricism because of non-availability of any technique to test it until the input-output analysis was invented. Leontief paradox came into lime light in 1956 when Leontief used the 1947 input-output tables of the US economy. He again repeated the test in 1956 for US imports and exports data for the year 1951. In support of Leontief's finding Prof. Robert Baldwin in 1971 used the 1962 US trade data and concluded that US imports were more capital-intensive than US exports. Tatemoto and Ichimura (1954) also supported Leontief's point of view in relation to Japan's international trade. Some other economists like Stolper and Roskamp (1961); Casas, Francois *et al.* (1984), etc. established that Leontief paradox is not universally true.

The present paper analyses the theory of international trade as developed by W.W. Leontief. It also examines the other supporting or contradicting studies related to the Leontief paradox. We have also tried to test the relevance of Leontief paradox in modern day economics, particularly the developing economics. The paper is divided into four sections, namely, introduction; explanation of Leontief paradox; relevance of Leontief paradox in modern trade; and lastly the conclusions.

Wassily W. Leontief was born on 5th August 1906 in St. Petersburg, Russia. He went to Berlin and received his doctorate in 1929. He spent a year in China as an economist advising the Government of China. Then he came to the United States and joined Harvard. At Harvard, he developed his theories and methods of input-output analysis. He received the Nobel Prize in economics in 1973 for the input-output analysis of America's production machinery. In 1953 he gave the famous Leontief Paradox. He passed away on 6th February, 1999. Some of the major studies carried out by Leontief are:

- The Structure of the American Economy, 1919-39, 1941.
- "Input-Output Economics", 1951, Scientific American.
- "Domestic Production and Foreign Trade : the American capital position re-examined", 1953, Proceedings of American Philosophical Society.
- "Factor Proportions and the Structure of American Trade: Further theoretical and empirical analysis", 1956, REStat.
- "Input-Output Analysis", 1965, Scientific American.
- Essays in Economics: Theories and theorizing, 1966.

- Essays in Economics, 1966.

LEONTIEF PARADOX: ITS EXPLANATION

Leontief's conclusion that the U.S., the most capital abundant country of the world by any criteria, exported labour-intensive commodities and imported capital-intensive commodities, was in contradiction with the Heckscher Ohlin theory. Leontief took the profession by surprise and stimulated an enormous amount of empirical and theoretical research on the subject.

To perform the test, Leontief used the 1947 input-output table of the US economy. He aggregated industries into 50 sectors, but only 38 industries produced commodities that enter the international markets, and the remaining 12 sectors were created for accounting identities and non-traded goods. He also aggregated factors into two categories, labour and capital. He then estimated the capital and labour requirements to produce one million dollars' worth of typical exportable and importable in 1947.

Capital Requirement		*Labour Requirement*
Exports	$ak_x = 2.55780$	$aL_X = 182.313$ man-years
Imports	$ak_m = 3.091339$	$aL_m = 170.114$ man-years

$$k_x = aK_x/aL_x = \$14{,}300$$
$$k_m = aK_m/aL_m = \$18{,}200$$

The US seems to have been endowed with more capital per worker than any other country in the world in 1947. Thus, the HO theory predicts that the US exports would have required more capital per worker than US imports. However, Leontief was surprised to discover that US imports were 30 per cent more capital-intensive than US exports, i.e.,

$$K_m = 1.30\ k_x$$

He observed that export industries used relatively more labour than do import-competing industries. Hence, the US exported labours-intensive goods and imported capital-intensive goods.

Several economists questioned the accuracy and the appropriateness of data used by Leontief. Buchanan (1955) criticized Leontief's measurement of capital; he argued that Leontief's capital coefficients were 'investment requirement coefficients' which did not take into account the durability of capital. Loeb (1954) argued that the difference in capital intensity between the export sector and the import-competing sector were not statistically insignificant.

Leontief refined his measurements and tried to answer this and some other criticism in a paper published in 1956 (Leontief, W.W., 1956). In his second study, Leontief used 1951 US data. He aggregated industries into 192 industries. He found that US imports were still more capital-intensive than US exports. US imports were 6 per cent more capital intensive, i.e.,

$$K_m = 1.06k_x$$

Leontief's paradox is explained as under :

(i) US was more Efficient

Leontief himself suggested an explanation for his own paradox. He argued that US workers may be more efficient than foreign workers. Perhaps US workers were three times as efficient as foreign workers. This increased efficiency of the American workers was not due to a higher capital-labour ratio, but due to some other factors such as level of education and skills, etc. He assumed that countries have identical technologies and hence identical capital-labour ratios.

It means that the average American worker is three times as efficient as he would be in the foreign country. Given the same k/L ratio, Leontief attributed the superior efficiency of American labour to superior economic organisation and economic incentives in the US. However, Leontief found very few believers among economists.

Trefler (1993) resurrects Leontief's theory and has proved that when quality indices of factors are incorporated, US exported capital and imported labour services in 1947. This still does not prove, however, that US exports had been more capital-intensive than its imports last year.

(ii) Factor Intensity Reversal

If a commodity is produced by a labour-intensive process in the labour rich country and also by the capital-intensive process in the capital rich country, then factor intensities are reversed in the production of that commodity. In the presence of factor intensity reversals, the Heckscher Ohlin theory cannot hold good for both countries, i.e. a Leontief's paradox always occurs in one of the countries. Thus, Jones and Robinson (1956) argued that factor intensity reversals could have been responsible for Leontief's paradox in US.

Another study compared trade patterns with similar countries in 1967. Capital-labour ratios are likely to be similar among developed economies and their resource endowments might be in the same cone of diversification (Moroney, 1967).

Thus, it can be said that while there has not been much empirical evidence about the possibility of factor intensity reversals (FIR), they are real. It may be important while comparing trade patterns between developing and developed countries (e.g. India and US).

(iii) Natural Resources

Leontief paradox can be explained on the basis of the treatment of the natural resources. According to some economists, Leontief paradox would not exist if natural resource-intensive industries were deleted from the analysis (Hartigan, 1981). In another study, Baldwin (1971) accounting for natural resources, found that the Leontief paradox was reduced but not eliminated.

(iv) Tariffs and Transportation Costs

Travis (1964) argued that tariffs may have been responsible for the Leontief paradox. However, tariffs tend to reduce trade volume but not reverse commodity trade pattern, US tariffs were and even today are higher *versus* labour-intensive goods. If all tariffs are removed the capital-labour ratio (K/L ratio) of US imports would be about 5 per cent lower than they currently are.

(v) Human Capital

Another factor that may be taken into account in explaining Leontief paradox is human capital. Human capital is created by education, i.e. by investment in human beings. Education, like investment in physical capital, requires time and uses up resources. Leontief referred to the greater productivity of American labour as a possible explanation for the Leontief paradox.

(vi) Demand Reversal

A demand reversal is perhaps a potential explanation of the Leontief paradox, when a capital abundant country is having a rising or very high domestic demand for capital-intensive product, it may have to import more of such product, then it contradicts with H.O. theorem. When import replacement of US are considered, it is quite logical that American import replacement production would be more capital-intensive than export production, since American production techniques are highly capital-intensive. Therefore, it may find it profitable to import such capital-intensive goods rather than produce them domestically.

(vii) Trade Imbalance

Leontief's data shows that US exports in 1947 amounted to \$ 16,678 million and imports were \$ 6,177 million. GNP of the US that year was \$ 198,688 million. Thus, trade surplus was more than 5 per cent of GNP. The H.O. theory is based on the assumption that trade is balanced. However, in reality it is not so. In general in the presence of trade imbalance a capital-abundant country may not export capital-intensive goods. With a trade surplus, a capital abundant country such as the US may not only export the capital-intensive goods but also the labour-intensive goods. Suppose that there are three goods 1, 2 and 3, so that $K_1 > K_2 > K_3$.

When trade is balanced, the US exports good 1; and imports 2 and 3. Then this trade would be consistent with the Heckscher-Ohlin theory. If the US is maintaining a large trade surplus then it implies that US consumers must reduce consumption of all three goods proportionately. In the presence of a large trade surplus, it is possible for the US to export the most labour-intensive good. That is, the US may export 1 and 3 and import 2. In this case, the average capital-labour ratio of the exports (1 and 3) can be lower than that in imports and a Leontief paradox occurs.

Balanced Trade

Industries	*Ki*	*Production*	*Consumption*	*Export*
1	2	400	200	200
2	1	50	200	–150
3	0.5	150	200	–50

Trade Surplus

Industries	*Ki*	*Production*	*Consumption*	*Export*
1	2	400	100	300
2	1	50	100	–50
3	0.5	150	100	50

$k_x = (300K_1 + 50K_3)/(300L_1 + 50L_3) > \text{or} < 1 = k_m = k_2$.

Among the 38 industries examined by Leontief, only three industries were importers in 1947. In the remaining 35 industries, the US was an exporter. Casas and Choi (1984) computed the trade pattern that would have prevailed had trade been balanced in 1947. They concluded that the US would have exported capital-intensive goods in the balanced trade situation. That is, US exports would have been more capital-intensive than US imports (www.econ.iastate.).

k_x = \$12,338 per man-year
k_m = S11,231 per man-year

Prof. Baldwin (1971) used the 1962 US trade data and found that US imports were 27 per cent more capital-intensive than US exports. The paradox continued.

$$K_m = 1.27\, k_x$$

On the pattern of Leontief, Bhardwaj (1962) made an empirical study of India's bilateral trade with US and found that Indian exports consist of capital-intensive goods to US and her imports from US consist of labour-intensive goods. This finding confirms the Leontief paradox. In this regard various explanations have been given: typical climate conditions, existence of a higher degree of disguised unemployment in Indian primary industries than in Indian manufacturing industries and extreme disparities in production technologies etc. (Mithani, 2000).

These are some of the possible explanations of the Leontief paradox. However, no conclusive inferences can be drawn. Some economists support while others contradict the paradox.

The Leontief paradox is not accepted as a fool proof method of refuting Heckscher-Ohlin's theorem. Leontief's study has been criticised on the methodological ground that it was basically concerned with exports industries and competitive import replacements rather than actual imports. Since, Ohlin's theorem is concerned with actual exports and imports, it is obvious that Leontief's conclusion is inapplicable to Heckscher Ohlin theory and so cannot disapprove it.

MODERN INTERNATIONAL TRADE AND LEONTIEF PARADOX

The modern world is a highly mechanized world. It is shaped by technological progress. The rapid progress of modern economic societies has become possible due to changes caused by technological and scientific advancements. Modern international trade is also influenced by technological changes to a large extent. It influences the composition of production functions, relative cost-price structure, demand pattern, use of resources, etc. The revolution in information technology, means of communication and transportation together with the concept of globalization and liberalization have radically changed the volume and mode of international trade world-wide. The expansion of global trade has received much attention because it has influenced the factor-markets of countries involved. Until recently in the international division of labour, the powerful and rich North was and still is assumed to be the workshop of the world, while the poor and subservient South is presumed to be forever the supplier of raw materials. The rise of countries like India, China, Korea, Brazil and 'Miracle Economies' etc. especially China in recent years is making this conventional world view questionable. The rise of China as the manufacturing hub of the world for many commodities, especially garments and consumer durables is a result of globalization and liberalization. Also it further reinforces the theory of comparative advantage as given by Ricardo and the H.O. theorem.

Besides the US, Leontief paradox has time and again been identified in other countries as well e.g. Canada, Japan, India, China, etc. In recent years, the developed and advanced countries of the world with their larger scale plants, more skilled workers, frequent technological innovations, etc. are not following the traditional norms of international trade especially the H.O. theorem. Their exports are not fully skill-intensive as expected. This fact reinforces the LP, although in a modified form.

The case of China is especially interesting. It has practically taken over the export of apparel, footwear, wire rods, copper-clad laminates, electric appliances, furniture, plastics, shampoos, toys, etc. Now it is ready to take over the export of higher-end products such as automobiles, cell phones, PCs, TVs, petrochemicals, advanced network gears, microchips, semiconductors, etc. In addition, many medium size firms and US multinationals are either outsourcing to or relocating their production mainly in China, besides India, Malaysia, Taiwan, etc. If this trend continues, the US would lose some 1.2 million non-factory jobs in 242 occupations by 2008 and 3.4 million by 2015. The same is the case with European countries too. The European trade deficit with China has almost doubled from $45 bn in 2002 to $86 bn in 2004 (www.global comment.com).

Now we take the case of India. It is a developing country with surplus labour and scarce capital. As per H.O. model, the concern of policy-makers in the field of international trade would have been to make all possible efforts to increase the exports of all those sectors which require high labour and low capital like handicrafts, yarn manufacturing, textiles and readymade garments, etc. Instead of that, the Indian economy has shown definite preference for the export of capital goods or the goods manufactured with huge capital investments such as machinery, transport vehicles and equipments and manufacturing of steel and other metals. It is clear from Table 1 that the decadal growth rate of capital goods mainly machinery, transportation equipments and steel manufacturing has remained by and large more than labour-intensive sectors such as handicrafts, yarn textiles and readymade garments etc. during the period 1960-61 to 2000-01.

During the 60s the capital goods exports increased by 800 per cent as compared to 563.63 per cent of handicrafts exports

TABLE 1

Export of Capital-Intensive Goods and Labour-Intensive Goods

Year	Capital-Intensive Goods		Labour-Intensive Goods			
	Machinery, Transport and metal manufactures Including iron and steel		Handicrafts (incl. carpets handmade)		Textile fabrics and manufactures, cotton yarn fabrics, made up, etc. Readymade garments of all textile materials	
	Amount	Percent Increase	Amount	Percent Increase	Amount	Percent Increase
1960-61	22	—	11	—	138	—
1970-71	198	800.00	73	563.63	295	113.76
1980-81	827	317.67	952	1204.11	1341	354.57
1990-91	3872	368.19	6167	547.79	8932	566.07
2000-01	31870	723.08	5097	–17.35	41508	364.71

Source: Government of India, Economic Survey, 2005-06, Ministry of Finance.

and 113.76 of textiles and readymade garments exports. During the 70's due to the more specific attention to labour-intensive sector exports of handicrafts increased by 1204.11 per cent and exports of yarn, textiles and readymade garment increased by 354.57 per cent, the growth rate of capital goods during this decade was 317.67 per cent. During 1980-81 to 1990-91, the labour-intensive sector's exports increased by 507.79 per cent (handicrafts) and 566.07 per cent (textiles, readymade garments) as compared to this the exports of capital goods increased by 368.19 per cent.

The era of economic reforms and liberalization opened the door of Indian economy for foreign investors; especially multinationals which made huge investments for the manufacturing of capital-intensive goods such as automobile sectors, aviation, petro-chemicals, communication and electronics, etc. These companies manufactured many items for exports. Majority of the industries adopted automation and modernization in a big way, as a result the export of capital goods during 1991-2001 increased by 723.08 per cent and exports of handicrafts decreased by 17.35 per cent. However, the export of textiles and readymade garments registered a growth of 364.71 per cent which is half than the growth rate of capital goods exports. Thus, this state of affairs substantiates the applicability of Leontief's paradox in developing countries such as India. Again the pattern of exports of recently developed and developing countries shows that these countries are trying hard to increase their exports so as to reduce their trade deficit in respect of adverse consequences on the pattern of employment growth and income generation. It is rather unfortunate that performance of external sector in India during the era of economic reforms and liberalization has remained by and large excellent without creating additional job opportunities (Sharma, 2004, pp. 1-10). The NSSO data of 55th, 56th, 57th, 58th and 59th surveys show that unemployment rate has increased in both male and female workers in India during 1990-91 to 2004-05.

Obviously, the situation is that a developing, labour-intensive country like China is exporting both unskilled and highly skilled intensive products to the US, while the latter is reduced to exporting oil seeds, grains, iron and raw hides, etc. The reason for this manifestation of LP is that today we live in a highly dynamic world where comparative advantages of countries are not only natural but can be acquired by skillful manipulation of opportunity costs, entrepreneurship, technology, innovation, the right monetary policy, skill, work discipline, purpose, incentives to delocalize, political will, etc. Developing economies seem to have understood this and have taken advantage of the globalization policy.

CONCLUSION

International trade is a highly complex phenomenon. The complexities are continuously increasing with the global expansion and dynamism of foreign trade. The traditional theories of international trade like the theory of comparative advantage, the H.O. theorem, the LP and others were mostly based on assumptions that are impractical in the modern world. LP results were drawn using the 1947 input-output table of the US. Leontief's study has been criticized on methodological grounds that it was basically concerned with export industries and competitive import replacements rather than actual imports. Further when measuring the capital-labour ratio embodied in US imports Leontief did not examine the factor intensity techniques used by foreign industries that exported commodities to the US. Instead, he examined factor intensity techniques used by US industries that were producing import competing commodities (Y.K. Kwok, Eden, S.H. Yu, 2005). Some empirical studies showed that Leontief paradox comes and goes from time to time.

In the end we can conclude that despite all the criticism and drawbacks of the Leontief paradox, the fact remains that it was a major study of its times, that questioned the static Heckscher Ohlin theory and started a different path for analyzing international trade with all its complexities.

REFERENCES

Baldwin, R.E. (1971), "Determinants of the Commodity Structure of US"; *American Economic Review*, Vol. 6, March, p. 126.

Bhardwaj, R. (1962), "Factor Proportion and the Structure of India-US Trade", *Indian Economic Journal*, October.

Buchanan, N.S. (1955), "Lines on the Leontief Paradox", *Economea Internazionale*, Vol. 8, November, p. 79.

Casas Francois and E. Kwan Choi (1984): "Trade Imbalance and the Leontief Paradox", Manchester School, 52.

Jones Robinson (1956), "Factor Proportion and the Heckscher Ohlin Theorem", *Review of Economic Studies.*

Loeb, G.A. (1954), "A Estrutura do commercio Exterior da, America do, Norte, Revista Brazileira", *de Economica,* Vol. 8, Dec., p. 81.

Leontief, W.W. (1956), "Factor Proportions and the Structure of American Trade: Further Theoretical and Empirical Analysis", *REStat.*

Mithani, D.M. (2000), *International Economics,* Himalaya Publishing House.

Sharma, Alakh N. (2004), "Globalisation, Labour Market and Poverty: Emerging Perspective in India", D.T. Lakdawala Memorial Lecture, 88th Conference of IEA.

Stolper, Wolfgang, F. and Karl Roskamp (1961), "Input-Output Table for East Germany with Application to Foreign Trade", *Bulletin of the Oxford Institute of Statistics,* Nov.

Tatomoto, M. and Ichimura, S. (1959), "Factor Proportions and Foreign Trade: The Case of Japan", *Review of Economics and Statistics,* Vol. 41.

Trefler, Daniel (1993), "International Factor Price Differences: Leontief was Right," *Journal of Political Economy,* 101, pp. 961-87.

Yun Kwong Kwok, Eden, S.H. Yu (2005), *Leontief Paradox and the Role of Factor Intensity Measures,* 2005.

Index